COMING TO TERMS WITH STUDENT
OUTCOMES ASSESSMENT

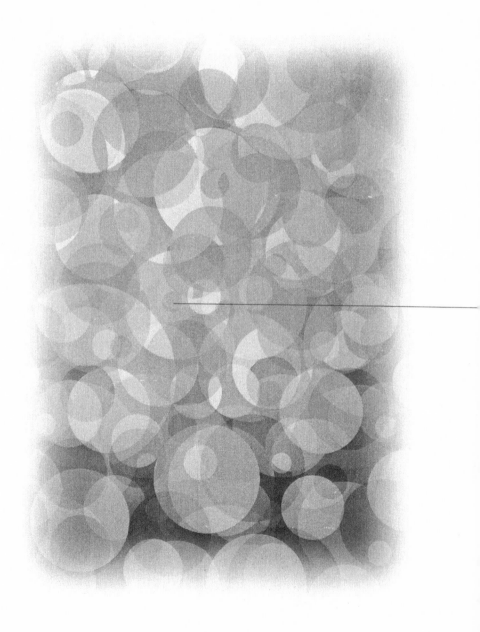

COMING TO TERMS WITH STUDENT OUTCOMES ASSESSMENT

Faculty and Administrators' Journeys to Integrating Assessment in Their Work and Institutional Culture

Edited by Peggy L. Maki

STERLING, VIRGINIA

Sty/us

Published by Stylus Publishing, LLC
22883 Quicksilver Drive
Sterling, Virginia 20166-2102

Library of Congress Cataloging-in-Publication Data
Coming to terms with student outcomes assessment : faculty and administrators' journeys to integrating assessment in their work and institutional culture / edited by Peggy L. Maki.
    p.   cm.
Includes index.
ISBN 978-1-57922-434-9 (cloth : alk. paper)
ISBN 978-1-57922-435-6 (pbk. : alk. paper)
1. Universities and colleges—United States—Evaluation.
2. Education, Higher—United States—Evaluation.
3. Educational evaluation—United States.   4. Educational tests and measurements—United States.   I. Maki, Peggy.
LB2331.63.C65   2010
378.1'07—dc22   2010005130

13-digit ISBN: 978-1-57922-434-9 (cloth)
13-digit ISBN: 978-1-57922-435-6 (paper)

Printed in the United States of America

All first editions printed on acid free paper
that meets the American National Standards Institute
Z39-48 Standard.

Bulk Purchases

Quantity discounts are available for use in workshops and for staff development.
Call 1-800-232-0223

First Edition, 2010

10   9   8   7   6   5   4   3   2   1

To colleagues across American higher education
who serve and have served
on the front lines of the assessment movement

CONTENTS

ACKNOWLEDGMENTS

I enthusiastically thank the contributors to this collection of essays for the realistic accounts of their institutions' journeys toward assessment and for their commitment to sharing their experiences with (sometimes through humor, which has a way of crystallizing reality), insights into, and reflections on integrating assessment into their institutions and programs. I hope readers view these authors' stories and perspectives, not only as documentaries of the assessment movement, but also as instructive accounts of institutional change in higher education: complicated, time consuming with periods of fits and starts, yet still possible when led by those whose commitment and intentionality are accompanied by patience.

INTRODUCTION

How has it happened that within the last 8 to 10 years, an increasing number of colleges and universities have come to terms with the assessment movement, shifting from an attitude of "say it isn't so" to actually developing institutional pathways that have drawn in faculty and other educators? For more than two decades, calls for higher education to demonstrate students' achievement have resounded from numerous sectors: the federal government, accreditors, legislators, funders, and other stakeholders. Until recently, however, responses to those calls had been spotty and limited, often consisting solely of students' and alumni's responses to satisfaction surveys. Over the last 8–10 years, however, assessment of student learning has made its way into institutional life primarily because of regional and national accreditors' increasingly focused demand that evidence of students' achievement of institution-level, program-level, and course-level learning outcomes be included as a major component of institutional effectiveness. More recently, national focus on assessment of student learning also increased dramatically in the exchanges and deliberations that characterized the federal Commission on the Future of Higher Education's work, leading to heated debates about how evidence of student learning should be comparably presented for external audiences such as legislators, parents and students, employers, and the federal government.

How have institutions managed to incorporate assessment of student learning into institutional ways of behaving? What has it actually taken to establish this movement on campuses? Having built a campus history, what do those on the front lines of their campuses' efforts have to share about their experiences, challenges, and successes and the obstacles that they faced? What lessons have they learned? Written in the first-person singular and plural by faculty and administrators who have served daily on the front lines of their institutions' efforts to integrate assessment into institutional life, this book consists of 14 essays describing institutions' and programs' journeys, including the ins and outs, ups and downs, and periods of ebb and flow that characterized day-to-day, month-to-month, and year-to-year developments.

Integrated into each essay are writers' observations, the lessons they learned, and their reflections on their institutions' or programs' journeys, as well as their personal journeys, which often led them to revise their own thinking about how to design and implement an effective and useful assessment process. These are firsthand accounts of the ways in which colleges and universities opened their institutions' doors to what many inside the institutions viewed as unwelcome, intrusive, and undesirable change in higher education.

Given that institutions now have a record of their entry into the assessment movement, and that they have built a history beyond that entry, now seems to be the right time to learn about how this change has come about in American colleges and universities. The chapters in *Coming to Terms With Student Outcomes Assessment: Faculty and Administrators' Journeys to Integrating Assessment in Their Work and Institutional Culture* were written, then, to describe how institutions began their journeys into the assessment movement; how they relied on or created processes, structures, committees, decision-making bodies, and forms of support to develop the commitment; and what they encountered in terms of challenges, obstacles, and often surprising positive developments and responses.

Collectively, then, the stories in this volume provide a documentary of representative efforts that have taken place in institutions of American higher education ranging from community colleges to 4-year colleges and universities. Representing community colleges are the College of San Mateo in California, part of the largest higher education system in the nation; Seminole State College of Florida, formerly Seminole Community College, a comprehensive midsize community college in central Florida; Valencia Community College, a large multi-campus college in central Florida; North Shore Community College, a three-campus community college in Massachusetts; and the Community College of Rhode Island, the only community college in the state of Rhode Island. Representing 4-year institutions are Clarke College, a small liberal arts Catholic college in Iowa; Coker College, a private liberal arts college in South Carolina; and Rhode Island College, a comprehensive public university. Representing the span of universities are a regional comprehensive university, Eastern Kentucky University; a large urban public university that is part of the expansive California State University system, California State University, Long Beach; the largest institution of higher learning in northeast Indiana, Indiana University–Purdue University Fort Wayne; a Carnegie doctoral research university, the University of Maryland, College Park; a comprehensive metropolitan public university, the University of Southern Maine; a public research-intensive university, the University of Rhode Island; a relatively young university founded in 1967 to serve junior, senior, and graduate students that became a full 4-year undergraduate institution in 1983, the University of West Florida; and the only university in the United States dedicated to serving deaf and hard-of-hearing students,

Gallaudet University. The final chapter in this book describes coordinated efforts among the three public institutions in the state of Rhode Island—the University of Rhode Island, Rhode Island College, and the Community College of Rhode Island.

Readers will probably immediately recognize and have personal experience with what stands out as the most consistent pattern that runs through all these essays: the overwhelming expenditure of human energy over multiple years and around challenges to gain faculty momentum in assessment—often preceded by years of inertia. That expenditure of energy manifests itself in multiple ways: numerous occasions for dialogue with individuals or departments; meetings upon meetings, initially to recruit faculty and then to work through subtasks of the assessment process; various campus convenings; workshop after workshop; individual department and program consultancies—illustrating how characteristically time consuming this work has been for campus leaders who have served on the front lines of assessment. Indeed, several chapter titles in this collection, such as "From Bereavement to Assessment: The Transformation of a Regional Comprehensive University" and "Slouching Toward Assessment: One Department's Journey Toward Accountability Bliss," characterize the difficulties of taking first steps into assessment, not to mention developing institution- and program-level processes and expectations to integrate assessment of student learning as a sustainable rhythm of institutional life.

As you read these essays on institutions' journeys, you will probably identify patterns of behavior that you have experienced on your own campus as you have worked to integrate assessment into institutional life: patterns of faculty resistance that range from initial mild discomfort to outright denial based on an enduring belief that grades themselves are the best documentation of student learning; that assessment is a fad that soon will pass; and that assessment is a bureaucratization of education, an invasion of academic freedom and individuality, a means to weed out undesirable faculty or programs with low enrollment, or a reductionist's approach to measuring what cannot be measured. Other challenges documented in these chapters may also reflect your own institution's journey, such as the challenge of articulating student learning outcomes, of identifying methods to assess those outcomes, of developing standards and criteria of judgment, or of interpreting results of student work. Or your own campus challenges may be reflected in these chapters in the authors' confrontations of issues such as how this new or additional assessment work will be rewarded, how it will affect faculty workload, and how—or even if—results will "really" be used.

These chapters illustrate how representative colleges and universities have forged pathways amid challenges—some of those internal, as with faculty, and others external, as with accrediting agencies and mandates from state boards of higher education. Clearly, the overriding push for assessment comes from these external forces; yet mandating behavior elicits immediate negative responses. How institutions translated those external demands into their cultures' behaviors, structures, processes, and procedures is the focus of these chapters. Although no two institutions used the same set of strategies or began at the same place or experienced the same kinds or levels of initial resistance, the sum of their experiences instructs us about ways in which assessment has been successfully drawn into institutions' lives. As you read these chapters, you also will learn about, if not identify with, the following successful strategies and processes that have brought faculty and other educators into the movement:

- Identifying a point of entry for the effort, for example, a desire or need to revise general education or the mission of the institution or a need to state explicit course-by-course student learning outcomes in syllabi
- Educating the community at large, including faculty, staff, and administrators
- Developing a top-down and bottom-up collaboration between administrators and educators
- Developing channels of communication at all levels and of all kinds that span an institution (from one-on-one meetings, to workshops, to the creation of assessment manuals or handbooks, to periodic faculty meetings as well as institution-wide meetings)
- Creating meaningful contexts for this work beyond the satisfaction of accreditors or state mandates—for example, by linking it to strategic planning, rewarding this work in faculty promotion and tenure, integrating it into program review, or integrating it into the scholarship of teaching and learning. This latter method may be accomplished by raising important institution-level research questions about learners so that assessment becomes useful and meaningful professional work
- Accepting time, accompanied by extraordinary patience, as an important ingredient in this work, advancing the commitment through dialogue, repetition, listening, hearing people out, and being able to respond to others who hold contrary positions or perspectives on assessment and the process itself

Amid the range of challenges that the authors of these chapters faced either initially or along the pathways that they forged to root assessment into institutional life, they have managed to leverage change in faculty perspectives, attitudes, and behaviors around assessment by chronologically and patiently addressing levels of misunderstanding and confusion and outright denial to foster understanding and openness to assessment. In the pages of this volume, you will read how faculty and administrators responded to faculty resistance while at the same time helping faculty develop a process that resonated with institutional, faculty, and other educators' values, as well as the mission and purposes of the institutions themselves. You will read the contributors' descriptions of campus breakthroughs or successes in the accounts of their work, such as discussions among faculty and other educators focused on examining the coherence underlying programs of study in general education and in their major programs of study; addressing how adjuncts can be engaged in this kind of discussion; identifying assessment methods that provide a chronological account of how well students are integrating, transferring, and applying their learning; and identifying patterns of weakness in students' achievement that lead to discussion and reflection on ways to improve those patterns. And you will also read about authors' own moments of reflection that led them to reconsider a strategy or direction to engage faculty and others in the work of assessment—often as a result of dialogue with their colleagues or as a result of recognizing that a particular approach to assessment simply wasn't working well or wasn't at all useful. Indeed, several authors see themselves becoming facilitators of the process or becoming coaches, recognizing their need to be flexible as they worked with and responded to their colleagues.

Now that campuses have made or are making pathways to incorporate assessment in their institutions, what needs to happen over the long haul so that this commitment will endure? There are four main issues, I believe, that loom over our colleges and universities: (1) sustaining this effort through annually dedicated human, financial, educational, and technological resources; (2) establishing institutionally agreed-upon times to report assessment results and recommendations to shape both program-level and institution-level planning, budgeting, and decision making so that there is timely implementation of recommendations to improve student learning; (3) prioritizing recommendations for action based on assessment results, such as changes in pedagogy, among other competing institutional priorities; and (4) developing promotion and tenure criteria for faculty and criteria for other educators who contribute to this work, such as professionals in the co-curriculum, that recognize and value the commitment to assessing student learning

Indeed, the institutions represented in this book have made and are making progress toward integrating assessment into their institutions' ways of behaving with considerable dedication of resources—human, financial, technological, and educational—initially to satisfy external forces. Can institutions continue these commitments of resources in light of competing institutional priorities and likely diminished resources? For example, maintaining a commitment to assessment requires that each year new and adjunct faculty be oriented to and perhaps even educated about the commitment. Can institutions rely on their centers for teaching, learning, and assessment or ask them to take on an educational role to fulfill the annual need to educate faculty and others in the absence of, perhaps, resources available for faculty to travel to national and regional assessment conferences to learn about developments in assessment? Can an increasing number of institutions invest in the assessment management systems that have also emerged over the last decade that enable institutions to track, store, and continually reflect on their assessment results and recommended changes?

Developing channels of communication and reporting calendars that bring to light assessment results and recommendations for changes in educational practices is a second need. Without clear communication channels for decision making and planning bodies at both the program and institution levels and without agreed-upon annual timetables for discussing and acting on results and recommendations, so that proposed changes can be implemented to improve student learning, assessment could run the risk of becoming an exercise without immediate student benefit. On that point, Jean Mach writes in Chapter 4 about the pressing need to align program-level assessment results requiring institutional resources with an institution's annual planning and decision-making timetable so that identified needs are immediately addressed to improve student learning. Scalability is the third large issue looming primarily over senior administrators. Will those who make institution-level decisions view recommendations emerging from assessment as an institutional priority, or will other institutional priorities take over and cancel out the value of this work, leading faculty and other educators to believe that this work has minimal importance or usefulness?

Finally, without a set of agreed-upon criteria for evaluating faculty and others for their commitment to this work, assessment runs the risk of becoming another one of those chores that faculty and others have to balance—perhaps even just a one-phrase entry on an annual list of responsibilities or accomplishments. Unless colleges and universities are willing to describe how the work of assessment will be recognized—perhaps even as a collaborative form of scholarly work—the likelihood of its becoming an even more useful endeavor to advance the profession of teaching will be diminished to a routinized mechanical accountability commitment. The time is right for determining how to recognize and reward this work: Focusing on our students' achievement has become a national priority. Thus, institutional and faculty governance leaders will need to determine how to support, reward, and prioritize this essential professional work.

I

ASSESSMENT IS LIKE A BOX OF CHOCOLATES

Lisa Maxfield
California State University, Long Beach

California State University, Long Beach (CSULB), is a large urban public university and one of 23 campuses in the California State University system. Identified by the Carnegie Classification of Institutions of Higher Education as a large master's college and university, CSULB enrolls approximately 36,000 students, making it one of the largest higher education institutions in California. Long Beach is an urban municipality of almost 500,000 people and was identified using 2000 U.S. Census data as the most ethnically diverse large city in the nation. Reflecting the diversity of the city of Long Beach, CSULB has a diverse student population (5.7% African American, 16.3% Asian/Asian American, 30.9% Caucasian, 18.6% Mexican American, 0.6% Native American/Alaskan Native, 8% other Latino/Hispanic, 7.1% Pacific Islander/Filipino, 12.8% unknown/other).

When conceptualizing this chapter, I first thought I wanted to say something provocative. If I were to sum up my experience with assessment, what would I say? Well, here's my attempt at provocative: I like assessment. Very few things that I've said in my professional life have garnered such baffled looks as those three little words. In selected venues, I've modeled it as a confession: "Hello, my name is Lisa, and I like assessment." I even like assessment more now than when I got involved in it. I also like chocolate, but the parallels between assessment and chocolate only begin there. Exactly how is assessment like a box of chocolates? The analogy emerged from reflection on the lessons I've learned in my own formative experiences with assessment, so I would like to provide some background and context before explaining the analogy further. Thus, I begin with a narrative about my campus and my role in its modern assessment enterprise.

Background

I am a cognitive psychologist with research interests in human memory and learning. In 2005, I accepted a 3-year appointment from the Office of Academic Affairs as the university's general education coordinator (a half-time position). The position had been vacant for over a year, during time which there were many changes in administration and other priorities were taking center stage. However, there was a need that had to be addressed and simply couldn't wait much longer. In 2002, our accrediting agency indicated that although the structure of our general education requirements was quite strong, we lacked a plan for evaluating the educational effectiveness of the program. My primary task, then, was to develop an assessment plan for our super-sized general education program (at the time of this writing, almost 700 courses).

Good intentions had never been enough. Our campus general education policy has had a requirement for program-level assessment since Jimmy Carter was living in the White House. Over the years, a variety of small-scale audits of general education were carried out to achieve specific purposes (e.g., ensuring a sufficient number of sections per course given student demand, examining enrollment trends to avoid bottleneck courses, ensuring that students take prerequisites). Yet no overall learning outcomes were articulated for general education, and no comprehensive assessment plan had been developed or implemented.

The GE Governing Committee, a standing committee of the Academic Senate, is the authority on the governance of general education. Historically, our GE Governing Committee has not enjoyed a particularly favorable reputation on our campus. Rightly or wrongly, the perception of the committee has been as gatekeeper, requiring faculty to jump through hoops to get courses certified for general education credit. Concern over enrollment targets has prompted undesirable competition among disciplines that offer general education courses, with each college strongly motivated to protect its content "territory." The general education governance process reinforced this turf battle. A primary judgment criterion essentially involved how well a course could fit into a single general education content category. Each course was allowed to define its own unique set of learning goals (at a modest 5 per course, we'd now have about 3,500 goals), with little consideration for specific program goals for the general education curriculum. The consequences have been far reaching. Both faculty and students have inherited a vision of general education as merely requirements to be fulfilled and checked off on a list, one course in lonely isolation at a time. It left little to the imagination as to why the idea of program-level assessment was never on the radar.

My Perspective on Assessment

As an experimental psychologist, I am naturally interested in the idea of assessment. It is an occupational hazard that I like to design research questions, collect data, and formulate explanations of patterns and trends. Although these skills have defined my approach as general education coordinator, they are not what drew me into this work. My vision for student assessment is grounded first and foremost in my devotion to liberal (general) education. My love of learning was resolutely shaped by my own general education experiences in college, when the general education course list looked to me like a menu of fascinating topics about which I couldn't wait to find out. I was a student who became easily distressed over picking just one major, when there were so many intriguing fields to sample. I discovered a passion for how psychologists think about things, and so I chose my major based on the intellectual challenge the discipline provided. However, my favorite courses were my general education courses: every semester offered something brand new to learn. As I reflect on this fact now, I realize it has shaped my belief that you need to be intrinsically invested in what you're assessing in order for assessment to succeed. People want to improve things that bear a relation to what they want to achieve.

Finding Energy for General Education Assessment

General education assessment can be a very tough sell. In major disciplines, faculty and students possess intrinsic motivation and passion for their field of study. People feel an inherent ownership of their own disciplines that general education does not necessarily enjoy. To take on assessment *and* general education has been, at times, as tantamount to adopting the path of most resistance as a career move. But I believe strongly in the potential value of general education. The focus that keeps me energized is always steering the dialogue toward issues of student learning. My essential goal is to design the assessment in service to what our campus can accomplish in general education. In my view, assessment is not a chore to be approached with the attitude of "Let's get this over with" but rather an essential tool for figuring out how to create powerful learning experiences for students. My vision has been profoundly shaped by LEAP (Liberal Education and America's Promise), an initiative of the Association of American Colleges and Universities (see www.aacu.org/LEAP). LEAP defines a set of essential skills that all students need to successfully navigate in their 21st century lives.

These essential skills include written and oral communication, critical and creative thinking, information literacy, teamwork, and intercultural knowledge and competence. Although LEAP can be applied beyond general education, what it brought into focus for our campus was the powerful potential of a cohesive general education curriculum. The LEAP skills clarify why general education should be the universal thread that runs through all our major degree programs. These skills have such interdisciplinary appeal: What major does not want its students to be proficient in written and oral communication? It is said that all great journeys start with one step. Adopting the LEAP outcomes as our general education program student learning outcomes was our singularly significant first step—away from a fragmented checklist of requirements to be gotten out of the way and toward a common purpose regarding what students can achieve through the opportunities of general education. To say that LEAP set the stage for us would be understating its influence. It was more like a booster rocket launching us into a universe where no one on our campus had gone before.

In 2006, I introduced LEAP to our GE Governing Committee; however, initially I did not make a decision to run with this commitment, as much as I was drawn to it, because I essentially had no authority to do so. If I were to describe the nature of my role as general education coordinator, I would say that I envision myself as a facilitator and resource finder. I bring some skills to the table that I think assessment "leaders" should have (e.g., experience working with quantitative and qualitative data), yet I take no authority beyond what I am given by being a member of the faculty. In fact, the reason our general education assessment program is moving along so well is that its oversight rests firmly in faculty governance. The GE Governing Committee consists mostly of faculty representatives from each of our seven colleges and the general education coordinator (also a faculty position), as well as adjunct faculty representatives, a provost's office designee (administrator), and the director of academic advising (staff person).

My general education coordinator position offers me the luxury of time to investigate and to filter ideas. I spent my first year researching a wide variety of assessment plans and brought ideas forward to the GE Governing Committee. On days when the ideas were not well received, I thought it was my responsibility to go back to the drawing board and rework them. No doubt I have been an instigator; yet I am also faculty, respectful of faculty governance and faculty roles. Common wisdom holds that the curriculum is the purview of the faculty. It seems only right that assessment of that curriculum, then, must come from the faculty.

Box of Chocolates Principles

In spite of this, there was certainly no clarion call for general education assessment from our faculty, or for any other kind of assessment for that matter. As on many campuses, our faculty still exhibit resistance to the idea of assessment, and many still have bruises from previous attempts to justify that resistance. Given that, and that I still liked assessment, I wondered what I had to lose by just admitting I saw potential value in it. One thing I thought I knew for sure was that if assessment wasn't as appealing as a box of chocolates, it would once again fail. So, at that point, I added "being a cheerleader" to the definition of my general education coordinator role. Let me grab my pom-poms and explain the ways in which assessment reminds me of a box of chocolates.

You Can't Eat All the Chocolates at Once. You Need to Know When to Stop

One of the most successful steps we took in starting a general education assessment program was to stop, literally, what we were doing. The workload of the process (reviewing 700 courses one by one) had drained us of any energy we might have had to remember the reason for the process. The GE Governing Committee and I agreed it was time for a culture shift in the way we thought about general education. As we explored new ideas brought about by our discussions about LEAP, we optimistically envisioned a very different world for general education governance procedures and wanted to keep the campus informed about our thinking. However, the business of general education had been so ingrained as background noise in a vibrant campus opus that to say we were doing something new and different made exactly zero people look up and take notice.

It was a great risk to stop doing general education business the way it had been done for years, but it was an investment in facilitating a true culture shift for our general education governance process. And the timing for the culture shift could not have been better. Our general education policy had been substantially revised in the late 1990s, and the new policy had gone into effect in 2000. Because of the sweeping changes, all existing general education courses had to be reviewed for compliance with the new policy. Because we had over 500 courses in 2000, and new ones were constantly being proposed, this amounted to a tremendous workload for the GE Governing Committee. Twice a month, each meeting involved review of a large stack of course proposals. The workload itself is not the ultimate issue here; it is the consequences of the workload that made the process unsatisfying. With just a few minutes per course, our discussion time was consumed largely by "housekeeping" issues.

Questions we constantly asked were ones such as, was the course in the right general education category, and did the attendance and makeup policies comply with university policy? There was no time to consider vital issues of curriculum. Questions we never asked were ones such as, what value did the new course add to the general education program, and what was occurring in the course to ensure the learning goals were achieved? In other words, we weren't talking about student achievement. And in our never-ending assembly line of course reviews, we had unintentionally nurtured an image of general education as a compilation of individual courses where each course might, at best, represent an "island of innovation." The GE Governing Committee was accumulating all this knowledge about what faculty were doing in these courses, but the knowledge was coming to no good use. That knowledge was compartmentalized, then filed away and lost until the course resurfaced at its next scheduled review (5 years later). Thus, we never had a chance to consider the greater purpose of our general education program as a cohesive, meaningful curriculum.

This issue was one of many discussed at a retreat held by the GE Governing Committee as the fall 2006 semester began. It was suggested that the real problem was that we had too many courses. Fewer courses would make the workload more manageable. Although it is likely that this was true, the committee as a whole resisted that solution for a variety of reasons. First, we are a large university with an extremely diverse student body. Our students have as many background experiences and interests as there are under the sun; we believe it is a strength of our general education program that they have as many choices of topics to explore as our diversely talented faculty can offer them. Second, it turned out that the data didn't support that conclusion. We looked at the other 22 campuses in the California State University system, and we found that several other campuses had a greater number of general education courses per student than we did. Third, it is a fact of life that departments depend on general education courses for enrollment. We wanted, then, to encourage broad participation in general education, not to make life impossible for our colleagues.

Serendipitously, fall 2006 turned out to be the perfect time for us to have raised these issues. We had now completed 5 full years of the general education policy adopted in 2000, and this policy required that all courses undergo periodic review every 5 years after original general education certification. So, as the first wave of courses that had been approved in 2000 came back for recertification, our stacks of paperwork were now largely course recertifications. The intent of recertification had, all along, been about course assessment. Faculty were supposed to provide us with data about how they knew that students had achieved (or would achieve) the learning outcomes of the course. We had, in fact, provided them with a form that asked them about that. It turned out that the problem was that we *only* provided a form; we had not included any instructions or guidance and absolutely no models for what we really wanted to learn. Why? Because we really didn't know what we wanted. Here was yet another aspect of the maintenance of the general education program upon which we had not had time to reflect.

After a number of weeks of doing business with this unguided, vagabond recertification procedure, we had accumulated an unimpressive stack of assessment reports that faculty had put real effort into and that, in terms of real assessment, didn't have much value. Personally, I felt awful. I felt I was an accessory to the crime of forcing my fellow faculty members to do the kind of meaningless administrative paperwork that the word *assessment* has legendarily represented. I admit that, with this as my impetus, I expanded my role from facilitator to instigator. In an executive session of the GE Governing Committee, I posed this challenge to my colleagues. I said that I thought we should stop. If we thought that this kind of recertification was truly the best we could do, we just shouldn't do recertification at all anymore. It wasn't a good use of anyone's time, including the GE Governing Committee's. On the other hand, if we thought we could do better, we needed to stop course review *entirely* for some significant period of time and concentrate on the work of planning for general education assessment and developing all the resources that would be necessary to make that work manageable and valuable.

And so we birthed the idea of a 2-year moratorium on new courses.[1] This was not an easy birth. At first, it was truly shocking, and that's just how the GE Governing Committee felt. How could we do that? How could we just stop the business of course review? That was our only function, right? We had this endless flow of new courses, and we couldn't just turn that off, close down the general education factory, so to speak. Could we? The campus would be outraged at such a hiatus. Well, now that was an interesting idea to consider. Here we were wanting to significantly change the culture of general education, and we didn't know how to get the campus to take notice. To stop doing the business we had implicitly taken on as our sole role, now, that would create some buzz. I need to mention at this point how dedicated my GE Governing Committee colleagues are. The committee took the risk of stopping the curricular process that was so familiar to the campus community. Furthermore, the purpose of doing so was to buy us time to develop an assessment plan for general education. How would the campus react when people found out we were concentrating on creating procedures that many of them did not want to do anyway, just so we could do it better? The GE Governing Committee took on the challenge and risk, and what has been achieved thus far could not have been done without their bravery. (I even underestimated them. When I raised the idea, I only envisioned a 1-year moratorium. The committee saw fit to extend it to 2 years.)

Let's revisit the analogy and examine the themes of this section. A box of chocolates might best be enjoyed slowly, one piece at a time. Assessment, too, takes time. Assessment involves abandoning unproductive activities, learning from them, and implementing more fruitful ones. A few valuable lessons about taking time to reflect are:

1. Be very clear and honest about why you are holding the moratorium. People will be inconvenienced by it; it is, therefore, wise to be respectful and explain to them why they are being inconvenienced.
2. Be your own role model for assessment by using the good lessons of assessment: Set very clear goals with a deadline for what will be accomplished during the moratorium, hold yourselves accountable for meeting those goals, and regularly update the campus community on your progress.
3. Seek input from the campus community throughout the hiatus. Recognize that your stakeholders know a great deal about curriculum. The GE Governing Committee benefited greatly from the wisdom of our colleagues, which allowed us to shape a plan for assessment that best fit our unique needs. Although we are not looking for some unattainable nirvana of full consensus (the GE Governing Committee maintains final voting authority on procedures), regularly soliciting input and inviting our colleagues to co-design the processes created buy-in in a truly organic manner.

Tasty Pieces Come in Many Different Shapes and Sizes, and You Get to Select the One That Looks Good to You

During our assessment planning process, we investigated a great number of models provided by other universities. Certainly, many had great attributes, and we were able to incorporate those aspects into our design in a unique synthesis that best fit our campus. Even so, we recognized that a one-size-fits-all model for general education assessment would be a disastrous one-note song. Variety is more than the spice of life. It provides the health of our general education curriculum, as evidenced by all 600-plus "learning experiments" (i.e., courses) that we've approved, and it is an important key to our assessment planning. Different faculty are in different places with assessment, ranging from being quite comfortable with it as a process (often found in majors with specialized accrediting agencies) to having absolutely no clear approach to getting started. As with students, teachable moments only occur when you attend to people where they are; therefore, no one should be made to feel disadvantaged simply because his or her field does not have established assessment procedures. Furthermore, we found it appealing that faculty would have some choice in defining their involvement in the assessment. To honor this, we developed a two-track model for assessment. To reinforce our culture shift toward outcomes-based assessment, we wanted a new brand (and marketing strategy) for what we were doing. We wanted our efforts to reflect a true culture shift, not merely a "new set of forms" (which is how many of our colleagues referred to it). We branded the two-track model SAGE, or Student Achievement in General Education. It is the name given to the process for assessment of general education courses at CSULB; participation in SAGE can fulfill the periodic recertification requirement for all general education courses. The objective of SAGE is to verify student achievement of the shared student learning outcomes of general education (essentially the broadly appealing LEAP outcomes previously described).

One primary goal of SAGE is to create guiding principles for assessment and uniform *standards* of expectations for the campus, rather than imposing a one-size-fits-all *process*. In my capacity as an experimental psychologist, I was inclined to approach this as I do science. There are uniform standards of how science answers questions (e.g., what constitutes good evidence for drawing conclusions) that still allow for a great measure of creativity in how one might study the variables of interest. For both of our assessment tracks we defined necessary standards such as:

1. Courses had to include assessment of the shared student learning outcomes of general education.
2. The assessment had to include direct measures (i.e., student performance data, not just faculty or student perceptions of courses).
3. Assessment had to be ongoing (even though the reporting was only periodic).
4. Evidence of implementation of improvements to courses made on the basis on the assessment data needed to be documented.
5. Documentation had to include a plan for communicating the results of the assessment to all instructional faculty.

The difference between our two tracks rests within the *how*, specifically *how* the assessment process proceeds. The single-course track allows faculty to design and to conduct assessment more or less independently. Courses in this track are still required to comply with GE Governing Committee assessment standards; therefore, faculty develop an assessment plan for courses in consultation with the committee. Once a plan is approved, faculty conduct the assessment on their own, in accordance with the plan. The GE Governing Committee has recommended this track for courses that have an assessment process currently in place that is working well (these are usually found in disciplines with outside accrediting agencies).

The collaborative track is truly innovative for our campus and is designed as a faculty learning community. The process begins with faculty identifying which of our general education program student learning outcomes (i.e., the LEAP skills) are most essential to their general education courses. They may select desired outcomes that they currently work toward in their instruction as well as ones they wish to further develop and emphasize in their courses. Faculty from all courses interested in one outcome or essential skill are grouped into a faculty learning community focused on that skill. Thus, for example, faculty from any number of disciplines who all share an intrinsic interest in the teaching of critical thinking form a learning community. The GE Governing Committee facilitates the work of the faculty learning community. Faculty participation is focused on the direction and implementation of the assessment only: Faculty determine what researchable question they want to ask about what our general education students are achieving in terms of the essential skill, and how the answers to that question will inform innovations uniquely defined for their courses. The GE Governing Committee and the general education coordinator, however, perform the actual assessment data collection and analysis. In this manner, faculty time is concentrated on the careful crafting of pedagogy. Thus, assessment data collection is centralized and streamlined, and removed from the shoulders of the faculty.

I don't mean to downplay the importance of data collection. I am a firm believer in the value of a culture of evidence and in fostering the development of a learning institution. I also believe that the need for evidence cannot translate practically into everyone needing to manage data collection and analysis. In the extreme, campuses institute a culture of assessment predicated on the belief that every student must be assessed for purposes of program assessment. One of the benefits of being on a campus with 36,000 students is that this approach never even entered my mind as a possibility. Investigating other institutions, I found that many good plans for assessment have been derailed when the process of data collection became too overwhelming. It is easy, when one is bogged down with data collection, to forget that student learning is the true end goal of assessment, whereas data collection is a middle step. The end goal is aligning our pedagogy to effectively achieve our outcomes.

The faculty learning community design is an exciting innovation for our campus, and its design is perfectly responsive to one of our needs. The culture of our campus is notoriously decentralized. It is easy to be anonymous in the big city that is our campus. Exemplifying how decentralized the culture is, my relatively large department (approximately 35 full-time faculty members) does not even hold faculty meetings (5 people are elected to advise the chair). My role in general education offered the first opportunities I had to engage in the campus community outside my department and college.

One positive aspect of doing university-level work is meeting great colleagues from across the campus; knowing that our general education assessment plan could fill this need and desire for more connection across the disciplinary "boundaries" that have limited our mindful (and even physical) exploration of the university became an exciting prospect. Thus, we may have enhanced the sustainability of the assessment plan by offering it in a collaborative format that has the simple value of just bringing people together. Is it too Pollyannaish to imagine general education assessment becoming a favorite social event?

Once again, we revisit the analogy and extract the themes of this section. Just as variety enhances the appeal of a box of chocolates, a variety of assessment techniques can make the process more palatable to more people. High content standards, complemented by flexibility in process, allow people to tailor assessment to best meet their own needs. Thus, a few valuable lessons here are:

1. Make the goals of assessment authentically relevant to the lives of students and faculty.
2. Facilitate assessment processes that allow experts to focus on what they do best.
3. Create mechanisms for flexibility in the methods of assessment as more and more people are invited into the process.

Packaging Is Important to the Sale

Assessment on college campuses has a sordid history, and it is fairly easy to find someone with a traumatic tale to tell. It is wise to respect that this reputation is well deserved. The nature of the assessment beast comes prepackaged with suspicion. When an institution fails to meet its goals, who will be blamed (or worse, punished) when precious resources are next doled out? Assessment can even merit contempt when it's *not* used. Faculty have logged many hours in good faith fulfilling "unfunded mandates" from administrations for which assessment reports are dutifully filed but never result in any apparent value or change. Campuses that have horror stories of their own should strive for assessment designs that provide transparent measures that conspicuously circumvent the causes of prior failures.

In addition, there are many notoriously bad ways to open a conversation about assessment. For instance, it may be the case that the administration wants assessment done because of an impending accreditation visit. This is a practical reason, but if it's the primary reason given, the assessment will probably not be genuine. We don't do our best work when it's done because someone is watching. And what happens when the specter of the accreditation agency leaves? Not much, perhaps. And so every 7 years we reignite the boom-and-bust cycle of assessment that may never get us closer to its intended true value: the informed design of pedagogy that most effectively meets our students' needs.

Our SAGE model is grounded in a simple question. The fundamental question we pose to engage faculty in the process of assessment is "What do you want to know about what your students are achieving?" We like the simple universal appeal of the question; all faculty are invested in student achievement. This question is the central driver of our assessment design. In our collaborative track design, it is the centerpiece of the faculty learning community.

Superficially, it may seem obvious to point out that we need to focus purposefully on student learning. Of course that's the focus. However, we found that, on close inspection, our intention didn't align with practice. We had been distracted by many tangents that distracted us from the work we should have been doing. In many previous attempts at assessment, we exhausted our limited time as we got caught up in policy tweaking. Policy is important, but shouldn't policy be driven by what we learn from assessment, not the starting point for assessment? How else would you know when the policy tweaking was successful? At other times, we debated what we knew about student achievement by looking at grades, even though invariably the conversation would degrade into dissatisfaction about the limitations of the value of grades as achievement indexes. In my opinion, during our most enjoyable attempts at assessing student learning, we were focusing on syllabi. Syllabi are useful for defining intent and priorities. And, of course, we can have a stimulating debate about outcomes and mission statements. However, syllabi alone cannot convey how those ideas translate into student perform-ance. To know about student learning, we must look directly at student performance.

Let's review the themes of this principle. Packaging is essential to any product, whether something tangible like chocolates or abstract like assess-ment. The messages regarding the purposes of assessment should resonate with the unique audience that is your campus community. As you build those messages, consider the following suggestions:

1. Develop a long-term vision for assessment that fits the unique needs and desires of the campus. Provide clear reasons why student achieve-ment of essential skills is a vital mission of assessment. Make clear why the essential skills are truly essential.
2. Develop and disseminate a common language about assessment that fits your vision. Do not assume that people are already equipped with that language, and take proactive steps to share the language to facilitate communication.

3. Focus the message on what you want students to achieve. If the message is inclusive and has wide appeal, it should have an impact on a number of your constituencies: students, faculty, staff, administrators, parents, accrediting agencies, and so on.

Chocolates Are Best Shared and Are Often Given as a Gift in Celebration of Special Occasions

Our general education program assessment plan is designed to identify the bright spots in the curriculum. We know, intuitively, that there are many good things happening on our campus. Part of what we would consider a successful assessment program for our campus is documenting those successes and sharing them with the campus community. This highlighting of success is crucial at all points in the assessment cycle, and arguably most crucial at initial stages, when it is important to establish that assessment is not the academic synonym for bad news. Assessment implies an aspect of troubleshooting, including a methodical process for distinguishing what works well from what might not be working well.

Despite my use of the box-of-chocolates analogy, I do not advocate sugarcoating issues to avoid addressing what needs to be improved (and there is always room for improvement). Programs, like students, benefit greatly from constructive feedback about ways to improve, and assessment reports should address patterns of weakness that are emerging. Even celebration should occur in moderation, and assessment results should address both strengths and weaknesses in a program. My point is that assessment carries some major baggage, including people's fears that assessment is merely a tactic to point fingers and lay blame for some (real or perceived) failure. There are valid reasons for this fear, and breaking this pattern requires proactive intervention. Use assessment in an open, transparent way that directly combats fear and suspicion. Programs should be lauded for identifying and effectively addressing weaknesses. Reward good work, and make that good work a reward in itself. Our colleagues liked the idea of the general education assessment efforts resulting in some form of electronic portfolio, a shared showcase of good ideas (e.g., distinctive teaching practices). This portfolio, to be maintained by the GE Governing Committee, provides us with a tangible goal that will require good stewardship of assessment data.

What major themes emerge here? Chocolates are associated with celebration, and so too should some aspects of assessment. Celebrate wisely; do not whitewash problem areas, but rather reward those who confront those problems and seek manageable, effective solutions that benefit the university and its citizens. Consider steps like the following:

1. Regularly share good news about assessment, even, or especially, during groundbreaking phases. Remember, good news comes in many

forms; the point is to validate the process and participation in it. When we made conceptual breakthroughs based on feedback we had received from the campus, we made a point of publicly thanking our colleagues for their cooperation and input. Be sincerely grateful when gratitude is due.

2. Find good news (even when you have to look hard for it), because momentum is based on tangible successes.

3. Be patient and learn to celebrate small victories as long as they are in the direction you want to head. Having a positive impact on the learning that takes place even in one course can have a profound effect on many students over time. Water those green spots, and showcase them where cross-fertilization may occur.

4. In assessment reporting, purposefully ask people to explain what is working well and how the work that they are doing makes a unique contribution to the experience of the university.

Chocolates Can Satisfy a Real Hunger

Reflecting on all the lessons I've learned so far about assessment, I wondered if I could pinpoint a particular piece of advice that truly shifted the way I conceptualized the design of the general education assessment plan. Though there have been many defining moments, my favorite piece of advice was posed to me in the form of a challenge from an overwhelmed and, despite or because of that, very insightful associate dean. He asked me, "Is there anything you can take *off* our plates, anything you can simplify?" It is a sincere and profound question worthy of serious consideration. In a world of endless information and demands on our time, could big, bad assessment be anything but another thing to do, let alone a process that takes something away? In thinking about the associate dean's challenge, I recognized that a pro-assessment culture could best be fostered by the design of an assessment process that fulfills a conspicuous need for the campus. When it came to general education, our campus was starving for a simpler course review process. Simply put, we needed to streamline the governance procedures.

Streamlining should be tailored for the individual campus. For our campus, streamlining was represented in two primary ways. First, a primary innovative aspect of SAGE's collaborative track is that it takes the burden of assessment data collection and analysis off the shoulders of individual faculty members and gives that responsibility to the GE Governing Committee. Second, the role of the GE Governing Committee is being recast. Although we cannot fully shed our gatekeeper mantle, we can use our position to offer valuable services to our faculty colleagues. As we search for the bright spots in the curriculum, we can be keepers of faculty wisdom. We recognize that, for its health and well-being as an institutional process, SAGE must produce tangible results that make our work lives more efficient and rewarding.

Once more, let's consider our analogy. What lessons does hunger provide about assessment? The work we often find most frustrating is that which fails to move us toward our goals. In other words, we loathe tasks that do not give us satisfaction—the sense that our time was well spent. Use assessment as you would other assignments, such that tasks fulfill a need or desire. Take into account the following suggestions:

1. Strategically use prevalent campus needs to inform the design of assessment programs.
2. Streamline the assessment process. Every task should have an obvious purpose. Honor the faculty workload in a genuine way, and people genuinely respond.

Concluding Remarks

So, can assessment really be like a box of chocolates? Or am I literally and figuratively sugarcoating a task that must be dreaded, an unfunded mandate from the administration that has no worth, except to measure the shortcomings of faculty? It seems certain to me that we won't find true value in any process that is framed in a negative way, so why not associate assessment with things we like? I think my positive attitude toward assessment has helped me stay focused on the work that needs to get done, and to discover viable ways to do it. My positive attitude has enabled me to develop personal skills and the disposition necessary to champion assessment. I have learned to be very patient, to be a good listener, to sincerely want to help my colleagues and students succeed, and to be persistent (even on days when I didn't want to be). However, I urge a strong note of caution here. Linking assessment to a box of chocolates does not imply that assessment is easy. I have endured angry meetings where people resisted and feared assessment, and I've had to return and continue to address their concerns. I have faced many of the common misconceptions about assessment (e.g., "We give grades, and that's enough"), and I have had to develop compelling answers to those points. I've been accused of being a sellout to the administration and told I would never be considered faculty again (that one really hurt, but again I had to show, and do so sincerely, that the charge was wrong). And when I started working on general education assessment, we really had nowhere to go but up. I mentioned that the GE Governing Committee consented to the moratorium in part because we were seeing the first wave of course assessment reports, and many were meaningless. Here are a few examples. One report read in full, "Amazing improvements in vocabulary, diction, confidence in engaging texts and expressing opinions and positions." No data. No methods. Another, from a colleague who wanted to provocatively spotlight the flaws in the process, read, "In meeting with myself, as the only instructor of record, I came to conclude that I had done a pretty good job the first time around."

Our reframing of assessment as a useful, manageable endeavor is fueling a genuine culture shift in general education on the CSULB campus that intends to provide meaningful coherence to our general education curriculum. SAGE, our comprehensive plan for outcomes-based accountability, represents a significant new direction for general education that will be refined and expanded for several years to come. The general education program will now be included in program review on a regular schedule and will submit yearly annual reports on assessment, as all other academic programs do. In addition, the new procedures will substantially strengthen the capacity of the GE Governing Committee to promote educational effectiveness. GE Governing Committee members will now be informed experts on general education and its learning goals, and the committee will be able to gather data that allow us to put a finger on the pulse of what is happening in general education as an entire program.

We still have a long way to go, and SAGE is still in the early rounds of implementation. But the path on which we are now headed is aimed precisely at what we want general education to provide for our students. And we've come a long way. While finishing this chapter, I attended a curriculum committee meeting of one of the colleges. Members had invited the GE Governing Committee chair and me to provide an update on SAGE, as well as to answer a few questions that they had. (We've done outreach to all campus constituencies that would allow us to do so: curriculum committees of each of the seven colleges; individual departments, particularly ones with many general education courses; faculty councils; faculty professional development workshops; the Academic Senate and the Senate Executive Committee; the associate deans; the Senior Management Council; Associated Students; etc.). At this latest meeting with the curriculum committee, we enjoyed a very collegial, stimulating discussion about student learning in general education. Members of the curriculum committee stated that they *like* the potential of SAGE and are looking forward to its continuation. Two years ago, members of this college committee said it would never work (for all the reasons that assessment has failed in the past). At this latest meeting, I was thinking, "Oh my goodness, we have created buy-in; now it's time to fulfill the promise of the plan." As the name of the Association of American Colleges and Universities' initiative clearly suggests, we are LEAPing forward!

How do you modify the inner workings and culture of a massive institution with minimal resources and even less authority (other than general education course approval), and thousands and thousands of talented people busy doing other things? It has been as though we are on a bullet train headed at top speed in one direction, and we are trying to create friction by waving our arms out the window. Our power is in the message. Our plans and our conversations focus fully on what essential skills we want our students to have, what students can actually do, and the faculty wisdom that gets them there. Our assessment is based on a process of discovery guided thoughtfully by the folks who are most intrinsically invested in its potential to explain why and how students succeed. These efforts are expected to facilitate, for the first time in the history of our campus, a common understanding among faculty and students of what general education is intended to add to the development of well-educated individuals.

Note

1. We did allow for a process of review through "curricular emergencies"—such as the hiring of a new faculty member who was promised that she would teach a new course—but it turned out that over the 2 years, the campus was very respectful of the moratorium, and these were fairly infrequent.

About the Author

Lisa Maxfield received her Ph.D. in cognitive neuroscience from Syracuse University in 1995. She is now a professor of psychology at California State University, Long Beach. Her cognition research interests are in human memory and language processing. Since 2005, she has been the general education coordinator at CSULB, a role that has afforded her opportunities to work on issues of assessment, program review, first-year experience programs, and accreditation. Her research now includes investigations of student success, particularly as it relates to traditionally underrepresented students and first-generation students. She is also currently involved with the Association of American Colleges and Universities' Compass Project. She serves as a member of the Substantive Change Committee of the Western Association of Schools and Colleges, Senior Colleges and Universities.

2

ASSESSMENT

Legacy, Culture, and Vision

Lynn Lester and Kate Hendel
Clarke College

Clarke College is a Catholic coeducational liberal arts college founded in 1843 by the Sisters of Charity of the Blessed Virgin Mary in Dubuque, Iowa. Clarke educates approximately 1,250 students at the postsecondary level in the liberal arts and sciences, the fine arts, selected professional programs, and graduate programs. Students come primarily from rural communities and towns within a 100-mile radius of the city. The college mission and Blessed Virgin Mary core values of education, freedom, charity, and justice inspire and guide the work of the Clarke College community. The legacy of Mary Frances Clarke, founder of the Sisters of Charity of the Blessed Virgin Mary and Clarke College, is claimed and celebrated by the community of learners and is reflected in her words to the community in 1885: "Leave the future to God. I have no fears, so long as you are working unitedly but that He will aid us as in the past." Remaining faithful to this sacred trust in the 21st century has challenged this community to even more intentionally unite its forces and engage in deeper reflection about and active responses to the global society of which it is a part.

Assessment is not unlike an unexpected legacy that one inherits from an unknown deceased relative—its arrival catches one off guard, its value is not readily apparent or understood, and its usefulness is questionable, at best! When the position of director of general education was created to facilitate and coordinate a newly developed liberal arts program, assessment simply became one more step in an already complicated arena of exploration and implementation of program components. At the same time, an outcomes-based assessment program was initiated for all major programs, and a director of assessment was appointed to provide support for continual implementation and improvement of the institution's academic evaluation and assessment practices. The director of assessment was also appointed chairperson of the Strategic Planning Committee and, as such, ensured that the program review process was an integral part of the college's evolving culture of assessment and strategic planning processes.

The self-study and subsequent comprehensive visit by the Higher Learning Commission of the North Central Association, which occurred almost simultaneously with the new appointments, provided these two directors with increased motivation to accept this inheritance with grace and to act expeditiously. Since their respective appointments, the director of general education and the director of assessment have become partners in their efforts to enhance and ensure the quality of assessment processes and ultimately to realize their common vision for student achievement. To assist these efforts, an assessment committee was established in 2004, and a general education advisory council in 2006.

Assessment practices of outcomes-based major and general education programs at Clarke College were conceived at different times and developed in different ways and progressed at different rates over time. However, because 17 out of 19 academic departments teach general education courses along with major courses, there have been many common efforts to learn about and implement effective assessment processes. Peggy Maki's book *Assessing for Learning: Building a Sustainable Commitment Across the Institution* (2004) was adopted as a guide for advancing a culture of assessment across academic programs. From fall 2003 through spring 2006, faculty participated in workshops that focused on writing student-centered outcomes based on Bloom's taxonomy, designing course syllabi that integrated department and course outcomes with assignment and assessment tools for measuring outcomes, creating authentic rubrics and performance products, and developing curriculum maps. These assessment workshops were key components in advancing a culture of assessment across academic programs and served as first steps for building faculty confidence and buy-in for new assessment processes.

By spring 2006, it had become apparent that faculty needed a forum designed specifically for the study, discussion, and practice of assessment; thus an assessment day was initiated. This forum, held each semester, has clearly enhanced the assessment skills of faculty and promoted the culture of assessment that permeates Clarke College today.

Assessment in General Education

In 2004, when the new general education program was initiated, faculty members had little or no outcomes-based assessment experience. Although many attended assessment workshops sponsored by Laverne College in Milwaukee, Clarke's academic and general education programs were significantly different and required a different approach. Consequently, the design of effective and efficient assessment processes has evolved as a byproduct of 5 years of trial and error, with attention to continual improvement shaped by formative assessments made at every step of the way.

The three-tiered design of the Clarke College general education program—consisting of foundational, divisional, and capstone levels—provided a structure in which general education outcomes were mapped and institutional assessment was tracked at designated points over time. At first the idea of matching the three-tiered program with three assessment levels—introductory, reinforced, and emphasized—appeared simple. Not true! Assessment at each level of the general education program required different approaches for measuring the four general education outcomes: writing, speaking, thinking, and spirituality. From the outset, it was obvious that general education outcomes would be assessed at the introductory level in the foundational core courses of the three disciplines (religious studies, philosophy, and cornerstone) that comprise that level. The cornerstone course focused on the communication outcomes of writing and speaking, philosophy attended to the thinking outcome, and religious studies addressed the spirituality outcome. Although this approach seemed straightforward, the faculty required time to learn to measure the newly created outcomes and implement the untested rubrics. Consequently, it was 2 years before reliable assessment results could even be expected.

Preliminary results of the assessment of writing provided a process on which many future assessments were modeled, including faculty-determined assignments, directions for establishing reliability, reporting forms and sampling guidelines, time lines for assessment (scoring, submission, and analysis), and subsequent reporting in the general education end-of-year report and sharing results with faculty. Finally, a general education curricular map was developed that documented the results of this evolutionary process and subsequent adaptations (see Appendix A at the end of this chapter).

While faculty teaching divisional courses at the reinforcement level waited for cohorts who had been introduced to the outcomes in foundational courses, they experimented with assessing the knowledge outcome at the divisional level. Divisional courses are designed to augment skills, knowledge, and values introduced in foundational courses and to broaden a knowledge base. Collectively, the two levels, foundational and divisional courses, were intended to provide students with opportunities to explore and integrate content within the skills (cornerstone) course; in religious studies and philosophy courses, which reflect the charisma of Mary Frances Clarke and its Catholic heritage; and in the fine arts, humanities, math and natural sciences, and social sciences divisions.

The four divisions identified desired outcomes and specific courses in which those outcomes would be achieved. An attempt to assess the general education knowledge outcome through divisional outcomes met with resounding failure. Outcomes were clearly too disparate to be compared across disciplines in each division and, consequently, a common assessment was declared impossible. However, the recognition that the divisional outcomes served as guidelines for how divisions proposed and selected coursework that would promote breadth and integration of knowledge was a byproduct of this otherwise feeble attempt at assessment. Moreover, it was decided that divisions would participate in institutional assessment by reinforcing general education outcomes (writing, speaking, thinking, or spirituality) and using the corresponding rubrics to support the acquisition of content knowledge.

Once two student cohorts had successfully navigated the foundational waters of the general education program, in which outcomes and corresponding rubrics were introduced, similar processes were implemented to assess reinforcement in courses at the divisional level. This new layer of assessment was not without its challenges. With more than 50 general education courses per semester, each requiring the services of a second scorer and specific reporting procedures as well as faculty readiness to use and apply the designated rubric, this proved unwieldy and burdensome. The first attempt to simplify the process involved the selection of a few courses from each division and the implementation of a 2-year rotation assessment schedule. This corrective measure was well received, but in an effort to establish reasonable limits, the adaptation created inequity among faculty, as some participated each semester, and some never participated. Furthermore, institutional assessments were becoming redundant rather than providing a variety of alternative forms of assessment at the reinforcement level. Finally, questions surfaced about whether or not information gleaned from these assessments actually informed instruction and improved student learning in meaningful ways.

With this in mind, a pilot study for assessing how general education outcomes were achieved in divisional courses was developed. This pilot study was based upon the premise that each general education divisional course includes at least one general education outcome, and a corresponding rubric is used for course assessment of one or more designated assignments. The new divisional assessment process eliminated the need for second scorers but requires instructors to review the assessment results and report on how well outcomes are achieved, where weaknesses lie, and what strategies will be used to address the areas of concern when the course is taught again. The reporting form was purposely limited to one page in order to promote specific, focused assessment and recommendations for improvement (see Appendix B at the end of this chapter).

In fall 2008, four faculty members teaching general education divisional courses piloted this new simplified process. When they submitted their findings, they indicated that they found the process simple and informative. In fact, some reported that they not only modified the assignment and syllabus for the course designated for this assessment but also made changes in other courses they taught. With this preliminary affirmation of the new process, it was expanded to all divisional general education courses in spring 2009 with the intention that the process would be reviewed and recommendations for further modification for implementation would be made in fall 2009.

Finally, the assessment of general education outcomes at the capstone level was initiated in spring 2006. Having learned from the efforts to assess divisional outcomes, faculty decided that the assessment must be a common assignment that students complete in major department capstones. Representatives from among the faculty assigned to teach capstone courses met and designed one required assignment for all capstone courses. Issues relating to the credit assigned for course grades, methods of preparation, and instructor review were also discussed. All agreed that the credit allocated for the common capstone assignment would range from 10% to 20% of the final grade, the rubric would be reviewed in at least one class period, and instructors would review a draft of the artifact one time before final submission. Capstone instructors would grade the assignment independently for course purposes, and the artifact would be submitted to the director of general education, who would prepare a random sample set of artifacts for scoring by all full-time faculty on assessment day.

With each assessment day from 2006 to 2008, it became increasingly clear that assessing every outcome in a single assignment for the purposes of institutional assessment was cumbersome, time consuming, inconclusive, and inauthentic. Balancing the values of faculty ownership and shared responsibility for assessment of general education outcomes with their uneven knowledge of and competence in scoring the artifacts was a major challenge. Despite these flaws, there is little doubt that the assessment of capstone artifacts on assessment day has provided rich opportunities for faculty to share perspectives and new learning about assessment. Faculty also developed skills for establishing interrater reliability in scoring with the rubrics. However, the question of whether we are improving instruction and student learning through this process remains. The frustration of dealing with this issue has led the college's assessment committee to seriously study an external assessment, the College Learning Assessment, an action that would have been unthinkable in the design and early implementation phase of the general education program. Even if the College Learning Assessment is selected to assess the communication, thinking, and integration-of-knowledge outcomes, how the institution will address the assessment of its spirituality outcome remains an issue to be resolved.

As stated earlier, these assessment processes were, in fact, a byproduct of 5 years of trial and error with serious attention to continual improvement. The following list summarizes some of the major accomplishments over the past 4 years:

1. Development and implementation of proficiency assessments and reporting processes
2. Implementation and use of rubrics for assessing general education outcomes
3. Improvement of instruction resulting from assessment of communication outcomes
4. Collection of baseline data for introductory-level assessments
5. Development of a cycle and process for assessing thinking skills and spirituality at the introductory and reinforcement levels
6. Collection of baseline data at the reinforcement level that documents positive progress in students' thinking skills and some development in students' perspectives about spirituality
7. Simplification of approaches and procedures to assess general education outcomes at the divisional level
8. Engagement of faculty across all disciplines in using and applying rubrics and developing skills for scoring artifacts for the purpose of interrater reliability
9. Creation, design, and implementation of programs and services to improve students' learning as they begin their college careers

These accomplishments demonstrate a strong emphasis on addressing the needs of first-year students, skill development and knowledge acquisition in foundational courses, and selected broad programmatic assessment initiatives. Over the past 5 years, comments from faculty have consistently focused on what students don't know when they begin upper-level coursework. Clearly, these remarks motivated the director of general education and her colleagues to focus and work proactively to improve the services and programs at matriculation and at the foundational level of the general education program. Data reveal that progress has been made in the provision of program components to address these issues, for example, in the Smart Start Program for underprepared students, the Advantage Program for entering honors students, and the writing and skills lab for students scoring low on the writing assessment at entrance. These initiatives and assessment data at the divisional level document in some measure—albeit small—that student learning has improved.

Not all initiatives have been successful or warrant continuation as currently articulated, and there are two issues that require substantive work and attention in the near future. They are general education rubrics and the capstone course. The general education rubrics have served the entire academic community as models and useful tools across the curriculum; however, it is time to review and simplify them. Equally importantly is the need for substantive reform of the capstone course itself. The intent of the capstone course, when it was implemented, was to provide students with a culminating integrative experience in which both general education outcomes and major outcomes would be assessed. At this time, most major capstone courses are senior seminars with a general education common assignment add-on. Although a few departments have made significant efforts to develop a capstone course that reflects the original intent, most have not. Consequently, the general education 2009–2014 strategic plan calls for establishing a task force, or using a standing committee such as the assessment committee, to explore and develop creative capstone designs and provide planning forums for engaging departments in a process that leads to redesigned capstone courses. Because capstone courses are only partially within the realm of general education, it is important that this process take place in a forum in which both general education and major department perspectives are represented.

From cornerstone to capstone, from planning to implementation, from outcomes and rubrics to data-informed decision making, this has been the picture of the assessment of the general education program at Clarke College over the past 5 years. Clarke College faculty, staff, and administrators have continued to work diligently to provide the necessary resources and to ensure that collaboration and substance characterize the general education program. As 2009 unfolds, the college community celebrates its successful assessment efforts in its general education program at the introductory level; continues to modify and streamline divisional-level assessment; and, like so many other institutions, continues to struggle with assessment at the capstone level.

Program Assessment in Major Departments

Major program outcomes and program reviews have been in place in academic departments at Clarke College for over 20 years; however, formalized and institutionalized assessment processes appeared only after an outcomes-based assessment program was initiated in fall 2003. As described previously, faculty began outcomes-based assessment by participating in a wide variety of professional development activities focused on the acquisition of the skills necessary for assessing general education outcomes. By fall 2006, academic departments had integrated the general education outcomes assessment model into major academic departments and programs. Within a year, systematic processes for advancing structured assessment plans were incorporated into major programs. Clearly, the comprehensive nature of the major program assessment processes has changed significantly and a culture of assessment has emerged.

Key to advancing this culture was the decision to devote one day each semester to assessment activities to further develop and refine assessment plans and processes. For example, on the first assessment day in spring 2006, goals were focused on improving program assessment procedures, policies, and plans. In morning sessions, selected faculty presented models of best practices in planning assessment. In afternoon sessions, departments adapted these models, establishing 3-year assessment plans for collecting, assessing, and reporting outcome data on student performance.

Subsequent assessment days provided time for breakout sessions and major department meetings. Activities up to the present have included designing specific elements of assessment plans and refining elements currently in place. Sample activities have included the following:

1. Aligning department mission, goals, and outcomes with institutional mission, goals, and desired outcomes
2. Refining student-centered measurable course outcomes
3. Adjusting curriculum maps to define when and where course outcomes are measured at introductory, reinforced, and emphasized levels
4. Designing course products and performances to match rubrics' performance indicators
5. Adjusting 3-year cycles for measuring department outcomes

At this point in time all academic departments have incorporated these five elements in their assessment plans.

In almost all departments, establishing reliability and validity of outcome data added complexity to the assessment process. The absence of reliable and valid data made meaningful and informed decision making impossible. Time and personnel were obstacles to the application of inter-rater reliability processes to department rubrics and the scoring of student performances. Ten academic departments had four or fewer members. Thus the dual-rater reliability process was time intensive. Several departments made progress toward analyzing data for driving pedagogical and curricular change to improve student achievement, and this continues to improve.

Each year department chairs complete an end-of-year report on progress achieved during the previous academic year. These reports include:

1. Department mission statement aligned with college mission
2. Department mission goals aligned with college goals
3. Desired program/department outcomes aligned with college outcome

4. Three-year cycle and time line aligned with program curriculum map
5. Statement of outcomes assessed during the current academic year
6. Assessment questions based on desired learning outcomes
7. Data on students, courses, assignments, and assessment tools
8. Data analysis, conclusions, and decisions processes
9. Actions planned to improve student performance
10. Time line for implementing action plans
11. Communication channels for closing the assessment loop
12. Pedagogical and curricular changes to improve student achievement

End-of-year reports are informed by course syllabi, curriculum maps, data reporting procedures, and rubrics. To standardize data reporting, a guide and model are included in materials distributed to departments. Sample questions provide direction for departments in reporting assessment processes, results, and future action plans; for example, departments' reports should include answers to the following questions:

1. What learning outcomes were measured?
2. What assessment tools were used to measure student performance?
3. What data were collected?
4. What decisions were made as a result of data analysis?
5. What actions were planned to improve student performance?

Methods for reviewing end-of-year reports and responding to departments have been standardized and continue to be applied at this time. The reports are reviewed independently by the director of assessment and the provost, and feedback is discussed with each department chair. The director of assessment completes an analysis of assessment processes and results in the end-of-year department reports and prepares an executive summary for review by the vice president of academic affairs as well as the assessment committee. This report provides direction for planning and achieving assessment goals during the next academic year as well as planning activities for assessment day. At the end of 5 years, each department prepares a program review that includes data gathered over that period of time. Annual end-of-year reports for the previous 5 years are examined. This yields evidence of trends and issues that have emerged during this period of time.

In addition to the significant change that has fostered the development of Clarke College's culture of assessment, these practices have produced a new legacy, namely, improvements in instruction and student learning, integration of the program review process into institutional strategic planning, and the introduction of assessment in student life programs. Clarke College has had many success stories; the following four examples were selected to represent the pervasive culture of assessment and how it influences decision making in every sector of the institution.

Example 1: Writing

The advancement of writing competency is an outcome goal that is embraced by most colleges and universities, and certainly Clarke College. Although the institution does not have a formal writing-across-the-curriculum program, there is growing awareness of and attentiveness to teaching and reinforcing writing. In a recent end-of-year report, the mathematics department stated, "We need [to] tighten up our plan for teaching writing as part of the mathematics curriculum. We will need to identify what is specifically germane to mathematical writing and to be sure we are teaching these skills and holding our students accountable for them all the time." To address this need, the department envisions that students will be given a writing guide in Calculus II. This guide will be referred to and writing will be assessed in each subsequent mathematics course. These initiatives will help shape the ongoing development of the rubric, and it will be used to assess requirements for the final paper in the mathematics department capstone course.

Example 2: Psychology

In the Psychology of Personality course, 16 class periods were devoted to instruction about 16 separate personality theories. After the lecture phase of the course, acquisition of knowledge was assessed in formal student presentations of theoretical-application papers on a designated personality theory. Approximately 5 weeks had transpired between the last lecture on the 16th theory and the assessment. Originally, the department made the decision to treat the assessment as a form of cumulative evaluation. In retrospect, the time delay between when the students heard the lecture and the assessment may have been too long and contributed to the students' poor performance.

Example 3: Program Review Process

As previously indicated, academic program reports are submitted to the Strategic Planning Committee for review on a 5-year cycle. As Clarke College's assessment processes have become more structured and reporting more standardized, the program review process has been revised and improved. Program review documents are now examined by a three-member subcommittee of the Strategic Planning Committee appointed by the chairperson and provost. The peer evaluators study the document in depth, meet with department faculty to pose questions and solicit clarifications, and present preliminary findings and recommendations to the full planning committee, at which time additional comments and suggestions are made. The report evaluation is finalized at a meeting of the Strategic Planning Committee and department chair, and subsequently submitted to the provost, who shares the recommendations with the department chair and to the president for final action.

This interactive process has heightened awareness of the importance of each step in the overall assessment process and prompted greater appreciation for how these assessments shape the department's story and vision. Furthermore, departments gain an understanding of how their work advances the purposes of the whole institution. This cycle of continuous improvement represents how assessment data at the course, department/program, and institutional levels are utilized to inform decisions, and thereby close the loop (see Figure 2.1).

Example 4: Student Life Assessment

After the initial steps of developing general education and academic program assessment processes, the vice president for student life challenged the staff to articulate desired learning outcomes appropriate to cocurricular departments. In 2005, Clarke College student life staff embarked on a unique process in which the missions and goals of the institution and the student life department were aligned, and desired outcomes with corresponding rubrics were designed. Seven student learning outcomes capturing the personal and social dimensions of student development were identified:

1. Self-understanding
2. Self-confidence
3. Leadership skills
4. Personal code of ethics
5. Spiritual values
6. Respect for people of different ethnic and cultural backgrounds
7. Skills and behaviors needed to achieve personal and professional goals

The staff developed a 3-year cycle for formal assessment of the seven learning outcomes for institutional assessment to supplement the informal, indirect assessment of the outcomes that occurs regularly in the Office of Student Life.

In spring 2006, seven of the eight areas of student life (athletics, campus ministry, career services, health services, multicultural student services, and student activities) engaged in the first attempt to assess learning related to the first outcome, self-understanding. Each division of student life selected a program or activity in which to assess this outcome, using the corresponding rubric.

FIGURE 2.1
Assessment Cycle for Continuous Improvement at Clarke College

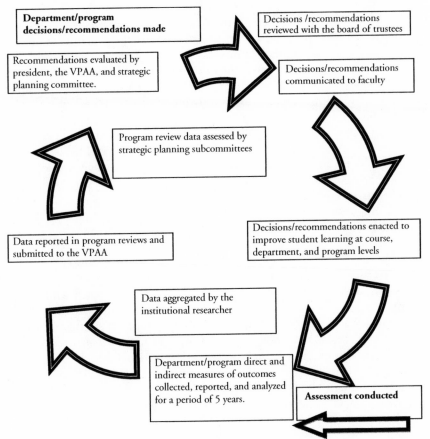

- The softball and basketball teams used the end-of-season evaluation based on multiple variables. The campus ministry employed post-service trip reflective essays.
- Career services synthesized reflections derived from internship experiences.
- Health services used a national screening inventory and correlated specific outcomes to categories of the self-understanding rubric.
- Multicultural student services surveyed Kwanzaa leaders.
- Student activities administered a self-assessment tool to class, club, and organization leaders.

- The counseling center compiled information gleaned from client exit interviews.

It was not surprising that the personal nature of self-understanding had an impact on the types of assessment used. Consequently, the direct quantitative measurements were informed by indirect measures and qualitative interviews. Student life department directors reviewed assessments in their respective areas, using rubrics, and collected and analyzed data. In addition to making recommendations for improving student services and refining student life outcomes and rubrics, staff also examined and evaluated methods used and issues related to validity and reliability that surfaced in this first experience with assessment. Like the faculty who first attempted assessment of program outcomes, the student life staff discovered that they learned more about the assessment process than about development of student self-understanding (see Appendix C at the end of this chapter).

During 2006–2007, two student life outcomes—self-confidence and leadership skills—were assessed through the use of corresponding rubrics. Student gains in self-confidence were identified in campus ministry, career services, the counseling center, and student activities. Campus ministry activities that centered on team building resulted in heightened awareness of and openness to diversity while challenging students to interact with people and situations previously foreign to them. "It taught me that community organizing is everything; . . . that we can teach each other; . . . that education is out there, but it is a choice." Career services noted an increase in self-confidence following mock interviews in which students used a self-reporting tool to report the impact of their experiences. On a 5-point scale, scores increased from 2.8 to 4.2 over a period of a year. The counseling center reported that all but three students who attended four or more counseling sessions increased their self-confidence, raising their scores on most indicators of the self-confidence rubric. Student leaders who used the self-confidence rubric indicated that serving as an officer had contributed to their confidence and leadership skills. Collectively, self-confidence ratings were high (3.6 on a 4-point scale), and the qualitative comments included in the assessment supported the data.

While assessing leadership skills, the student life offices that work directly with student leaders—namely, campus ministry, career services, multicultural student services, residence life, and student activities—assumed responsibility for conducting the assessments. Growth over all categories of the leadership rubric was noted in each student life area; however, two specific leadership qualities surfaced consistently: level of cooperation and openness to feedback. This was particularly true among younger leaders in the first and second years who worked more closely with staff. It appears that staff might be operating under the assumption that upper-class students require less direction. Consequently, providing all student leaders with more frequent or more regular meetings or opportunities to exchange ideas and observations with experienced staff was identified as a need in the action plans of all student life departments.

Program changes in the multicultural center and residence life have focused mostly on student employees. Responding to assessment results related to the self-confidence of these students, staff developed systematic strategies to acclimate new employees to the work setting while simultaneously building their self-confidence. These included (1) a newly designed first-day-of-employment orientation; (2) goal-setting, self-assessment, and evaluation meetings with an employer at designated periods (2 weeks into employment and in the seventh week of employment); (3) regularly scheduled individual and group meetings between student employees and employers focusing on leadership development and providing more in-depth training; and (4) the use of sociograms as part of the employee effectiveness evaluation in residence life.

The summary of this first-ever formal assessment of student learning outcomes in student life revealed specific areas in which the ways that the student life staff assists students in developing greater self-understanding, self-confidence, and leadership skills, as well the assessment process itself, could be improved. Recommendations based on the analysis of assessment data included:

1. Communicating learning expectations to student participants in a more deliberate manner
2. Modifying current assessment practices to ensure that future assessment will be more closely aligned with desired learning outcomes
3. Improving the way that student learning outcomes are measured through the use of rubrics and qualitative data
4. Making specific changes in student life programs and activities to ensure that student learning is taking place

As assessment of outcomes in student life increases, communication about the learning outcomes for student life is becoming more pervasive. New approaches and assessment tools are being developed that require students to reflect on and assess their own progress. Student life departments have adopted a wide variety of surveys, pre- and post-tests, and qualitative interviews, as well as adapting existing evaluation tools. The Council for the Advancement of Standards in Higher Education's professional standards have been adapted for program review processes across all student life departments.

These examples are but a few strategies and processes that are being used in student life to review, refine, and inform assessment future practice.

Moreover, these efforts represent tangible ways in which the legacy of assessment has been shared and used to bridge student learning in the academic setting and learning outside the classroom, thus emphasizing the culture of assessment throughout the institution.

Much has happened since 2004, when the general education program was launched and outcomes-based assessment infiltrated the academic major departments across disciplines. The surprising, and perhaps unwelcome, bequest of assessment has become a constant companion to all members of the Clarke College community of learners. In the past 5 years, faculty and staff have produced a new legacy and vision. They have developed the ability to ask and embrace challenging assessment questions and seek alternatives in response to both successful and unsuccessful attempts to engage in meaningful assessment of student learning. This culture of assessment permeates the fabric of how we work together "unitedly" and shapes how we envision a future that ensures Clarke College students are prepared to become academic, moral, and spiritual leaders in our evolving, globally diverse society.

References

Maki, P. (2004). *Assessing for learning: Building a sustainable commitment across the institution.* Sterling, VA: Stylus.

About the Authors

Lynn Lester serves as assessment director of academic departments and is an associate professor of education at Clarke College. Lynn holds an M.A. in teaching mathematics from San Francisco State University, an M.A. in educational computing technology, and an Ed.D. in educational leadership in private school education with a minor in educational computing from the University of San Francisco. She began her teaching career in secondary math education and taught mathematics at St. Paul High School in San Francisco for 24 years. For the last 13 years, she has taught secondary math methods to undergraduates, and educational technology to graduate students at Clarke College. As director of assessment, she conducts faculty development workshops and oversees assessment of learning outcomes across academic departments.

Kate Hendel serves as dean of adult and graduate studies and directs the general education program at Clarke College in Dubuque, Iowa. Kate holds a B.A. in music from Mundelein College, Chicago; an M.M. from Arizona State University; an M.A. in pastoral liturgy from Santa Clara University; and a Ph.D. in music education from Louisiana State University. She began her teaching career in elementary and secondary music education. For most of her 28 years at Clarke College, she served as director of music education and then as Music Department chairperson, with additional service in campus ministry and teaching religious studies and education courses. Serving as a visitor and consultant for the National Association of Schools of Music, as a consultant evaluator for the Higher Learning Commission of the North Central Association, and as director of general education are among the primary experiences that have shaped her work with assessment.

APPENDIX 2.A
Clarke College General Education Curriculum Map

			General Education Courses		General Education Outcomes					
	Dept./No.	Course Title	Credit Hours	Writing	Speaking	Thinking	Spirituality	Breadth of Knowledge
FOUNDATIONAL LEVEL (Introduce/Reinforce)	GNED 110	Cornerstone I	3	I	I			I
	GNED 111	Cornerstone II	3	I	I			
	PHIL 110	Fundamentals of Philosophy	3			I	R	I
	PHIL 212	General Ethics	3			R		I
	PHIL 213	Western Political Thought	3			R		I
	PHIL 225	Applied Ethics	3			R		I
	PHIL 230	Philosophy of Religion	3			R		I
	PHIL 240	Philosophy of Peace and War	3			R		I
	PHIL 250	Asian Philosophy	3			R		
	PHIL 270	Philosophy of Women	3			R		I
	RELS 100	Foundation of the Spiritual Life	3	R			I	I
	RELS 200	Spiritual Growth	3				R	I
	RELS 204	Faith Communities	3				R	I
	RELS 206	Introduction to New Testament	3				R	I
	RELS 208	Sacramental Experience	3				R	I
	RELS 212	Spirituality of Christian Marriage	3				R	I
	RELS 216	Contemporary Catholic Faith	3				R	I
	RELS 218	Ethics for Christian Living	3				R	I
	RELS 219	Faith Development	3				R	I
	RELS 222	Multicultural Faces of Jesus	3				R	I

APPENDIX 2.A (Continued)
Clarke College General Educational Curriculum Map

| | | | General Education Courses | | General Education Outcomes | | | | |
	Dept./No.	Course Title	Credit Hours	Writing	Speaking	Thinking	Spirituality	Breadth of Knowledge
HUMANITIES DIVISION	ENGL 121	Approaches to Literature	3	R				I
	ENGL 215	British Literature	3	R				R
	ENGL 218	American Literature	3		R			R
	ENGL 219	World Literature			R			
	ENGL 222	Short Fiction	3		R			R
	ENGL 231	Literature of Diversity	3	R				R
	ENGL 232	Popular Literature	3	R				R
	PHIL 200	Our BVM and Clarke College Heritage	3			R	R	R
	PHIL 260	Philosophy of Sex and Love	3			R		R
	RELS 210	Biblical Literature	3				R	R
	RELS 220	World Religions	3				R	R
	SPAN 103	Intermediate Spanish I	3	R				R
	SPAN 104	Intermediate Spanish II	3		R			R
	SPAN 111	Span. Convers., Comp. & Grammar	3	R	R			R
	SPAN 112	Adv. Span. Composition & Grammar	3	R				R
	SPAN 160	Latin Am. Literature in Context	3	R				R
	SPAN 235	Civilization of Spain	3	R		R		R
	SPAN 246	Latin American Civilization	3	R		R		R
	SPAN 260	Approaches to Hispanic Lit.	3	R		R		R

APPENDIX 2.A (Continued)
(Continued)Clarke College General Educational Curriculum Map

			General Education Courses	General Education Outcomes				
Division	Dept./No.	Course Title	Credit Hours	Writing	Speaking	Thinking	Spirituality	Breadth of Knowledge
FINE ARTS DIVISION	ART 101	Studio for Non-Majors (hands-on)	3			R		R
	ARHS 133	Art of the Western World I	3	R				R
	ARHS 134	Art of the Western World II	3	R				R
	ART 215	Ceramic Sculpture (hands-on)	3			R		R
	ART 217	Ceramics I (hands-on)	3			R		R
	ARHS 152	Art in the United States	3	R				R
	ARHS 253	PreColumbian Art	3	R				R
	ARHS 257	Renaissance Art	3	R				R
	ARHS 260	African Art	3	R				R
	ARHS 261	Native American Art	3	R				R
	DRMA 108	Oral Interpretation (hands-on)	3		R			R
	DRMA 123	Great Plays Analysis	3	R		R		R
	DRMA 140	Introduction to Theatre	3	R				R
	DRMA 243	Shakespeare I	3			R		R
	DRMA 244	Shakespeare II	3			R		R
	MUSC 105	Chorus (Ensemble) (hands-on)	1		R			R
	MUSC 305	Chorus (Ensemble) (hands-on)	1		R			R
	MUSC 124	Art of Listening	3			R		R
	MUSC 126	Music in World Cultures	3	R				R
	MUSC 225	Music in the United States	3		R	R		R
		"Hands-on" limited to total of 3 hours						

APPENDIX 2.A
Clarke College General Educational Curriculum Map

| | General Education Courses | | | General Education Outcomes | | | | |
	Dept./No.	Course Title	Credit Hours	Writing	Speaking	Thinking	Spirituality	Breadth of Knowledge
MATHEMATICS & NATURAL SCIENCE DIVISION	MATH 110	Math as a Liberal Art	3			I/R		R
	MATH 117	Precalculus with Algebra	4			R		R
	MATH 220	Statistics	3			R		R
	MATH 223	Discrete Mathematics	3			R		R
	MATH 225	Calculus I	4			R		R
	BIOL 101	Introduction to Life Sciences	3	R				R
	BIOL 102	Biology of the Human Body	3	R				R
	BIOL 115	Fundamentals of Cell Biol. & Genetics	4	R				R
	BIOL 116	Diversity and Ecology	4	R	R			R
	BIOL 204	Environmental Biology	4		R			R
	CHEM103	Applied Chemistry: Focus	3	R				R
	CHEM 107	Gen., Organic, & Biochem.	4	R				R
	CHEM 110	General Chemistry I	4	R				R
	CHEM 111	General Chemistry II	4	R				R
	PSYC 101	Physical Science	3			R		R
	PHYS 105	Intro. to Astronomy	3			R		R
	PHYS 110	Elements of Physics I	4			R		R
	PHYS 111	Elements of Physics II	4			R		R
		1 Lab Science Required						

APPENDIX 2.A (Continued)
Clarke College General Educational Curriculum Map

	General Education Courses		General Education Outcomes				
Dept./No.	Course Title	Credit Hours	Writing	Speaking	Thinking	Spirituality	Breadth of Knowledge
BUEC 120	Principles of Economics	3	**R**				**R**
HIST 101	Western Civilization I	**3**		**R**			**R**
HIST 102	Western Civilization II	3		R			R
HIST 107	American Civilization I	3			R		R
HIST 108	American Civilization II	3			R		R
POLI 120	American National Government	3			R		R
POLI 210	Global Challenges	3	R				R
POLI 213	Western Political Thought	3			R		R
PSYC 111	Introduction to Psychology	3	R				R
PSYC 121	Child and Adolescent Psychology	3	R				R
PSYC 122	Adult Development	3	R				R
SOC 101	Introduction to Sociology	3			R		R
SOC 201	Social Issues	3			R		R
SOC 202	Race and Ethnicity	3	R				R

SOCIAL SCIENCE DIVISION

			General Education Outcomes				
Dept./No.	Course Title	Credit Hours	Writing	Speaking	Thinking	Spirituality	Breadth of Knowledge
DEPT 499	Capstone	1–3	E	E	E	E	E

CAPSTONE

APPENDIX 2.B
Divisional Instruction and Assessment of General Education Outcomes
Reinforcement Level

Dept./No.:	Course Title:
Section:	Faculty Name:

Outcome reinforced:	Check only one:	
	Writing	
	Speaking	
	Thinking	
	Spirituality	

Outcome as stated in the syllabus

Outcome assessment artifact (Assign ment) as stated in the syllabus

RUBRIC USED	CHECK ONE	CATEGORIES USED IN THE ASSESSMENT (Check all components of the selected rubr ic that are assessed in this assignment.)						
Writing		Purpose	Audience	Content	Organization	Style	Correctness	
Speaking		Topic Choice	Introduction Conclusion	Organization	Voice	Body	Lang. Skills	
Thinking		Purpose	Information	Reasoning	Creativity			
Spirituality		Life Ques., Beliefs, Values		Life Decisions				

Average Rubric Scores Assigned Artifacts	In spaces below each rubric score, insert the number of students receiving that score on the rubric.						
	4	3.5	3	2.5	2	1	Class Average

After reflecting on the results of this assessment of the general education outcome designated above, briefly comment on one rubric component in which the students demonstrated a reasonable or expected level of success.

After reflecting on the results of this assessment of the general education outcome designated above, briefly comment on one rubric component the students demonstrated a lack of or least developed skills.

Identify one instructional strategy that you will use to assist students to improve in this skill component the next time you teach this course.

APPENDIX 2.C
Student Life Self-Understanding Rubric

Learning Indicators	Self-Understanding			
	Beginning 1	Developing 2	Accomplished 3	Exemplary 4
Increases POSITIVE THOUGHTS	Begins to recognize defeating thought process	Recognizes self-defeating thoughts and explores ways to change those thoughts	Identifies and corrects self-defeating thoughts in a timely manner	Consistently has positive and healthy thoughts
Increases feeling of SELF-CONTROL	Becomes aware of loss of self-control	Recognizes loss of self-control and finds ways to regain control	Is aware of the situations in which loss of control occurs and makes changes to avoid those situations	Consistently feels in control
Increases sense of WELL-BEING	Begins to understand components of well-being	Recognizes ways in which one sabotages one's own sense of well-being	Implements strategies for creating a sense of well-being	Has consistent feelings of well-being
Increases ACCURATE PERCEPTIONS of situations	Begins to understand that we create our own feelings through our perceptions	Recognizes one's own tendencies toward thought distortions and the situations in which they occur	Learns and implements strategies for correcting thought distortions	Consistently has accurate perceptions of situations
Increases HEALTHY AND SATISFYING RELATIONSHIPS	Begins to understand the principles and components of self-defeating patterns of interaction	Recognizes own self-defeating patterns of interaction	Implements correct perceptions and appropriate behavioral changes	Creates positive methods of developing and maintaining healthy and satisfying relationships

3

SOME UNCERTAINTIES EXIST

David A. Eubanks
Coker College

Coker College is a small private liberal arts college in Hartsville, South Carolina. With a day and evening enrollment totaling about 1,100 over four sites, the college offers traditional liberal arts programs as well as professional programs like business, education, criminology, and social work. The mission includes an emphasis on analytical and creative thinking and effective speaking and writing. Coker's accreditation was reaffirmed in 2005 by the Southern Association of Colleges and Schools. Recent institutional expertise in assessment includes systematic documentation for accreditation data, a "simple as possible" ePortfolio system, general education assessment, and helping students bridge the gap in writing expectations from high school to college.

Back in the early 1990s, after the Berlin wall became something to celebrate, but before the age of ubiquitous online computing, I began a career as a math teacher at Coker College, having been newly robed into the ranks of teaching faculty. There certainly is a lot they don't tell you in graduate school. An understanding of things such as rules of order and what committee to join became as important as knowing how old the lettuce in the salad bar was. But in the rearview mirror, before the Assessment Party came to power, with all its talk about accountability, those days seem stress free.

Until recently, when I took a position at Johnson C. Smith University as dean of academic support services, I taught continually for 17 years and always thought of myself as a faculty member first. Slowly, however, I got seduced into more and more administrative work, until I looked up one day and realized that my summer vacations had vanished. I have not yet found my way back into the classroom in my new position, so I tell people I'm the director of exotic plumbing, which comes as close as anything to my actual job description.

However, this account is not really about me, but rather about every professor who encounters learning outcomes assessment for the first time. Each of us has our own stories of survival and loss, our secrets we never share, our ways of coping. It is my hope that others will derive some benefit from the account that follows. So here, in three acts, are the good, the bad, and the unmet standards.

Genesis

Coker's 10-year accreditation cycle was on the fives, and so as 1995 approached, I found myself invited to be on our regional accreditation committee as a department chair. In particular, someone had seen fit to invite me to join the editing committee for the report, which was at that time a self-study with over 400 individual standards to be addressed. I got the impression that the purpose of writing the report was to create the literary equivalent of poison mushrooms. I amused myself by estimating how many dollars per hour it was costing the college to perform this exercise. It's still a fun thing to do in a large committee meeting—would you pay a consultant $300/hr to decide whether a preposition is something to end a sentence with?

As part of the standards, each academic program was supposed to have an assessment plan. In that sentence you have the total instructions I received regarding what an assessment plan is and how to do one. An assessment plan, you say? I can say in all honesty that my heart was not in the job. But as department chair, I had to put on a good face about it and helped write the one we would adopt for the mathematics program. It included things like plans to interview past majors to see what they thought of their education. Anything that might have looked like a learning outcome was far from my mind. Here's what the first report from 1993 contained: a program review, a curriculum review, a goal of improving pedagogy, and an objective to help prepare students for employment after graduation.

A note that I wrote in the conclusion is guaranteed to grab the attention of any reviewer: "This report does not completely address all of the items listed as "assessment procedures" in the assessment plan. However, it would be a waste of time to perform all of those surveys every year anyway." Note the scare quotes around "assessment procedures," as if the author were handling the concept with a pair of tongs in order to avoid getting his hands dirty! The final sentence punts the responsibility down the road as far as possible: "It is the recommendation of the mathematics faculty that the assessment plan document be amended to imply a periodic rather than constant nature of monitoring various aspects of the program."

I think it's fair to say that the plan and the report were done to satisfy the requirement and nothing much more came of it. But we did heave a long collective sigh of relief and happily banished the thought of assessment from our minds for a year. I think it took me about 40 minutes to write the whole report.

The following year we had to do another report because it wasn't 1995 yet. This time I employed a hoary old method of procrastination: create more plans. With an entirely straight face, I wrote: "What follows is a list of questions raised by the 1993 assessment that have not been answered. Each item is accompanied by our plan of action." A list of items followed (which demonstrates that the curriculum review hadn't been done very well, by the way) with duty assignments for the faculty. I'm quite sure I never did mine. Item 5 demonstrates another method of not doing anything: foist it off on someone else:

> Q: Is the campaign to increase communication skills working?
> A: The General Education Committee is working on a college-wide procedure to assess written work through portfolios. No further action is required on our part at present.

But my crowning achievement in these first skirmishes with the assessment mandate was the following:

> No attempt has been made in the past year to conduct oral interviews with a sample of mathematics majors after graduation. As stated in last year's assessment report, work must be done to develop an appropriate question list. Uncertainties about who will and how to conduct these interviews also remain.

This last sentence might serve as the rallying cry for my generation of faculty upon being confronted with assessment: Uncertainties exist about how to do this and who will do it! Note the passive voice—no author is left to taint this purely existential sentiment. Even the dangling "who will" in the original is a reflection of how far anyone really wanted to get involved in this project.

So this was my contribution to the assessment plan and the report. My colleagues' work comes off better, and there are a few bits here and there that are related to learning outcomes. For example, we had started doing oral presentations and oral exams with students specifically to develop their confidence in this format. But we never wrote that down as a learning objective. It just wouldn't have occurred to me in 1993. Later on, I realized that one can get to goals by working backward from actions, a trick that other consultants have said they use too. Here's how it works:

1. List all the changes you've made in the last year that relate to teaching and learning (for example, introducing a public speaking component to senior classes).
2. For each of those, write down what you observed that led you to take that action. (We noticed informally that some students were not confident in solving problems at the blackboard, which is a particular problem not only for future teachers, but also for future grad students.)
3. For each action, write down what you hoped to achieve (develop students' public speaking skills and their ability to think, literally, on their feet).

This, my friends, is the assessment loop. It's just upside down. Turn it over like an egg, and you have your goal, assessment, and action loop. This is good for two things: One is to discover what your most important goals are (what you act on), and the other is to create out of thin air assessment reports based on implicit rather than explicit goals. It would be, of course, unethical to claim that the goals were written down before they actually were. I'll leave others to explore the metaphysical implications of predetermined intentionality versus these natural assessment loops that happen all the time.

After 1995, the bad assessment karma I'd created gathered like a cumulonimbus over my head. I had assumed the position of institutional research (IR) director in addition to the teaching gig, and the chair's mantle rotated on. I spent happy days immersed in great globs of data—retention, grades, finances, and predictive models—the usual fodder for IR. I hadn't realized, however, that no one is more likely to get sucked into the accreditation tornado than the IR director. And so I found myself taking one of the phone calls where you can't say no and ended up as the SACS (Southern Association of Colleges and Schools) liaison and lead toad on the 2005 reaffirmation project. The air was thick with irony.

Job

We had no furniture in the living room, so that night I hauled a table out of storage and started spreading out material to begin to educate myself on my new job. It was, frankly, terrifying. The accrediting standards had changed, and there was only limited prior art to review on the new model. But even a tyro like me could see that there was a lot of stuff about institutional effectiveness and learning outcomes. There were program outcomes, general education outcomes, and even outcomes for non-academic units. The more I read, the more the dread crept up my limbs. Shortly thereafter, my young daughter adopted the name "Big Stupid Report" for the project.

Unfortunately I seem to have lost the letter I dashed off to the college president that night. The sentiment was something like, "Holy bleep! We're screwed!" But, of course, this sentiment was expressed in careful language explaining how my institutional research role presented potential conflicts of interest in gathering data and simultaneously writing reports, and the like. I tried to weasel out of the assessment part—to no avail.

A trip to the national SACS convention did not ease my sense of dread. I can say unequivocally that there is no comfort in being around either your peers who are just as terrified as you are or the ones who have blissful years ahead of them before their next accreditation visit. The powers that be were grinding their collective teeth over the watery assessment sauce that had been ladled up by the likes of me for the last decade. They were grouchy about it, and the winds of change swirled through the sterile conference center. Or maybe that was just overloaded air handlers evaporating all the sweat off the attendees.

I went to sessions about learning objectives and its new big thing, the quality enhancement plan. I flipped through the draft copies of the new *Principles of Accreditation*, learning most of the sections by heart. The ones on learning outcomes were scary. I puzzled over the general education requirement, which stated that institutions had to set standards and show that students met them. How in the world was I going to pull that one off? And the thought of telling the faculty—people like me—that they'd have to really, truly, do this assessment stuff . . . well, it made my blood run cold.

I began to puzzle over some of the new terms I was hearing. Words like *rubric,* which I thought meant a red-lettered title, were being used as an incantation to keep citations away, as in "We mapped our curriculum and have rubrics for all our general education outcomes." Those who uttered such things seemed terribly sophisticated in their application of assessment. I was like the country mouse coming to the city. Much of what was presented was abstract and couched in this new lingo. It sounded precise and scientific, all this talk of benchmarking and measuring outcomes. My problems were practical, however. How was this all going to get executed? For awhile it was as if the two halves of my brain were arguing with each other over the means of assessing general education. On the one hand, there was all this nice theory about finding a measurement tool and applying it, I presumed, in order to see that students measured up to the mark to satisfy what was Section 3.5.1. But every time I felt like it was beginning to make sense, the ideas would slip way into infeasibility. I was having trouble really seeing how this could be done. So I took the easy way out.

There are products on the shelf for all your needs, including assessing general education. Coker had used the Academic Profile standardized instrument in the past, so I figured that would at least solve one of the dozens of

problems I had. Notice that there was no such thing as an assessment committee to take on these tasks—I wasn't smart enough to set one up and also
felt like there was no time to waste. So I made a pitch to the academic
chairs for the Academic Profile, listing all the merits the marketing material
provided me. Reliability, validity, blah, blah. I could figure out what reliability was, but validity was a mystery. The following semester we administered it.

To say that the administration of this instrument was not confidence
inspiring is an understatement. We sent a very stern letter to freshmen and
seniors about this mandatory test. Out of about 150 seniors, perhaps 20
showed up. A disaster. One of those took a flip through the test booklet,
scribbled a bit, and walked out. We got the results a few weeks later.

Okay, I thought, now we have measured the minds of our students.
Even if there was some shadiness going on with the sample sizes, the graphs
went in the right direction—up. There was a nagging sensation, though. We
hadn't really set standards, just tried to assess accomplishments. My mind
reeled at what would be required to actually execute Section 3.5.1. It would
mean creating a way of testing seniors and refusing to let graduate those who
failed it. Something like that had happened in Coker's primordial past, and
there were still active antibodies about for any such idea. The legal problems
were easy to imagine too. We'd have to have utter confidence in this test.
Finally I started asking around discretely, trying not to sound like an idiot.
How do you assess general education? Do you set standards? The answer was
Kafkaesque. It turned out that SACS reviewers didn't look for a minimum
standards model at all—they wanted to see a continual improvement model
of assessment and learning. I couldn't believe this until I'd asked more than
one vice president and several veteran committee members. It was true. All
anyone cared about was continual improvement—the opposite of what the
standard actually said. That solved one problem and created another.

It was no longer necessary to use the standardized test to show that
standards were met. Instead we were expected to act on the information to
make improvements. That was an easy one—I sent copies of the reports to
the department chairs and said, "Here, figure out how to improve general
education." Bear in mind that assessment of general education was only one
of many problems awaiting a neat solution. The other, bigger, problem was
learning outcomes in major programs. Even though we'd supposedly been
doing assessment loops for a decade, only a rare program or two had anything concrete to show. My program had a report from 1993 and another
from 1994, and those were openly antagonistic to the process.

I gave the standards to the departments. I instructed them to set some
goals, gather some information, and act on the information. There was
wording in the standard that left it open to doubt as to whether one actually
had to demonstrate improvements or whether one just had to show actions
that could plausibly lead to improvements. I wrote letters to SACS about

this, and years later they finally changed the wording (the effect of my letters is unknown).

In leaving the construction of assessment plans in the hands of faculty with no detailed instructions, I committed a big mistake. It wasn't fair to them, and it ultimately cost us a lot of wasted effort. I was, of course, involved in the construction of the new and improved mathematics assessment plan, but it didn't improve much from the 1993 version except for one thing. That one thing, however, turned around my whole idea about how useful assessment activities could be.

While the departments were busy beavers wasting their time on poorly wrought plans, I worried about general education some more. Clearly the standardized test scores, however useful as statistical Play-Doh in creating graphs that go up, were not useful for measuring learning. First of all, one would have to establish that what the instrument tested aligned with what we taught. That was by no means clear. Worse, the scores gave no clue about what needed to be changed to improve them. This, together with my bad experience in administering the thing, made me question the whole epistemological foundation. Was this really and truly measurement, like weighing a sack of potatoes or applying a yardstick to an ear of corn? I read (about half of) *The Philosophical Foundations of Neuroscience,* by Bennett and Hacker (2003), which confirmed my suspicions. The word *measurement* has been more or less hijacked to lend weight, if you will, to the interpretation of the results. This was, of course, a statement about validity. I began to wonder, "What was the ultimate source of validity for abstractions like analytical thinking, which was one of our general education goals?"

Well, I mused, what if we could hire a bunch of experts—very learned people—to visit campus for a few weeks just to observe our students as they worked? They could observe carefully as students participated in class, rate their homework and tests, and then give their opinion about the cognitive skills of each student studied. This sounded like a very good way to really estimate the complex behavior that we associate with higher-order thinking skills. As an added attraction, this is how assessment is done outside the academy. When Stanislav gets a job at the orange juice factory, the boss will judge her new employee's thinking skill by what she sees in practice. If Stanislav can't concentrate, he'll be let go.

This idea is far removed from the usual ways of looking at assessment, which often is positivist: "We say that a sentence is factually significant to any given person, if and only if, [she or] he knows how to verify the proposition which it purports to express—that is, if [she or] he knows what observations would lead [her or him], under certain conditions, to accept the proposition as being true, or reject it as being false" (Ayer, 1946). It owes more to a simpler, more social definition (which I have simplified further by omitting context): "The meaning of a word is its use in the language"

(Wittgenstein, 1967). It's like the difference between an experiment and a conversation.

Of course, it would be prohibitively expensive to go out and hire a bunch of experts to descend like crows on the campus. But why do that at all? We already paid a cadre of experts, and they already did all the tasks needed to form impressions of Stanislav. All you had to do was go to the dining hall at lunch and listen to the table talk. "So-and-so is a good writer, while so-and-so was a good student until he started hanging out with the math crowd." It became obvious that this was a valuable source of assessment data that could be obtained with almost no effort. So in addition to the other accreditation problems to be solved, I dived headlong into what became the Faculty Assessment of Core Skills (FACS). The four core skills were analytical and creative thinking and effective writing and speaking. After a semester of trying things out and getting faculty input, we converged on a successful model:

1. Each faculty member decided which of the four skills he or she should or could assess (not necessarily teach—an important distinction) for each class.
2. For each syllabus, the professor wrote up a simple rubric for each of the skills to be assessed in that class. The ratings were standardized at "remedial," "freshman- or sophomore-level performance," "junior- or senior-level performance," and "ready to graduate." The use of this scale, rather than a more usual "meets/doesn't meet standards" scale, was very important because we could naturally track ratings relative to expectations.
3. At the end of the semester, faculty logged into a portal and entered their ratings on a web form. I did it many times myself, and it takes just a few minutes per class.

The advantages of this approach quickly became obvious. Because the faculty really did care about the liberal arts mission, it wasn't a hard sell to convince them of the importance of the project. Once the rubrics were written, the actual ratings were very simple and quick. It generated lots of data—roughly two ratings per class per student in the traditional program (we had a harder time with adjuncts). The usefulness of the rubric was that it got faculty members to think up front about their objectives, and not so much as a technical application of the rubric during the rating of students. This effort yielded thousands and thousands of separate observations about our students. We now have 6 years of longitudinal data.

The original motivation for creating FACS was the accreditation, but it took on a life of its own. The results poured in, and the lines on the graph went up as they were supposed to (even accounting for survivorship), and so I happily distributed charts and graphs and grids of numbers to the teaching faculty. But I nursed a guilty suspicion that got worse over the months that followed. What if it was (or were) all crap? I did interrater reliability studies and saw that raters agreed on the same score more than half of the time, which was impossible to explain by chance. The writing effectiveness scores correlated with books checked out in the library. The score averages correlated with grades. The scores were gathering some kind of information. But try as I might, I couldn't figure out how to link these nice averages and error bounds to anything meaningful in the classes I was teaching. I'm embarrassed to say how long it took me to realize what the problems were.

First, it may not be obvious when we talk about learning outcomes, but we can assess things we can't change. That's obvious if you think about, say, the stock market or the weather, but it's true of students too. We might be able to get good agreement on the big fuzzy blob we call analytical thinking, but that doesn't necessarily mean we can do anything about it. If the first problem was philosophical, the second was technical. I was reporting out scores as averages and error bars (2 standard errors plus or minus). This is a really awful way to look at learning outcomes. The faculty were appreciative when I could show them that average seniors were better than average freshmen, but like me, they hadn't a clue about how to actively use this information. One of the psychology professors had told me right at the beginning that I should use nonparametrics instead, but it took a long time for me to turn to that method. It was the difference between night and day. Instead of reporting that the art program's creative thinking average was 2.9, or .4 better than the college average, I could show them that one of their seniors consistently scored at least one "remedial" in that skill each semester and had never scored higher than "freshman- or sophomore-level performance." The only time I've heard gasps in an assessment presentation was when I showed that a small portion of the graduating seniors were still scoring at least one "remedial" in analytical thinking in their final year.

But this is really an account of assessment from a faculty perspective, and it is as a faculty member that I finally came to see the value of assessing and was finally able to sort through the nice theories to find what actually worked for me. As someone wise has said: In theory, theory and practice are the same; in practice they're not.

Exodus

Because of the FACS, we at least had the four liberal arts outcomes embedded in courses all across the curriculum. In my math and computer science classes, I always rated analytical and creative thinking, and sometimes the communications skills, depending on classroom activities. The act of creating rubrics for the thinking skills was the beginning of a revelation—the most important thing I've learned about teaching math.

What is creative thinking in mathematics? Certainly, some students have a spark of understanding that seems miraculous. I get chills when I see a student demonstrate a leap of intuition from problem to solution, knowing that I'd never seen it. Why hadn't I made that connection myself, and why was he unable to explain where it came from? They don't talk about this kind of thing in graduate school. They'd look at you funny and then go back to their chalky ciphers.

Why, for that matter, are some courses consistently harder than others? Why does one student sail through Introduction to Analysis and another change majors to accounting?

It so happens that I inherited very good learning objectives from the mission of the college, where these four core skills are written. If it had been "critical thinking" instead of "analytical and creative thinking," I don't think I would have gotten anywhere.

Because we had to each create our own definitions for the core skills rather than having one given from on high, it created a natural dialogue. What do you think it is? Despite this lack of standardization, the reliability was there. My original idea had been to create standard definitions for each area, but after a few meetings I saw that this was futile. In that case, faculty intransigence saved the day. The expert raters should be independent to do their own thinking. In my case, dialogue with my colleagues in the mathematics program produced a remarkable insight.

We associated analytical thinking with a deductive process—following rules. Rules can be simple, as in long division, or more complicated, like those for solving a system of linear differential equations. In either case, however, there is a step-by-step process for getting from the problem to the solution. When students arrive on our doorstep, they are used to this kind of thinking. "Just tell me what I need to do," they say. And they can get through calculus with just deductive thinking, provided they apply enough effort to learn all the rules. But then the game changes. Very suddenly students are expected to read and write proofs, where there is no usable recipe for reaching a solution. This is a different mode of thought requiring creativity. As an example, look at the puzzle below and see if you can write the next line. Only first grade math is required.

$$
\begin{array}{c}
1 \\
11 \\
21 \\
1211 \\
111221 \\
\underline{312211}
\end{array}
$$

How do you get to a solution? If you're like me, you'll take a guess at the pattern and then test it against the evidence in front of you. The first part is creative, you might even say random. The testing part is straightforward deductive reasoning—does my rule compute to the given numbers? This back-and-forth between creative insights and precise deductive testing is the heart of mathematical thought. I never consciously thought of that until I started applying these ideas to my courses. Immediately I had explanations for the behavior I'd seen and thought of ways to help students succeed.

We had been suddenly requiring creative thought after years of training students to be deductive. With no warning! No wonder they had trouble. So I discussed the syllabus with students, explaining that some problems would be marked as "creative," and that they'd probably find them harder at first. I sketched out the math curriculum and showed which courses were going to be heavily creative. We talked explicitly about ways to approach these hard problems—that it requires persistence more than anything else, but that it also requires a very good understanding of the deductive rules. If you have trouble with exponents, you'll have a terrible time writing a correct proof because you can't accurately check your own work.

I could begin to have deeper conversations with students about the course content. Suppose you want to find two numbers that sum to 16 and have a difference of 4. The least creative approach is to try to exhaust the possibilities. Is it 10 + 4? No . . . With more creativity, a student might see that the average of the two numbers must be 8, and so it must be 6 + 10. The concept of a "brute force" solution and an "elegant" solution exists in all sciences. It is a high compliment to say to a biologist, "Your experiment is elegant."

I'd like to tell you that I precisely measured the success rates of students before and after implementing my new teaching methods, and that there was a clear difference. I don't have that evidence. Perhaps that study could be done with sample sizes bigger than what I was dealing with, but for me there is no doubt that the students benefited. They understood the types of thinking, how they would measure their own success relative to them, and how it fit within the bigger picture of the curriculum. We routinely used the new vocabulary in class and in discussions among faculty. The absence of graphs going up to show the effectiveness of this assessment-based dialogue with students is probably important to some. But it leads me to my final observation about learning outcomes assessment in the classroom: It isn't measurement and it isn't science. We might say that:

$$\text{classroom assessment} = \text{teaching} + \text{paying attention.}$$

Simply setting some goals and really thinking about them, inviting dialogue with students and colleagues, can be an engine for positive change; the most powerful and discerning assessment tools anywhere are the minds of the classroom teachers. A little focus and encouragement can go a long way, assuming that the faculty you hire care about teaching. There are, on the other hand, a large number of ways to make the process harder—I have a long list of failures to my credit. For example, the more we talk about assessment as an activity distinct from teaching, the more irrelevant it becomes. Every time we create extra bureaucratic hurdles, we reduce participation. It's a common complaint among assessment directors that the faculty have only to use the beautiful systems they've put in place—often elaborate and complicated ways of keeping track of "artifacts" and detailed rubrics that everyone is supposed to adhere to. A better role for an assessment director is as a resource and a coach and, above all, an advocate for the faculty perspective.

Okay, you probably want to know the answer to the puzzle if you haven't figured it out. It took me about 5 hours, as I recall. I was taking a flight somewhere and spilled my drink all over the guy next to me at the point of "Aha!" The sequence is something called run-length encoding, which is a data compression technique for data with a lot of constant runs. Despite that imposing introduction, it's very simple. Just read the lines aloud, one by one, to see the pattern. Each line describes the one above it. So the blank line would be one 3, one 1, two 2s, and two 1s: 13112221. Notice how easy the deductive part—checking my answer—is now. It's the inductive/creative step that's challenging.

References

Ayer, A. J. (1946). *Language, truth, and logic.* London, England: V. Gollancz.

Bennett, M. R., & Hacker, P. M. S. (2003). *The philosophical foundations of neuroscience.* Malden, MA: Blackwell.

Wittgenstein, L. (1967). *Philosophical investigations.* Oxford, England: Blackwell.

About the Author

David Eubanks earned his doctorate in mathematics from Southern Illinois University and held a variety of positions at Coker College for the following 17 years. He currently serves as dean of academic support services at Johnson C. Smith University, working on planning and effectiveness, technology, library, faculty development, and of course exotic plumbing when the need arises. He blogs regularly about these issues at highered.blogspot.com.

4

WANTED

Nutrient-Rich Environments for Genuine Assessment

Jean Mach
College of San Mateo

The College of San Mateo (CSM) is one of 110 colleges in the California community college system, the largest system of higher education in the world. CSM's spectacular location atop a hill overlooking the affluent San Francisco Bay Area gives little indication of both the rewards and challenges of providing a high-quality college education to the 11,000 students—widely diverse in age, socioeconomic background, and college preparedness—whom it serves. This essay tells the story of an assessment effort that crossed over department and division barriers in order to assess students' learning as demonstrated in their writing.

At CSM, nearly everyone would agree that assessment of student learning—at least the recently introduced mandated species—has taken hold in many forms, quickly adapting to the environments of different disciplines and causing relatively mild discomfort in the settled educational systems of curriculum, pedagogy, and programmatic planning. Our accrediting agency, the Accrediting Commission for Community and Junior Colleges, is happy with our progress and no longer breathing down our backs. A few years into this endeavor, we've written student learning outcomes for virtually every course and program, assessed a majority of them, and duly posted the results. But has this impressive effort really made a difference in how we teach or how our students learn? Has our whole institution improved because of it? Perhaps not much. A few species of assessment introduced here have been beneficial and meaningful, at least for the teachers and students involved. They are the most endangered. This chapter tells the story of one such species.

CSM is a midsized California community college typical of other community colleges in the wide diversity of its students and their needs, the serious financial challenges that it faces, and its underdeveloped relationships to transfer institutions. It's a good college, ranking 15th out of 108 California community colleges in its transfer and degree completion rates for the years 2002–2005. The general education courses that our students take to transfer or complete associate degrees are dictated, to a large extent, by transfer articulation agreements. Those courses and sequences have changed very little in the 20 years I've been teaching in our district.

Yet the world has changed. Just about everyone working in the community college system questions whether students are learning as they should be or whether their learning is adequate for the needs of our global society today. We bemoan the fact that students drop out in appalling numbers. Indeed, almost half (46%) do not return after one semester. In addition, our students frequently do not follow a consistent trajectory through one community college in 2 or 3 years to one transfer institution, completing a bachelor's degree in a total of 4 or 5 years. In contrast, they may attend two or more community colleges (sometimes simultaneously) and move back and forth between 2- and 4-year institutions, quite often taking semester- or year-or decade-long breaks. This phenomenon, often referred to as "swirling," makes it extraordinarily difficult to track individual student progress, to identify a culminating stage in the educational journey, or even to find a point at which the institution can try to assess what its students are learning over a period of time. It's extremely challenging to look at our students' learning in a holistic manner.

It's not surprising, then, that most of our assessment efforts look at student work in relation to desired student learning outcomes that simply reflect what we're teaching in individual courses. Often we assess students' essays or tests—near the very end of the semester—when a third of the students may have already dropped out. Students leave for a multitude of reasons, but in any case, we are often assessing only those who have persevered. Our assessments don't tell us much about the students who have vanished, and those students—the ones who are definitely not benefiting from our efforts—play almost no part in the whole assessment effort. We don't know the role of our curriculum or pedagogies in the failure or disappearance of these students. Yet poor persistence is perhaps our college's most serious problem.

A Focus on Assessing Students' Writing

I am a professor of English who has found great personal satisfaction in teaching, in an interdisciplinary fashion, the required sequence of composition courses, from basic skills to advanced levels. Assignments in a composition classroom seem, to some degree, arbitrary, based on the likes and dislikes of individual instructors. Assignments do not necessarily reflect what students need to know to make connections to other disciplines or to write successfully in a wide range of situations. Yet composition course requirements are justified by the idea that students need those writing skills to succeed in college, in jobs, and in life. Thus it makes sense to me to make interdisciplinary connections in teaching writing. I have seen that teaching also comes alive in other disciplines when we look at our students' education as an ecosystem in which all the parts are interrelated and interdependent. Because of my enthusiasm for the interdisciplinary nature of learning communities and writing-across-the-curriculum programs, I have been involved with them for years. I have long understood that we need to document and assess such work in order to defend its existence and promote institutional support. So assessment, in general, has seemed like a worthy idea. I have also become hungry for information about how such programs affect students' learning and attitudes, for better or for worse. In these interdisciplinary endeavors, I have worked with many innovative and curious faculty members who share this desire to track the impact of their efforts on students' learning.

So, in 2007, roughly 15 members of our faculty from mathematics, English, philosophy, ESL, sociology, political science, and biology, many of them already familiar with interdisciplinary learning communities and eager to gather data and information on student learning, agreed to collaborate on a new project. It was one that seemed likely to gain support at our college, especially as the official push for assessment was becoming hard to ignore. The Writing Across the Curriculum program (WAC) at CSM also became the basis for our acceptance into the Carnegie Foundation's CASTL (Carnegie Academy for the Scholarship of Teaching and Learning) Institutional Leadership Program. As described on the Carnegie Foundation website,

> The CASTL Institutional Leadership Program builds on the influential work undertaken by colleges and universities, campus centers and educational organizations, scholarly and professional societies, and CASTL Campus Program Leadership Clusters, to facilitate collaboration among institutions with demonstrated commitment to and capacity for action, inquiry and innovation in the scholarship of teaching and learning. Participating institutions are organized to address specific themes important to the improvement of student learning, as well as the development and sustainability of a scholarship of teaching and learning. (Carnegie Foundation for the Advancement of Teaching, n.d.)

We were honored to be among approximately 100 institutions selected for the program; it seemed that the external connections to the Carnegie Foundation and to the other seven campuses in our cluster would lend credibility as well as valuable sources of expertise to our project. WAC, for us, grew out of an all-too-real problem: We knew that, other than in the English composition sequence, students do little writing in transfer-level courses on this campus. This is understandable, as the weak writing abilities of many of our students have discouraged instructors from assigning writing tasks. Furthermore, most of our classes in disciplines other than English *have no prerequisite for college-level writing* and would undoubtedly suffer untenable enrollment losses if they did. Thus asking for college-level writing in those courses is problematic. We set out to address an important research question, one that perhaps addresses issues central to California community colleges: Can WAC function as a teaching and learning tool for below-college-level writers who are enrolled, along with more advanced writers, in courses with no writing prerequisite? We planned for assessment right from the beginning because we simply did not know the answer to our question and felt our college could not begin to grapple with the problem of underprepared students until we understood more about how to encourage and support writing in all classes.

After nearly a whole semester of dialogue, which was necessary to build trust, practical working relationships, and an understanding of different disciplinary needs and conventions in writing, the team was ready to collaborate on many aspects of teaching writing in non-composition classes. We had discussed everything from prompts to plagiarism, brainstormed ways to scaffold the assignments, developed rubrics, standardized our marking practices, and compared our grading scales. We were ready to send teams of faculty from a variety of disciplines into classrooms. In those classes, we planned to conduct writing workshops with drafts and discuss the strengths and weaknesses of anonymous student writing samples. These were exciting activities, and we needed to know how all of them affected students.

As we thought about an assessment model that would depict how our program and our students were doing, we had a slew of questions to be answered on an ongoing basis, every semester, for the 3 years of our CASTL project. We realized we needed baseline, formative, and summative feedback. We wanted quantitative and qualitative information. We also knew that none of the information we needed was readily available on our campus. We couldn't just tell a research department what we needed; we would have to develop most of the assessment tools ourselves.

Relevant Research Questions

We returned to our central research question: Can WAC function as a teaching and learning tool for below-college-level writers who are enrolled, along with more advanced writers, in courses with no writing prerequisite? Our discussions led us to a variety of tools for identifying students with weak writing skills very early in the semester and then to see if our various WAC strategies were helping them succeed at greater rates in transfer-level courses. We were interested in the affective results of our enterprise as well. Could the various signals we were infusing into these classrooms, signals that seemed to support the idea that all disciplines value, teach, and support writing development, help our students succeed? Could we use our college's general education student learning outcomes (GE-SLOs) to make students aware of the educational goals of the college and to engage them intentionally in reaching those outcomes? Could we use the WAC program to start to understand the needs of the students we were losing as well as those who were succeeding? Given that the WAC classes were populated by some students in their last semester before their transfer to a 4-year university—as well as those just beginning their college education—could WAC give us an opportunity to assess student progress toward the GE-SLOs? Could we also formalize some ways to capture faculty experience?

We got to work. Mathematicians, philosophers, biologists, and sociologists worked alongside English and ESL instructors; everyone pooled ideas that often reflected differences in our approaches to writing in each discipline. We had to acknowledge, consciously, that the first version of each tool might need revision, to give ourselves permission to achieve less than perfection, in order to try unfamiliar ideas. A spirit of adventure and collaboration permeated our meetings.

Multiple Sources of Evidence

The WAC faculty designed and began to implement the following five assessment tools: diagnostic writing sample and profile, student survey, end-of-semester student ePortfolio assessment, student success data, and writing center student record form.

Diagnostic Writing Sample and Profile

We decided that we wanted to use a prompt that invited students to give us a self-assessment of their writing and reading skills at the very beginning of the semester, noting their perceived strengths and weaknesses and the kinds of support that they would like to have in order to succeed in a class that required significant writing. On an attached sheet, we also asked them to list the various English and ESL reading and writing classes they were currently enrolled in or had taken in the past along with the grades they had received (this was optional). The original prompt read as follows:

> Faculty at CSM are looking for new ways to help students succeed. You are enrolled in a class in which you are expected to have college-level writing and reading skills, and sometimes students do not succeed because of

weaknesses in these areas. Your feedback today will help us understand what help students need and want.

Please describe, in some detail in one or two paragraphs, your strengths and weaknesses, as you perceive them, in writing and reading. What do you struggle with? What comes easily?

Then, in another paragraph or two, please discuss the kinds of support you would find helpful, or strategies you already use on your own, to help you succeed in this course. Don't limit yourself to what support you now believe is available on this campus, as we want to hear your ideas.

Student Survey: Educational Gains Made at CSM

We wanted an additional student self-assessment tool to be administered near the end of the semester. The survey questions we wrote broke down our college's five GE-SLOs into 14 specific aspects and asked students to rate their own progress toward these educational goals. On the survey, we also invited general comments. The five GE-SLOs are as follows:

1. Effective communication: The ability of students to write, read, speak, and listen in order to communicate effectively
2. Quantitative skills: The ability of students to perform quantitative analysis, using appropriate resources
3. Critical thinking: The ability of students to analyze information, reason critically and creatively, and formulate ideas/concepts carefully and logically from multiple perspectives and across disciplines
4. Social awareness and diversity: The ability of students to recognize cultural traditions and to understand and appreciate the diversity of the human experience, past and present
5. Ethical responsibility: The ability of students to make, with respect to individual conduct, judgments based on systems of values

We used a 4-point scale ranging from "no progress" to "major progress" for students to rate their own gains toward these outcomes, broken into 14 bits. This survey was given to a control group before the first semester of our WAC program so that we had a baseline for comparing our students' perceptions of what they were gaining in the WAC program. The survey results were tabulated anonymously.

End-of the-Semester Student ePortfolio Assessment

The end-of-the-semester student ePortfolio assessment had three components:

1. Assessment of writing chosen by students and posted on ePortfolios developed in the WAC classes

2. Assessment of student progress toward specific GE-SLOs in the ePortfolios
3. Assessment of ePortfolio reflection, a piece of writing in which students discuss how the posted writing demonstrated progress toward the selected GE-SLO

Our decision to use student ePortfolios as our central assessment tool—as the centerpiece for both faculty and students in our desire to make learning visible and intentional—resulted from our work in the Integrative Learning Project (2004–2006), a program sponsored by the Carnegie Foundation for the Advancement of Teaching and the Association of American Colleges and Universities. Its goal was to support and promote integrative learning in undergraduate education by working with "10 selected campuses to develop and assess advanced models and strategies to help students pursue learning in more intentional, connected ways" (Carnegie Foundation for the Advancement of Teaching, n.d.-1). In particular, our admiration for the ePortfolio programs at LaGuardia Community College and Portland State University inspired our effort. We envisioned ePortfolios that combined the qualitative assessment capabilities of the Portland State model, which requires students to post artifacts that demonstrate their progress toward the goals of their freshman inquiry, such as communication, inquiry and critical thinking, their understanding of ethical issues and the variety of human experience, and the learner-identity emphasis of LaGuardia's model, which includes "Welcome," "About Me," and "Educational Goals" pages.

However, despite numerous efforts to share our enthusiasm, we failed to interest our administrators and instructional technology people in the concept of ePortfolios or to obtain financial or technical support. Faced with the potential failure of our program only a few weeks before our first semester of implementation, we had the kind of inspiration that comes from desperation: We decided to use the Carnegie Foundation's KEEP Toolkit (n.d.), "a set of web-based tools that helps teachers, students and institutions quickly create compact and engaging knowledge representations on the Web." We had experience making web pages with KEEP in the Integrative Learning Project. It had levels of privacy; it gave us the ability to provide students with a template of our own design and to elicit postings of the materials we wanted to assess. We could adequately introduce students to the tool in one class session, and we could gather together galleries of student ePortfolios that would simplify the logistics of the assessment sessions. It was also extremely easy to use. But most important, given our lack of a budget, it was free!

So, using KEEP, we designed a basic template to include the five GE-SLOs and places to link WAC artifacts as well as individual student learning plans and educational goals (see Figure 4.1). This template was made available to all the instructors involved, many of whom further refined them for their own classes. We realized that we needed separate rubrics to assess the posted writing and the students' reflective pieces, to document the students' posted artifacts as evidence of progress toward the GE-SLOs. Unsure of what we were really going to be looking at, we kept the initial rubrics very simple. We would ask pairs of instructors to read the ePortfolios, discuss them, and score them together with the rubrics. After one semester, we added a rubric that gauged the faculty's perception of each student's progress toward the GE-SLOs—which, we found, did not always correspond to the student's perception (see Figure 4.2). Because there was no other impetus behind

FIGURE 4.1
WAC ePortfolio Template Using KEEP Toolkit

ISLO snapshot template (sent from gregory@smccd.edu)   file:///Users/jeanmach/Desktop/snapshot%202/index.html

COLLEGE ᴼᶠ SAN MATEO

My ePortfolio :

Student Name

About Me

My Educational Goals

My Resume

GE-SLO# 1 Effective Communication: The ability of students to write, read, speak, and listen in order to communicate effectively.

no current link
Enter evidence of effective communication in the form of a document, photograph, movie, or sound bite.

GE-SLO# 2 Quantitative Skills: The ability of the students to perform quantitative analysis, using appropriate resources

no current link
enter evidence of quantitative skills in the form of a document, photograph, movie, or sound bite.

GE-SLO# 3: Critical Thinking: The ability of the students to analyze information, reason critically and creatively, and formulate ideas/concepts carefully and logically from multiple perspectives and across disciplines.

no current link
Enter evidence of critical thinking in the form of a document, photograph, movie, or sound bite.

student or project group photo
student or project group photo

The Assignment

photo of our presentation
photo of our presentation

My Class Project for Course XXX

First Draft of the Project

Reflection on the Project Process
What I learned in the process of this project... What I would do differently if I could do it again...How this project relates to my other course work...

Final Draft

GE-SLO# 4 Social Awareness and Diversity: The ability of students to recognize cultural traditions and understand and appreciate the diversity of the human experience, past and present.

no current link
Enter evidence of social awareness and diversity in the form of a document, photograph, movie, or sound bite.

GE-SLO#5 Ethical Responsibility: The ability of students to make, with respect to individual conduct, judgments based on a system of values.

no current link
Enter evidence of ethical responsibility in the form of a document, photograph, movie, or sound bite.

FIGURE 4.2
ePortfolio Evaluation Rubrics

WAC Project Keep Toolkit Evaluation Rubrics

WRITING	A	B	C	D
Focus Organization/ Structure	Clearly stated main idea or thesis. Logical organization. Good structure to supporting paragraphs.	Thesis stated with reasonable clarity. Organization apparent, even if somewhat clunky. Supporting paragraphs have some apparent structure.	Thesis vague or poorly stated. Some sense of organization. Structure of supporting paragraphs sometimes weak.	No main idea. No apparent organization. Paragraphs not focused or structured.
Clarity of Ideas/ Concepts	Clearly articulated key ideas and concepts	Few mistakes in key ideas, little confusion in evidence/ explanation	Key ideas often mistaken, some confusion in evidence/ ideas	Substantial mistakes in defining key ideas, substantial or fatal confusion in evidence/ explanation
Coherence	Reasoning flows logically and is easy to follow. All relevant steps/ideas included.	Logical sequence. Relevant steps/ideas included.	Generally logical in development. Some errors in sequencing or connections/ relationships.	Reasoning does not flow logically. Relevant information missing or replaced by irrelevant information.
Completeness/ Development	Main elements are completely and accurately presented, explained, and/or supported. Conclusion fully realized.	Main elements are presented with reasonable accuracy and completeness. Conclusion reached.	Main elements are present but not complete. The knowledgeable reader is able to fill in the gaps.	Main elements are missing or incomplete.
Mechanics	No spelling or grammatical errors. Correct citations included as needed.	Few spelling or grammatical errors. Correct citations included as needed.	Some spelling and grammatical errors. Incomplete citations.	Multiple spelling and grammatical errors. Needed citations lacking
Fluency	Good language flow, transition, and paragraph cohesion	Generally good language flow.	Inconsistent fluency. Some difficult to read sections.	Difficult to read. Jumpy. Paragraphs not focused.

Formative reflection: evidence of student recognition of connection between work and GE-SLOS	substantial	moderate	some	none	n/a

Evidence of student having met GE-SLOs:	(3) substantial evidence	(2) some evidence	(1) no evidence	(0) n/a
Effective Communication	substantial evidence	some evidence	no evidence	n/a
Quantitative Skills	substantial evidence	some evidence	no evidence	n/a
Critical Thinking	substantial evidence	some evidence	no evidence	n/a
Social Awareness and Diversity	substantial evidence	some evidence	no evidence	n/a
Ethical Responsibility	substantial evidence	some evidence	no evidence	n/a

introducing student ePortfolios at the institution, our ePortfolio assessment included no control group.

Student Success Data

Our college research department does produce generalized student success and completion data, but we needed information on particular WAC-identified sections that could be compared to control groups, with all the data broken down to show which courses students had successfully completed in the ESL and English writing sequences.

Fortunately, one of our WAC faculty members was familiar with writing the code needed for such a request. Because of her efforts, the protocols for this research were successfully created.

Writing Center Student Record Form

The writing center student record form was intended to be used to track students' use of the writing center but could also be used to aid communication between the WAC classroom instructor and the writing center faculty.

Additional Assessment Tools

We added two more pieces to our assessment tools after the first semester, when we found we needed even more refined information: Faculty reflection papers were developed to capture faculty perspectives on the program, and the diagnostic tracking grid was developed to track the relationship of writing weaknesses on the diagnostic writing sample to student completion of the course (see Figure 4.3). With this grid, we hoped to discover any correlation between particular areas of writing weaknesses and lack of success in WAC transfer-level courses.

What We Learned

Our WAC program assessment continued over four semesters, with 15–19 sections of transfer-level classes participating each semester. Well over 2,000 students were involved in the program. Without question, the most important lesson we learned from and about the process of assessing was that we needed more than one strategy to understand the impact of our program, as originally designed, as well as to see what modifications were needed in the program and what formative conclusions could be drawn as we proceeded. Furthermore, we needed a prompt and an ongoing feedback loop, from the assessment results to faculty planning efforts to actual activities in the classroom, semester after semester, to sustain the process of change that we had

FIGURE 4.3
Diagnostic Tracking Grid

PLEASE MARK AREAS OF WEAKNESS								
Students (paste roll sheet)	Focus Organization/ Structure	Clarity of Ideas/ Concepts	Cohesiveness	Completeness/ Development	Mechanics	Fluency	Current/ Last English/ ESL Course	Course Completion (W-date C or higher? Yes or No)

embarked upon. Finally, we needed a campus climate that supported problem solving and the initiation of change. When our assessment revealed a need for modifications in campus support systems and structures outside the WAC program, the dozen or so WAC faculty members could not by themselves effect such change. For example, creating a learning center that would provide help for students writing in any discipline would require new college funding; adding writing prerequisites to transfer-level courses would require entire departments to endorse a change that might reduce enrollments; and, finally, taking the assessment results and recommendations from a temporary interdisciplinary program would require new educational planning systems outside the traditional departmental and division pathways—a change that can be perceived as a threat to those accepted pathways.

A more detailed summary of what we learned from the combined assessment tools follows.

1. The majority of WAC student survey comments were significantly more positive than the responses in the baseline non-WAC control group; the self-assessment ratings seemed to indicate greater self-awareness of inadequacies in writing and more realistic perceptions of writing needs, but improved self-confidence in other areas of learning and more positive outlooks on college learning in general.

2. Survey comments also indicated that in-class writing interventions by the WAC faculty team were effective in conveying the importance of writing.

3. Use of the writing center to support WAC was insufficient to justify the classes' hour-by-arrangement requirement. Students, for various reasons, including limited writing center hours, rigid scheduling, and insufficient cross-disciplinary support and expertise, were making little use of that resource.

4. Students concurrently enrolled in ESL classes were the group most likely to benefit from and take advantage of supports available to WAC students. They also succeeded in somewhat greater numbers than ESL students in the non-WAC control groups.

5. Students identified as having below-college-level writing skills did not succeed at any greater rate than those in the control groups; requiring writing in their transfer-level courses may in fact have contributed to even more significant retention problems for them.

6. Specifically, those students identified as having weak grammar and sentence skills on the diagnostic writing sample were at highest risk of not completing the course. These students were most likely to be the "disappearing students."

We also noted the following serendipitous findings, which were not measured but were repeatedly observed; they were mentioned in some of the faculty reflections.

1. Although our assessment did not focus specifically on reading skills, nor did the project measure incoming reading levels, quite often reading issues surfaced in the faculty discussions of written work. Instructors often felt that weaknesses in written work reflected poor comprehension of assigned readings. The WAC faculty team all agreed that this problem merited further attention at the college.
2. Faculty observed the development—among faculty and students alike—of a community of teaching and learning. WAC provided opportunities for faculty from different disciplines to learn together and talk about common educational concerns in a collegial and supportive atmosphere. Students saw that writing matters in all disciplines.
3. Faculty reported anecdotally that, in most classes, the WAC support strategies developed within the group were essential for successful implementation of their structured writing assignments. It would be difficult to maintain the writing emphasis without the support mechanisms WAC had provided.
4. Faculty felt that the presence of writing support in the classroom showed promise of changing students' attitudes toward seeking academic support in general.
5. Faculty felt that WAC was an effective professional development experience. Through collaborative sharing of different perspectives on writing, all faculty members involved learned a great deal about the role of writing instruction in teaching and learning.

We thus concluded that the WAC program did help reinforce the value of writing in student learning. The new interventions, pedagogical strategies, and support mechanisms were constructive and could become increasingly important as the writing skills of even more entering students prove to be inadequate for the demands of college work. The WAC program alone could not reverse the distressingly poor success and retention rates of students who are underprepared yet enrolled in transfer-level courses. It did, however, document and offer important insight into what was happening to those underprepared students.

Final Recommendations and Reflections

The following recommendations came out of these assessments and experiences:

1. Programmatic and institutional curricular changes (examples might include prerequisites for reading, writing, or both; focused basic skills

programs; re-envisioned and expanded reading support) are needed if the college wants to increase the success rates of developmental students (i.e., students entering college with below-college level skills in writing, reading, and/or mathematics). Such changes, if shown to be successful, must be institutionalized.

2. Writing support should be extended in additional ways to be available to students in any class, not just those enrolled in English or ESL.

3. Additional new reading strategies and interventions are needed across the curriculum.

4. Assessment of ePortfolios, which pairs two instructors looking at the same student work and encourages collegial discussion about the artifacts viewed, is an invaluable process for initiating dialogue about what students are and are not learning at a college.

5. Most important, a large-scale cultural shift among students, faculty, counselors, and administrators is needed at CSM to create a learning environment in which writing is recognized as a central component of a college education. Students in all classes must have access to academic support that is comfortable with different disciplinary expectations and conventions. Such a shift will take time and support, but it is essential to meeting college goals for improved success and retention.

We started to run into some difficulties after the end of the first semester during which we used our assessment tools, when the delivery of the data we wanted from the college research department lagged months behind the data we were accumulating and analyzing ourselves. Without the student success and completion data, we were relying solely on the qualitative aspects of our assessment (primarily from the survey and the ePortfolio assessments) to modify our strategies the following semester. But the hard numbers that would help us identify the writing levels (ESL/English course completion or placement test scores) of students who had disappeared and were thus not represented by the survey and ePortfolio data, came to us well into the next semester, too late to affect our strategies that semester. The second year, the institutional data stopped coming at all. Other institutional needs took priority for the overworked and understaffed research department. Research required for the state and for the accrediting commission, understandably, trumps research desired by a cohort of faculty for the improvement of student learning. But most important, our WAC program's research needs did not fit into institutional planning and program review, with their supporting research structures, all of which are aligned with divisions and departments.

Nevertheless, we had collected enough assessment data to start to answer our own research question and to understand that underprepared students need additional support or special programs on our campus, beyond what we could provide through WAC, if they are to succeed in greater numbers. We hoped that formally presenting our results and conclusions would be the first step in initiating positive change on the campus, change that would extend beyond what a dozen or so faculty members could do on their own. We hoped for administrative help in finding ways for the college as a whole to use the knowledge we had gained and to grapple with our seemingly unsolvable retention problems. The WAC assessment efforts opened our eyes to the need for changes in instructional design, pedagogy, and technology; for collaboration with student services and counselors; and for access for students enrolled in any class on campus to tutorial support in our writing and reading labs. But we found that the institutional environment was not one in which our assessment findings—which indicated a need for changes that cut across institutional boundary lines—were welcome.

It should be understood that CSM does take seriously its commitment to assessment, as required and understood by the Accrediting Commission for Community and Junior Colleges. Administrators and faculty are all strenuously working for full compliance at the course level. The expectations and procedures for program review, required of all departments, have been modified to include a description of a department's assessment of SLOs, including which courses or programs were assessed, how they were assessed, and the findings of the assessment. At the same time, faculty remain wary, in part because of a requirement to link assessment to faculty evaluation, a connection that is not clearly understood and that most faculty think should be subject to union contract negotiations. Assessment is also more work—indeed, a significant additional burden on an already stressed college—so a desire to keep it simple has often prevailed at all levels of the institution. In addition, few people on campus feel that assessment should lead to significant change in the way we go about the business of educating our students.

Yet faculty in the WAC program at CSM have learned much about the value of assessment that tries to look at student learning beyond the course level in an integrative, interdisciplinary way. Our efforts have made us aware of both the potential and the limitations of rich and meaningful assessment measures. We share a genuine desire to study the impact of our teaching and our curriculum on our students' learning. But we now recognize that our institutional environment is not one in which new approaches like ours can easily take root and thrive.

An educational environment must be willing to confront real questions that it really does want answered, and students must be involved in the whole process. If finding answers requires changes that extend beyond a single course, institutions must be willing and able to support both the collection of data and college-wide discussions of all relevant educational structures, despite the traditional territorial boundaries that make such discussions difficult. Finally, the immediacy of the feedback loop is essential. Combined with collaborative faculty discussions about new strategies, tweaking and assessing and tweaking and assessing again can foster dynamic teaching and learning environments that can truly make a difference in how students learn.

I will let two of my colleagues share the value of such an environment, one in which assessment is rooted in real questions and real needs:

> What I have experienced as a participant in the Writing Across the Curriculum initiative is the building of a community, a community involved in learning more about the practice of good writing. To begin with, we assumed different roles in this community, but ultimately we were all learners, learning from each other and from the students.
>
> Like members of other communities, we participants in the WAC community have had to learn to trust each other. We have trusted each other enough to show our work—assignments, rubrics, drafts—and share our reactions, and in response we have received respect, not judgment. We have worked on a vocabulary, a language for discussing writing issues and responding to writing. Both in our meetings and in the classroom working with students, this has sometimes resulted in epiphanies.
>
> When we as teachers have responded to student writing as readers rather than as evaluators, students have been eager to imitate this behavior. They have welcomed our comments and become willing to see their own writing from a new perspective. In one class I visited, a student who had been vocal in his critical evaluation of one paper revealed to me after class that he had been critiquing his own paper. In another class, once teachers had begun to comment, students tentatively began to voice their own reactions. They showed evidence of developing confidence in their ability to help each other.
>
> Working with other colleagues on this initiative has given me an opportunity to appreciate more deeply what they do. When I reacted to student drafts in Dave Danielson's philosophy class, I realized that his midterm assignment provided students a model for the way he expected them to come to a conclusion. The assignment did not dictate the conclusion but modeled for students a logical way to move from evidence to conclusion, a path to good thinking. When I worked with students in Mike Burke's [mathematics] class on his global warming assignment, I saw how this assignment encouraged students to realize what they could discover from certain data and what they still did not know. Both assignments helped students develop their thinking by requiring them to write.
>
> For me, the experience of working on the Writing Across the Curriculum initiative has expanded my understanding of the community in the community college. Whereas before I saw myself as a member of the Language Arts Division and a member of the foreign language and ESL departments, now I see myself as part of the writing community, working with

colleagues from many different disciplines to provide support to students, working with students both in the classroom and in the writing center, so that these students can become more confident writers. I am hopeful that students will begin to see all of us as resources, willingly seeking us out for feedback on their assignments. To make that happen, I hope to be present in classrooms when the writing assignments are given out so that the students there will see me as a potential coach and so that from the beginning I have a clearer understanding of the class instructors' expectations for the assignment.

Like other communities, this community will undoubtedly develop in unexpected directions, leading to surprising insights for all of us. My hope is that the participating students will see themselves as members of this writing community, recognizing that we too are striving to get better at this skill, some as apprentices, others more practiced, but all valuing the effort that good writing requires. (D. Musgrave, personal communication, 2007)

We have learned about prompts and rubrics, and that has been very helpful. We were already convinced that students should write about the meaning of the mathematics they do, but WAC has given us the tools to implement writing in mathematics. In the other direction, I think that one of the most useful results for (at least some) people in English is [the recognition] that the requirements for successful writing differ by discipline. That, at least, is the short version. (K. Brown, personal communication, 2008)

My colleagues' words suggest that assessment itself is not the point; we must protect and value the whole environment in which genuine assessment can be nurtured. The somewhat unsupportive institutional environment I have described here is not, I believe, idiosyncratic to my college. California's community colleges operate in an impoverished ecosystem, starved for continually dwindling resources, struggling merely to survive. The introduction of mandated assessment seems like yet another competitor for already inadequate time and money for reform. But I believe that if assessment is nurtured in forms more native than invasive, it can infuse new health and life into the entire system.

References

The Carnegie Foundation for the Advancement of Teaching Institutional Leadership Program: (n.d.-1). www.carnegiefoundation.org/scholarship-teaching-learning/institutional-leadership-program

The Carnegie Foundation for the Advancement of Teaching Undergraduate Education: (n.d.-2). www.carnegiefoundation.org/previous-work/undergraduate-education

KEEP Toolkit. (n.d.). *Home.* www.cfkeep.org/static/index.html

About the Author

Jean Mach is professor of English at the College of San Mateo. She earned her M.S. in English literature and creative writing from the University of California, Berkeley; her M.A.T. in English from the College of Notre Dame; and her B.A. in English from the University of Washington. She has coordinated CSM's Learning Communities, Writing Across the Curriculum, and Scholar programs. She has enthusiastically used ePortfolios for assessment in WAC, learning communities, and creative writing classes and has seen that integrative learning (i.e., fostering connections of all kinds in students' learning) helps students find purpose in their education and in their lives. It also helps teachers renew their interest in their fundamental charge of educating students. A published poet, she is the recipient of the first *Inside English* Article of the Year Award and the Jack London Writing Conference Poetry Award.

5

FROM BEREAVEMENT TO ASSESSMENT

The Transformation of a Regional Comprehensive University

Rose Perrine, Charlie Sweet, Hal Blythe, Paula Kopacz,
Dorie Combs, Onda Bennett, Stacey Street, and E.J. Keeley
Eastern Kentucky University

Eastern Kentucky University (EKU), a regional comprehensive university located in Richmond, has an enrollment of about 16,000. Serving a student body from diverse socioeconomic backgrounds, many of whom are first-generation college students, EKU offers 168 degree programs, relatively small classes, and more than 200 student organizations.

I n "The Passing of Arthur," Tennyson uses the phrase "The old order changeth, yielding place to new" to describe a familiar rite of passage. Lately, EKU has seen the passing of an old order and the advent of a new era—the assessment movement. As when any way of doing things dies away, before the new way is established, people must go through a grieving process, which, as Elisabeth Kübler-Ross (1969) explains in *On Death and Dying,* is a natural phenomenon. Whether the event is the death of a loved one or divorce, the process evolves through five interrelated steps: denial, anger, bargaining, depression, and acceptance. Much to our surprise, traces of these same psychological states presented themselves at our institution as we trudged toward establishing effective assessment protocols.

At EKU, we spent 1997–2007 implementing changes geared toward earning reaffirmation from the Southern Association of Colleges and Schools (SACS). The assessment movement has grown stronger nationwide, and university leadership saw early on the need to create effective assessment protocols to monitor the success of our changes. Our desire to improve has forced us to analyze our effectiveness on many levels of student learning and to work toward maintaining a culture of assessment at the program, departmental, and institutional levels. Importantly, our philosophy has evolved into one in which assessment results provide information for decision making regarding the future direction of the institution.

As a result of our decade-long journey, EKU employs a unique approach: assessment of student learning outcomes and other objectives takes place within the framework of the university strategic plan. Whereas strategic planning seeks to answer the questions "What should we be doing, and how will we do it?" assessment seeks to answer the singular question "How well are we doing what we are supposed to be doing?" In essence, our strategic plan's mission drives all assessment processes. Our goals and objectives link directly to our mission; assessment, then, informs us on our progress toward achieving that mission.

The current plan for assessment at EKU is as follows:

1. All units (college, department, academic/teaching, and academic support) assess progress in meeting both planning objectives and educational objectives.
2. Units describe what has occurred, why it has occurred, and what it means.
3. Units enter objectives, measures, criteria for success, results, and use of results for improvement into a centralized database.
4. In the database, units link planning and educational objectives to their college's and the university's goals and strategic directions.
5. Units prepare annual reports that include:
   a. An explanation of faculty/staff involvement in assessment
   b. A summary and explanation of outcomes
   c. Adjustments made to the unit's strategic/action plan
      i. Significant improvements made based on assessment results
      ii. Plan for assessing effects of improvements
   d. Priorities for next year
   e. Strategic budget requests

A decade ago, assessment at EKU reflected a top-down model, but administrative directives rarely achieve idealistic goals. We realized early on that until the entire university community began to respect and engage in the spirit of assessment rather than adhering to its letter, the lofty aims of assessment would not be realized. At this point, evidence of the Kübler-Ross model surfaced.

A university culture does not change quickly or without resistance. The key to constructive change was the implementation of good systems and a commitment to continually asking and answering the questions necessary for sound assessment practice. Approaching assessment under the umbrella of strategic planning offered the context necessary to develop excellent processes and to promote its role in the overall campus culture. At EKU we progressed neither quickly nor smoothly in fostering a culture of effective assessors. And as in any grieving process, the transformation has come with some pain. To illustrate our recent transformation, we have created a fictional unit that we use to focus on the amalgam of problems the university encountered and the solutions we attempted; this fictional unit also provides anonymity for colleagues and protects us from recriminations. We have also created faculty personae to express representative attitudes. As our university is probably fairly typical, we hope that our experience will offer guidelines for other universities attempting similar transformations.

Denial in the Department of Literature: "This Can't Be Happening"

For several years prior to 2003, the director of institutional research, Dr. Foresight, made various attempts to get departments to develop student learning objectives, or desired educational outcomes. Typically the Department of Literature treated Dr. Foresight like a gnat—the buzzing was annoying, but it was fairly easily shooed away. This buzz-shoo dance lasted for a number of years: Dr. Foresight reappeared periodically to preach the importance of student learning outcomes, and the Department of Literature continued to deny that any change was necessary. Finally, in 2003, upper-level administrators began to get nervous about the upcoming SACS visit, and the burden to convince departments to assess educational outcomes was no longer on Dr. Foresight's shoulders alone. The Office of Institutional Effectiveness (IE) was created to spearhead the development of the university strategic plan, and it boldly and creatively integrated student learning outcomes and planning outcomes into the university's strategic plan. Departments were subsequently required to link both planning outcomes and student learning outcomes to the university's strategic planning goals. Upper-level administrators in concert with IE began singing the same tune—"You must create and assess student learning outcomes."

When the Department of Literature held a faculty meeting in fall 2003, its response to this mandate was denial. Professor Delay claimed, "We already do assessment. We give grades. Why should we do anything differently? If you want to know how much students are learning, look at their grades." Professor A. Pathy assured her colleagues, "Oh, don't worry. This is just a fad. It will pass." Professor Typical shook his head and said, "This is a clear infringement on academic freedom. This top-down mandate of administrators telling faculty what to do with our courses is not going to fly around here." Professor Drone slumped in his chair, thinking, "Well, it's not my job. I wasn't trained to do this assessment stuff, so I'm not taking on anything else." Chair Martina Nett, like her fellow chairs around campus, continued to deny the need to think about, or do, assessment. Thus, initially no one in the Department of Literature took responsibility for assessment much less admitted to its urgent need. Chair Nett was avoiding an even bigger problem. The literature teaching option, a shared program with the College of Teaching and Learning, was preparing for its periodic state and national review. The program coordinator in the department, Professor Lucy Guse, had been inundated by e-mails from colleagues in the College of Teaching and Learning, but she was so busy attending conferences and writing articles in her quest for tenure that she couldn't seem to find the time to get involved in the process. Surely, the faculty would just take care of it, she assumed. Besides, the secondary education majors all had good grades in their literature courses, so the state board and national reviewers would be satisfied.

Assessment personnel were very much aware of the department's inaction. Pondering this challenging situation, IE staffers Dr. Kev Larr and Ms. B.P. Vest realized that they had to break through the denial before progress could be made, and they needed both top-down and bottom-up support. First, they worked on obtaining commitments to the assessment process from upper-level administrators, including the provost, vice presidents, deans, and directors of professional units. Second, IE tackled changing faculty culture through multiple avenues of professional development, such as workshops to provide information and teach skills, and forums to discuss the benefits of assessment to individual faculty members and to units.

In the first workshop, Professor Delay gave voice to most faculty members' confusion: "We already assess students. We give grades. Why do we need to do anything differently?" Dr. Kev Larr explained that grades are an amalgam of all class requirements—tests, papers, homework, attendance, participation, and so forth. As an example, he asked faculty to think about a single assignment for which students are asked to find relevant information, summarize that information, and integrate that information with class material. "A student who competently completes some, but not all, of those tasks," he continued, "may earn a B or a C, but the grade provides no information about which parts of the assignment were good and which parts were weak. Assessment allows us to disaggregate the tasks to determine how students do on each part of the assignment. Faculty can then use this information to adjust their lesson plans in order to reinforce the weak parts, while leaving the other parts alone."

"How many of you cook?" Miss B. P. Vest asked. "If you taste a dish and decide it's not quite right, how do you know which ingredients to adjust? This is the question that assessment seeks to answer for student learning."

Anger in the Department of Literature: "Why Me? It's Not Fair"

Once all the reasonable objections had been addressed, what remained was a powerful emotional resistance fueled by anger. On a daily basis, faculty in the Department of Literature could be heard complaining in the halls and exploding in the faculty lounge as professors railed against their new bête noir.

Professor Delay bellowed, "They're dumping this assessment stuff on us, and we don't have time to do it. Besides, those 'experts' don't know what it's like in the real world. They don't deal with our students. They don't have the time demands we do."

Professor A. Pathy thundered, "This is useless paperwork, the job of an administrator, not someone with a Ph.D. in my field. This is pure 'educationese'—the College of Teaching and Learning is taking over the Department of Literature."

Professor Typical angrily roared, "What about my academic freedom?" And he placed photocopies of the American Association of University Professors guidelines in every department member's mailbox.

Professor Drone whined, "Why do you want this information? Are you going to evaluate my performance? It's not fair to rate me on how my students do—you know how unmotivated our students are these days."

Professor Paranoia, although quiet, knew what was really going on—his chair was out to get him.

Finally jerked out of her denial, Chair Nett realized that someone had to be responsible for assessment in the department. She commanded Professor Solo: "Make it so!"

Professor Solo exploded, "What part of my job do you want me to give up to do this assessment stuff?"

Chair Nett shook her head and sighed. "Just do it! I'm sorry, but I don't have any resources to compensate you." Begrudgingly, Professor Solo, believing herself a paragon of efficiency, quickly threw together some assessment items for each course and told faculty to include the items as part of the final exam.

The other faculty members were angry that they had to include extra items, and, besides, they did not like the items Professor Solo had developed. Professor Delay responded with practiced passive aggression: "The heck with this; I'll just teach to the test and show them how great I am."

On the day of the final exam, Professor Typical told his students, "Items 30–45 are assessment items that we were forced to include. Do your best, but don't worry; I won't count these as part of your grade." Predictably, most students performed poorly on assessment items, except for Professor Delay's students, who performed unrealistically well.

When Professor Solo presented a summary of the collected data at a faculty meeting, Professor Typical protested, "Of course students did poorly. Those assessment questions were not fair. Maybe some people teach that stuff, but I sure don't."

Professor Delay retreated inward, stating: "I'm going to continue teaching to the test. There's nothing wrong with that. My students learned what we wanted them to learn."

While on a research trip to nail down documentation for an article that would aid her bid for tenure, Dr. Guse forwarded Chair Nett's e-mails to the instructor of the literature methods course, Professor S. Choir. She reminded him that the methods course objectives had to be aligned with national and state standards, that he had to demonstrate how each is assessed, and that he had to show how the program used these assessments to improve. Seeing more work and red, S. Choir pounded his keyboard, reminding his dean and chair of the university's policies regarding academic freedom, and threatening to sue.

Desperate to quell faculty anger about assessment processes, IE sought out champions—true believers among the faculty, those already involved in assessment in their departments. IE knew that people were more easily persuaded by their peers, and these champions were "just like us," dealing with the same teaching, scholarship, and service loads. Thus, it was harder for faculty to dismiss these champions than it was to dismiss "those blankety-blank administrators."

IE also partnered with the University Assessment Committee (UAC), a committee that had been established before the student learning assessment hubbub and was already active in assisting departments with various assessment activities. IE and UAC personnel went to departments in pairs to help faculty develop learning objectives, answer faculty questions about assessment, and help them enter assessment information into the university database. IE and UAC felt it was essential to send their personnel in pairs because they were "non-expert" faculty members, and some were hesitant to go to departments alone. More importantly, sending faculty members delivered a strong message to departments that their peers were concerned about assessment and willing to spend their time helping colleagues. This step proved to be beneficial to faculty and to the advancement of assessment alike. Faculty felt freer to complain to colleagues and to express fears and concerns that they may have been reluctant to express to IE personnel, who were perceived

as "experts." Thus, the partnership between the faculty peers and IE personnel provided faculty with both emotional and informational support in the
assessment process. Having competent, patient IE personnel was a key to
defusing the anger. They consistently emphasized their role as facilitators
and expressed the attitude "We will do anything to help you."

Change is never quick or easy, and some faculty continued to angrily
denounce the process.

Professor Chekkedout argued, "I teach creative writing. I can't use
multiple-choice tests to find out if my students can write a short story."

Professor Methods added, "I'm not interested in how well they write
poetry or they know the conventions of an Italian sonnet. I want to know if
they can teach high school students to understand a sonnet."

IE calmly reminded them, "This is your curriculum, these are your
courses, and you do not want administrators doing this for you or to you.
And assessment is not just about a traditional test. It's about designing consistent scoring guides to evaluate various types of student performances."
For the Professor Typicals of the university, one message had to be repeated
often: "*You* get to decide what is important for your students to learn, and
how best to measure that learning. Thus, *you* have the opportunity to ensure
that assessment does not infringe on your academic freedom." Furthermore,
providing opportunities for faculty to express their anger gradually helped to
dispel that anger so that emotional energy could be directed toward achieving positive outcomes.

Bargaining in the Department of Literature: "If I Do This, What Will You Do for Me?"

The subsiding tide of anger cleared the way for more rational, though often
selfish, negotiation. As faculty began to think about assessment, they saw
that it could be used as leverage. Part of the bargaining process involved
coming to an understanding about how assessment data were to be used.
Chair Nett saw assessment as an opportunity to evaluate individual faculty
members. Her agenda for assessment was to "ferret out" the faculty who
were not performing well in the classroom, and she not-so-subtly communicated this agenda to others. Thus, Professor Paranoia's perception that her
chair was out to get her was somewhat true. The professor certainly was not
alone in her fear that assessment data would be used to judge individual
faculty members, and the department urgently needed intervention. When
IE heard about the department's misunderstandings and concerns, staff conducted a series of workshops that sought to educate administrators and faculty about the ethical collection, summary, and use of assessment data. These
workshops placed all aspects of assessment within the context of its primary

purpose: informed decision making regarding, and enhancement of, student learning.

IE's role in educating faculty was necessary, but it still wasn't enough to transform the campus culture. IE could remove the "stick" by telling departments they should not use assessment data in a punitive manner, but they also needed "carrots" to encourage assessment efforts. Departments had to have motivation to tackle the hard work of assessment, and one bargaining tool that IE created was assessment grants. Departments were encouraged to apply for assessment grants to fund various assessment activities, such as purchasing standardized exams, paying faculty to develop assessment items or scoring rubrics, buying equipment necessary for assessment activities (e.g., video recorders for oral communication courses and music courses), and providing stipends for faculty time spent scoring assessment instruments.

Of course, the Department of Literature as a whole did not apply for an assessment grant in the first year because Chair Nett and the faculty had relegated assessment responsibilities to Professor Solo, who was still resentful of the extra work. Professor Solo thought, "Why should I spend my time writing a grant proposal that is not going to benefit me?" However, one faculty member in the teaching program, Professor Collaborative, jumped on the opportunity to get some help redesigning his adolescent literature course. He requested a stipend for himself and another faculty member to create an assessment instrument that would meet all these different standards required for the looming national and state reviews. When his grant was funded, Professor Collaborative thought, "I guess the university really does want to help us with assessment tasks. This stipend will push me to get this project completed, and it definitely improves my morale about doing the extra work."

In order to disseminate information about assessment issues and assessment grants themselves, IE asked departments and individual faculty members receiving assessment grants to share their grant-funded assessment experiences via poster presentations at the IE Assessment Exemplar Conference. Being quite careful not to add to the burden of assessment, IE made the poster presentation as easy as possible by creating the posters themselves, with information sent by the departments, and by setting up the posters at the conference. All departments had only one task—send a representative to answer questions. Significantly, the Assessment Exemplar Conference provided additional professional development as departments learned about various assessment activities in which others were engaged, pitfalls to avoid, and benefits to be gained.

The Assessment Exemplar Conference convinced Chair Nett that assessment was here to stay; other departments were benefiting from their assessment efforts, and she was aware her department could reap similar rewards by fully engaging in the process. Importantly, she also realized that the

Department of Literature, too, could bargain for what it needed to conduct assessment, and faculty did not have to let all assessment efforts "come out of their hide." She also recognized that Professor Solo's style of working independently had turned off faculty to the process.

Adding to the pressure, the dean of the College of Teaching and Learning called Chair Nett to get a report of how the student learning objectives in literature courses aligned with the goals of the department's teaching program option. Returning from a trip to a distant library with her research complete, Lucy Guse was surprised to find nothing had been accomplished in her absence. Chair Nett was chagrined that she had resisted the assessment process for so long because it was now clear that participating in an ongoing assessment process would eliminate the pressure of these last-minute report demands. How many times had IE told her that there was no need to develop a separate set of objectives and assessment procedures to meet various needs? Instead, data from a single set of objectives could be multipurpose, meeting the needs of various levels of assessment—course, department, program, accreditation, and university. And how many times had IE told her that if data were entered into the university's database, then reports could be printed as needed?

So Chair Nett took two very important actions: she bargained with the dean of the college to allow reassigned time for a faculty person to coordinate assessment efforts, and she asked Professor Consensus to take over these duties. Professor Consensus, she thought, was a wise choice because he had some assessment experience and was well liked by the faculty in the department. Professor Consensus immediately called a meeting and asked faculty for their opinions regarding the assessment process.

Professor A. Pathy ventured, "I don't believe this is going to be useful, but at least someone asked for my opinion."

Professor Drone added, "Thank goodness someone besides me has to do this. What do you need from us?"

Professor Consensus engaged the faculty members in a meaty discussion about what they viewed as the most important learning objectives for their courses. He reminded them to look at the standards that they needed to address for the teacher education accreditation process as well. Groups of faculty who taught the same courses eventually agreed on a small set of common objectives.

Professor Typical was quick to underscore, "I can add other objectives that are unique to my course!"

Because of Professor Consensus's inclusive approach and reassurance that he would be the facilitator and collector, faculty members were able to calm down and agree on an assessment process.

Professor Delay asked, "Why don't we all just teach to the test? What's wrong with that, anyway?"

Professor Consensus calmly responded, "There's nothing inherently wrong with teaching to the test, but it depends on the nature of the test. If our assessment items included everything we want students to know and be able to do, then teaching to the test would be reasonable. However, as we have included only a sample of things that we want students to know and do, teaching to the test is akin to holding students responsible for learning only a small part of the course material. Nevertheless, we should teach to all our objectives."

Professor Drone said, "But if we set the bar low, students will do well, the department will look good, and we won't have to change anything. I certainly don't have time to modify my courses."

Professor Consensus was not riled; he understood that temptation. Instead, he appealed to the faculty's professional ethics: "That is one approach to assessment, but I suspect that none of us would be very proud of our students, or ourselves, if we took that approach. And you have to remember that assessment results that are poor can provide a wealth of information regarding what we might want to change."

"And what could be even worse," Professor S. Choir chimed in, "is if our students make high grades on our assessments but don't score well on the teacher licensure tests, they might come back and sue us!"

"That's right," said Chair Nett. "Some of these assessments ought to predict success or failure on those tests too. Remember, those IE people are always saying that there are two ways to win with assessment: if we achieve our goal, we win, and if we do not achieve our goal, we devise a way to help our students improve. In either case, we win by gaining important information about student learning that we can use to improve our curriculum. Over a period of time, our accreditors don't expect our students to score perfectly—just to show improvement." Faculty in the Department of Literature decided that assessment should be embedded in the course and be part of the students' grades.

Professor Typical was quick to point out, "You can't tell us how to weight the assessment items, though. I still have some academic freedom left."

The College of Teaching and Learning dean offered to pay for an outside consultant, Dr. Geta Long, to facilitate a planning session. He had a special grant that could be used to pay the faculty stipends and provide meals for those who participated in the workshops. Chair Nett invited both literature and education faculty to the workshop and sweetened the pot with promises of reassigned time as well as funds to purchase materials and resources.

In short, the administration, IR, and IE made many bargaining chips available to departments—professional development, assessment grants, assessment conferences, multipurpose assessments, stipends, and database-produced reports. All these chips served to increase the motivation to do assessment and improve faculty morale about spending the time necessary to do it well. All departments had to do was take the deal.

Depression in the Department of Literature: "I Don't Care Anymore"

At the end of the semester, Professor Consensus presented a summary of the assessment data at a department meeting. The data continued to show weak performance by the students. He asked faculty, "Now that we have used these assessment items, do you think they might need some tweaking? Are they a fair assessment of what we want our students to learn? If the items are okay, then we need to think about why our students do not seem to be learning what we feel is important."

Professor Delay shook his head and said, "Look, we've wasted enough time on assessment, and for what? These results are discouraging, and I just want to go on break and forget about it for awhile."

Professor Drone agreed and added, "It's obviously the students' fault. You know how unmotivated our students are. I don't know what we can do about it. I had high hopes for this assessment stuff, but it didn't work, and I don't have time to figure out what to do differently. I can barely keep my head above water."

Professor Typical rang the same bell. "Our job is to give students the information. If they don't take it, it's not my problem. The weak students deserve to be weeded out; not everyone is going to make it in college. I remember the days when our grades had to conform to a bell curve."

Professor Oldschool, who was close to retirement, simply shook his head and sighed. "The field has changed so much since I got into it, I don't feel I can be effective any longer. Our students were so much better when I first started here. I would rather retire early than deal with this assessment mess anymore."

Professor S. S. Minnow agreed. "I'm leaving this sinking ship. There is too much to do. We're asked to do more every day. I can't keep up."

Even Professor Consensus was depressed. "I gave it the old college try as departmental assessment coordinator, but everyone expects me to do all the work. They won't talk about how the results could translate into something positive, and I feel I'm all alone on this disappearing island with no one to listen to me or appreciate me."

This time Chair Nett was prepared to spur faculty out of their funk and get them thinking productively again. She was finally convinced that assessment was tied to the budget. The university was poised to reallocate funding to programs that validated their needs through the strategic planning process. The days of "the squeaky wheel getting the grease" were over.

The new game plan was "plan, do, check, act"—*plan* by developing objectives that would benefit the students and curricular programs, *do* by implementing the plan, *check* by assessing whether the objectives were met, and *act* by using the assessment data to improve the program (closing the loop). Administrators needed to determine that money was spent wisely, which meant that budget requests had to support the department's and university's strategic plan. Thus, Chair Nett encouraged her faculty to withhold judgment until after the workshop with Geta Long, at which they would discuss what the department should do with its assessment data and how the data could be used to improve the program.

Acceptance in the Department of Literature: "Finding a Way Forward"

At the end of the semester, the faculty gathered at Geta Long's workshop. They sat down together reluctantly and started to share their experiences over fresh "crowsants." Professors Delay and A. Pathy were not eager to change the projects they had developed and perfected over the past 10 years. But even Professor S. Choir exclaimed, "The food's not bad, and the extra pay will cover the cost of my lawyer's retainer fee!" They all agreed to listen to what Dr. Long had to say. She assured the faculty that they themselves had the expertise to accomplish effective assessment. In fact, she pointed out that faculty routinely make adjustments to a course when it is clear that students aren't learning the material; here they were being asked to think about the same issues, but at the program level. Dr. Long went on to facilitate a discussion of course sequencing, topic coverage across the curriculum, and the possible addition of a new course, all in light of the findings from their assessment. The IE staff sat in the back of the room and smiled. Sometimes you need someone from the outside to make these points for you.

Chair Nett surveyed Geta Long's workshop in amazement. All the literature and teaching faculty were there—and they were talking with each other! Professors Typical and Collaborative were excitedly discussing an assignment for a Shakespeare lesson plan analysis, and the two of them quickly figured out that this assignment could be used to demonstrate not only students' skills in lesson planning and teaching methods but their knowledge of the specific Shakespearean play being studied. Before they knew it, they had designed a scoring guide that could be used to evaluate each student's knowledge and skills as well as provide ongoing data about how effectively the program was meeting national and state standards. Even soft-spoken Professor I.D. Savant asked naively, "Can I take this out of my course if it's not working?" and "Is there a reason for our department to continue to require courses like Sanskrit in Translation?"

Pondering the next chairs' meeting, Chair Nett announced, "I'm going to start sharing our plan with other chairs and see what they have been doing. I know several departments have received funding because they developed effective assessment strategies. I finally feel like we are all in this together, and maybe we can partner to help each other succeed."

The IE staff thought the real winners were also the students, who ultimately provided services as professionals in their communities, and upper-level administrators, who now saw the necessity of a combined top-down, bottom-up process.

Assessment nirvana had been attained . . . almost. The truth is that the assessment process is never over; the loop is closed as new ideas born of previous assessments create more data that are fed into the loop. Up ahead on the road to perfection lies another SACS visit, another accreditation . . .

Recommendations

After a decade of erratic progress, we can look back on our successes and failures with a new perspective and wish we had known then what we know now. In that spirit, we offer these recommendations to provide you a shorter, straighter path to assessment nirvana:

1. Create an organizational structure that promotes effective assessment.
   a. Tie assessment to the institution's strategic plan and to units' strategic plans. Budget allocations should be based on assessment data.
   b. Upper-level administrators must communicate to deans and chairs the importance of tying assessment to strategic plans. Deans and chairs who have operated via the "squeaky wheel" principle will need to be convinced that assessment data will be used to allocate resources.
2. Educate, educate, educate!
   a. Provide professional development to administrators and faculty. Make use of a variety of approaches—IE/IR-led workshops, IE/IR question-and-answer sessions at departmental meetings, faculty-led workshops, faculty learning communities, newsletters, fireside chats, personal support, and on-campus assessment conferences.
   b. Make resources known so that units can share. Encourage collaboration within and across disciplines. We found, for instance, that assessment rubrics designed in the English and Communication Department could be easily adapted to evaluate written and oral assignments in many courses.

3. Provide incentives and support.
   a. Our assessment grant is an example of how departments can get resources necessary for doing assessment. Provide stipends for assessment activities that are more time consuming—for example, reading papers in large required English courses, developing/refining grading rubrics, and watching videos for oral communication courses. Even a small stipend or gift certificate to the campus bookstore or computer store tells faculty their time is valuable and appreciated.
   b. Personal support is crucial. Form partnerships between people who are assessment savvy and those who need help. IE/IR personnel must be perceived as available, supportive, and patient. Support from other faculty "just like us" helps to increase knowledge and improve attitudes about assessment.
4. Use assessment data and use them responsibly.
   a. Faculty need to believe that assessment data will not be used against them. IE/IR, deans, and chairs must earn the trust of faculty by demonstrating ethical use of assessment data.
   b. Help faculty maintain, review, and analyze the results of assessments. Help departments close the loop by maintaining constant communication among upper-level administration, IE/ IR, assessment committees, deans, chairs, and faculty.
   c. Faculty must believe that assessment data will be used to improve the curriculum. Deans and chairs need to ensure that faculty are expected, and given time, to discuss assessment data and possible changes to the curriculum. When faculty own the process, they are empowered to make informed decisions. When faculty are shown that assessment makes both teaching and learning better, they will feel excited to teach students this way while at the same time working toward the university's larger goals.

As Woodrow Wilson wisely stated, "It is easier to move a cemetery than to effect a change in curriculum." When faculty can put their personal preferences aside, they can pool their resources to create assessments that not only measure student and program success but also become real-world motivational and instructional tools. Ultimately and at its best, the assessment process truly facilitates student learning.

References

Kübler-Ross, E. (1969). *On death and dying.* New York: MacMillan.

About the Authors

Rose Perrine is a professor in the Department of Psychology at EKU, where she teaches research methodology. She also serves as the university's coordinator of general education and assessment.

Charlie Sweet is a foundation professor of English and co-director of the university's Teaching and Learning Center at EKU. With Hal Blythe, he is the coauthor of more than 700 publications, including 10 books, critical articles in literary studies and educational research, and popular fiction.

Hal Blythe is a foundation professor of English and co-director of the Teaching and Learning Center at EKU. With Charlie Sweet, he is the coauthor of over 700 publications.

Paula Kopacz is a foundation professor of English at EKU. She has been teaching for over 30 years, and she publishes mainly in the field of early American literature.

Dorie Combs is a professor in the Department of Curriculum and instructor at Eastern Kentucky University. A member of the Kentucky Board of Education, she teaches middle-grade curriculum and reading/language arts.

Onda Bennett is currently interim dean of University Programs and an associate professor in the Department of Occupational Therapy at EKU. Having held administrative positions in higher education for the past 15 years, she focuses her research and teaching on evidence-based practice, community mental health, and pedagogy in higher education.

Stacey Street is the assistant director of assessment and strategic planning in the Division of Institutional Effectiveness and Research at EKU.

E. J. Keeley is the executive director of institutional effectiveness and research at EKU. With extensive leadership experience in public, private, and for-profit universities, he has published extensively in the areas of student learning assessment, using data to improve retention/graduation performance, and predictors of academic success.

6

HOW IT TOOK
A WHOLE VILLAGE

Eileen Matthews
Gallaudet University

Gallaudet University, founded in 1864 by an act of Congress, takes great pride in its uniqueness. Unlike any other university in the world, Gallaudet's academic programs are designed to provide deaf and hard-of-hearing students with a comprehensive liberal education at the undergraduate and graduate levels. Gallaudet is a bilingual community in which students, faculty, and staff are expected to achieve a specified level of proficiency in American Sign Language and English. The Education of the Deaf Act of 1986 changed Gallaudet from a college to a university, but teaching deaf students remains its core value. Research and dissemination of knowledge about deafness as well as discipline-based research are high priorities for the university, but if one were to track the dollars, one would see that the heart of Gallaudet University is its investment in the undergraduate education of deaf and hard-of-hearing students. The diversity of Gallaudet's student body is another source of pride. Not only does Gallaudet reflect the national increase in students from diverse racial and ethnic backgrounds, but its students possess a wide range of signing skills and knowledge of sign languages from around the world. This presents a challenge and a richness to the community that distinguish Gallaudet from other higher education communities. Just as one cannot claim to be a scholar of African American history without having spent considerable amounts of time in the Moorland-Spingarn Research Center at Howard University, one cannot claim to be

The author wishes to thank Olugbenga Aina and Janice Johnson for their contributions to this chapter, and Jiayi Zhou, who helped develop Figure 6.1.

a scholar of deafness without having studied, conducted research, attended workshops, or taught at Gallaudet University. The Gallaudet experience is an essential credential for those aspiring to work in the field of deafness and with deaf and hard-of-hearing students. Gallaudet enjoys the distinction and the enormous responsibility of being in a class of its own.

I arrived at Gallaudet University with 10 years of teaching and curriculum development experience under my belt and remained for another 27 years. During my first 7 years at Gallaudet, I worked with students in the developmental English and math program at Gallaudet's satellite Northwest Campus (NWC) on Kalmia Road in Northwest, Washington, D.C. As a part of our continual effort to improve teaching and learning, a team of NWC faculty and staff visited Alverno College in Wisconsin. After my third visit, I was hooked on assessment as teaching. I became passionate about assessment as a transformational means of pedagogy capable of improving teaching and learning.

Fortunately for those of us at Gallaudet's NWC, our dean, Dr. Ann Davidson Powell, was both an administrator and a student-centered educator. She provided opportunities for faculty and staff to learn more about assessment and sharpen our pedagogical skills. When Gallaudet decided to offer an associate's degree program, I was asked to lead the initiative at the NWC. If you ever have the opportunity to build an academic program from the ground up, go for it! It is an exciting and energizing experience. With an army of highly motivated, caring, and innovative faculty, faculty and staff from the NWC created an assessment-based associate's degree program for office technology that emphasized:

1. Assessment as learning
2. Student learning outcomes
3. Timely feedback
4. Student self-assessment and peer assessment
5. Rubrics
6. Engagement of students in learning
7. Use of videotaping to capture students' growth
8. Interdisciplinary approaches to instruction
9. Shared accountability for student performance

That was the good news!

The bad news was that when the NWC closed and faculty members were dispersed to their discipline homes on the main campus, most, if not all, of our synergy, assessment work, and innovative practices were lost in new committee work, politics, and the university's lack of interest in associate degree programs. Teaching, learning, and assessment at NWC had truly been a team effort. The breaking up of the NWC faculty and staff made it much more difficult, if not impossible, to continue our practices. I returned to the classroom and, within this comparatively limited scope, continued to use Angelo's and Cross's (1993) techniques to inform myself how I was doing and what my students were learning. I developed rubrics. I designed varied assessment instruments that allowed students to demonstrate what they knew and could do. I kept up with the work of leaders in the assessment field. Unfortunately, what I and others from NWC were doing was only a drop in the proverbial bucket. And then, bingo! I became the new associate dean of the Center for Academic Programs and Student Services (CAPSS) and a new door opened up to me, offering an opportunity to search for ways to link assessment efforts across departments.

The Missing Link

As the associate dean of CAPSS, I was responsible for academic support offices—the Academic Advising Office, Tutorial & Instructional Programs, the Office for Students with Disabilities, the Career Center, the First Year Experience Program, the Mentoring Program, and the Office of International Programs and Services. Many of the individuals in these offices thought of themselves as support staff. I knew they were teachers, and within 3 years, all units were assessment based and produced semester reports with evidence of what students who used their services had learned. Much to our pleasure, the "Evaluation of the Periodic Review Report of Gallaudet," prepared by the Middle States Commission on Higher Education (MSCHE), acknowledged the work of CAPSS and its implications for the entire university in the section on "Evidence of Outcomes Assessment." Specifically, the commission commended CAPSS for an assessment plan that linked its six academic programs to the center mission of CAPSS and the university's strategic goals—a model by which a university-wide assessment infrastructure could be developed. The review team was encouraged by the creation of a position responsible for coordinating assessment efforts across the university, although that position had not yet been filled when the periodic review report was compiled. In short, the necessary components were in place—a coordinator role, a model from which to build, external accreditation standards, and a range of internal tools that were already in use. What the MSCHE did not see during its accreditation visit was a coordinated implementation of assessment across the institution or a clearly defined process for making appropriate use of assessment data. This lack of a coordinated university-wide assessment planning process was the reason why Gallaudet did not meet MSCHE's assessment standards. This finding, along with deficiencies in other areas, threatened our accreditation. Developing a comprehensive university-wide assessment process was no longer optional, but mandatory! Addressing the team's findings about weaknesses in our assessment process became one of the main reasons why the incoming provost asked me to assume responsibility for coordinating efforts to implement a university-wide assessment process—one that would lead to results that could be documented, shared, and used for improving student learning. For the second time in my career, I was placed in a position that enabled me to pull together individuals interested in and enthusiastic about building something from the ground up.

Under normal circumstances, developing a comprehensive university-wide assessment process for the entire university would have taken at least 5 years, but these were tumultuous times: During this period students had taken to the streets and closed down the campus over the selection of a new president; faculty and staff had voiced grave misgivings about the presidential selection process; the media portrayal of these events exacerbated the confusion; GallyNet-L, a Listserv, provided a platform for anyone and everyone who had real or imagined unresolved grievances with Gallaudet; and the university heard from unhappy alumni as well as foundations. Furthermore, enrolled and prospective students and their parents wanted to know if we were accredited or not. Amid all this, the Gallaudet community was visibly shaken by the knowledge that the university did not meet 8 of the 14 standards for accreditation. The Gallaudet spirit deserves accolades, because this disquiet was exceeded by its determination to do what was necessary to preserve the university for future generations of deaf and hard-of-hearing students.

For those of us who have removed our blinders, it is easy to see that establishing an assessment process is mandatory for all in higher education. The university poured resources into summer work, faculty overload, faculty and staff reassignments, development of a new general studies curriculum, the new Office of Institutional Research, and the new Office of Assessment to ensure that we met all assessment standards within the time allotted us by MSCHE. Nine months later during the MSCHE's final visit and exit report, the Gallaudet community packed the Swindells Auditorium to learn our fate. Every time the MSCHE's site visit team chair acknowledged that a standard had been met, hands went up into the air and we cheered. Then quickly, we collapsed into silence for news of the next standard. I leaned on my colleague for support when we arrived at Standard 14 and I heard Gallaudet University's assessment process described as "superb" and "a model for other universities." We had done it! We'd come out on the other side twice as strong as when we entered. The task and the timelines were of such a magnitude that it would have been impossible for an assessment office that consisted of only two people (i.e., an executive director and a program coordinator) to accomplish this feat. Every faculty member, every staff person, and every administrator at Gallaudet contributed to this victory.

How Did We Do It? Our Strategies

How did Gallaudet University move from being one of many universities without a concrete assessment mechanism to being a model for other universities? In the heat of the moment I would probably not have been able to tell you, but now, in hindsight, I can recollect successful and not-so-successful strategies, plus some hindrances. Here are some of the strategies that fueled our efforts.

Strategy 1: Identify Experts on Your Campus

Every campus has faculty and staff experts on assessment. Find them and engage them. I asked 12 of those individuals to serve on my initial advisory board, and only 2 were unable to accept my invitation. The board met weekly during the heat of July and the first part of August, when most faculty were not on campus, but these individuals made the sacrifice and gave time to this effort. They were instrumental in paving the way for our later success and were acknowledged by name on the assessment website. The assessment advisory board became a sounding board for me. We hammered out the meanings of words, concepts, and processes. We discussed what made sense for Gallaudet. Before disseminating any information or making any presentations, I received critical feedback from the advisory board. They assisted me in producing the college's assessment handbook and other written and electronic materials that would be used by the community.

Strategy 2: Tap Into Experts

Tap into the knowledge of experts in the field through their books, their websites, and materials from assessment conferences. I saw myself as a resource. I opened an assessment resource room within my office suite and invited members of the campus community to borrow any resources they wanted. The assessment resource room had over 150 resources, which the program coordinator gathered within 2 months. Unfortunately, the assessment resource room was not the success I had hoped it would be, primarily because I could not find the time to market it aggressively; it simply could not be a priority during the start-up year. Also, the program coordinator did not have time to become the librarian for this room in addition to her normal duties. Books were checked out on the honor system. Very few books were returned to the room, and I suspect that had more to do with memory than a lack of honesty. There was an open house and the community was invited to munch on pastries and browse through the materials. A lot of people came during the open house, but not many came after that. With the benefit of hindsight, I would do several things differently. First, I would have a committee to review each book and share their critiques with the campus community. Second, I would start a book club to read and discuss these books over a brown bag lunch. Third, I would promote these books during my presentations and bring them with me to give people the opportunity to scan the books for topics recently discussed.

Strategy 3: *Share and Share and Share Information*

And when you think you have shared with everyone, start all over again. When the academic year began, I was ready to share information about the cyclical assessment process that was accepted in the field of higher education and that should be adopted by Gallaudet. Only a few with political agendas thought that the process for assessing student learning should look different. The provost opened the door to his Academic Affairs Management Team. The deans opened doors to meetings with their chairs, and the department chairs in turn opened doors to their department members. The vice president of administration and finance opened the doors to his business offices. CAPSS continued to be a model. I gave interactive workshops to faculty in the Division of Academic Affairs, to staff in the Office of Student Affairs and academic support units, and to employees in administration and finance. During these workshops, participants wrote or revised unit mission statements, developed student learning outcome statements, identified various assessment tools, and discussed how assessment results would be used to improve student learning. I operated on the premise that everyone at a university shares the responsibility for educating its students. Some on campus are responsible for teaching general studies, major courses, and graduate courses; others are responsible for teaching about multiculturalism, student civic responsibility, sportsmanship, and college survival skills; and still others are responsible for teaching students how to protect themselves on campus or how to make the most out of a local or international internship experience. Ultimately, everything happening at an institution of higher education should foster student learning, and once the concept was introduced, staff readily saw how they were supporting student learning.

I usually requested 3 to 4 hours for a workshop presentation that gave an overview of the entire assessment process, and I asked that as many people from the unit as possible attend. Once departments started the process, I was occasionally called in for an hour-long department meeting to answer questions or explain a specific component of the assessment cycle, as show in Figure 6.1.

did, I used and disseminated their work as models. Early in the process I posted on our web page a list of campus consultants and their areas of expertise, thereby reinforcing the notion that individuals on campus were already engaged in assessment and willing to support the efforts of others. The Office of Assessment published a booklet entitled "Exemplary Assessment Practices," which contained some of the best departmental models that documented complete assessment cycles, including how change was being implemented.

Strategy 8: Spark Interest in the Use of Rubrics

Rubrics became a topic of great interest at Gallaudet. In addition to bringing in a specialist to present on rubrics and consult with departments, the Office of Assessment also produced models of Gallaudet faculty–developed rubrics that could be modified to fit the purposes of other departments.

All these strategies resulted in a critical core of believers and users of the assessment process. Signs of a transforming university could be found in discussions of our mission, bilingualism, diversity and learning outcomes. We were working toward leaving behind the former tendency for beautifully written reports that were left to gather dust and moving toward a culture of evidence, empiricism, results, assessment, and student learning outcomes. We were absolutely on the right track and needed only to follow our own advice about sustaining this momentum.

Assessment Allies: Couldn't Do Without Them!

During the 2007–2008 assessment trek, the university carried a lot of baggage that had to be jettisoned and faced some new realities: a new emphasis brought in by a new administration, another report, more action plans, the start of a new strategic plan, and one more climate study revealing some rather unfavorable snapshots of us. Although many of these developments were new, they were viewed as part of an established cycle of window-dressing initiatives that had honed report writers' adeptness and that the jaded campus community was all too familiar with and tired of. If this assessment effort were not to be any different from past efforts, individuals and departments wanted to know up front so they could waste as little time on it as possible. Our task therefore was to confirm the credibility of the assessment process, establish that assessment as university culture was here to stay, and win the confidence of the community in the process. All this allowed us to get to first base.

Learning by faculty, staff, administrators, and the Office of Assessment took place throughout the process. Some, particularly within the graduate school, had been involved in assessment for many years and easily merged into the flow. Conversely, knowledge of assessment as a cyclical process varied in most undergraduate academic departments. Meanwhile, academic support programs were accustomed to evaluating program success but were less likely to work along the lines of assessing student learning outcomes. Ten months into the development of our campus-wide assessment process, a minimum of 87% of the academic programs and academic support programs had a written mission statement, desired student learning outcomes, learning opportunities, and assessment tools. In addition to this foundation, departments had assessed learning outcomes, identified results and how the results would be used, and shared the results with the campus community on the assessment website. This exceeded my expectation of 50%–60% engagement, which would have been acceptable as evidence of a serious effort to our accrediting agency. Achieving this critical mass was the key enabling the university to move forward and enable the holdouts to convert to assessment practices. That 87% of the undergraduate departments traveled around the assessment cycle in two semesters is phenomenal—a tribute to the faculty, staff, and administrators, who love what they do and aspire to do better. A lot of credit for this success goes to the administrators at Gallaudet. If you are in a situation where you don't have at least one administrative champion, you might find more helpful information in other chapters of this book. At the beginning of Gallaudet's journey, provost Stephen Weiner opened a new assessment office that reported directly to him. Given his time in the classroom, he knew this was a necessary administrative structure to validate the importance of assessment and the need for a more student-centered approach to teaching and learning. The deans also listened carefully, believed in the transformation, and gave me access to chairs' meetings for presentations. At least half of the deans attended one of the national conferences on assessment during this time and offered financial support enabling individuals within their units to attend assessment conferences. The deans were always willing and eager to communicate information to their faculty and staff on my behalf. Whenever outside experts were invited to campus, they met with the president and the provost. The deans would usually attend their campus-wide presentations and join them for a lunch meeting. Their invaluable support facilitated our speedy arrival at a university-wide assessment process.

Knowing the prevailing cynicism on campus toward reports and endless committee work, I avoided talking about accreditation and loss of accreditation as the primary reason for engaging in assessment. I framed discussions and actions regarding assessment around teaching, learning, and assessment as a process that yields valuable information:

> What do students who have completed your course know? What can they do? What do they value? How do you know students are achieving desired

outcomes? How do academic support units know that students are learning anything when they go to academic advising, the tutorial center, or the career center? How are we doing with diversity? Is the climate more conducive to learning this year for students of color than it was 5 years go? Are students of color being outperformed by their White counterparts? Do residential programs reinforce and supplement what students are learning inside and outside the classroom? Are our answers to these questions based on gut feelings or evidence?

When communicating with administration and finance, I talked in a language they understood, referring to their national benchmarking standards. Offices of administration and finance were also able to inform us of their contribution to student success at Gallaudet:

Are students being prepared for future careers in business through our internship program? Is the cafeteria providing meals that nourish the body and mind? Can female students, gay men, lesbians, and students of various religions walk our campus free of the fear of physical harm or verbal or signed abuse?

These questions are examples of the kinds of critical inquiries that Gallaudet raised. The answers, if we use them properly, are the return on our investment in appropriately assessing learning outcomes, not the sum total of hours spent serving on countless university committees. Gallaudet's assessment process provided the university with an empirically based mechanism for discovering evidence-based answers to many of these questions. The process also led to other questions that needed answers. Most important, it led departments to changes that improved student learning.

The Simple Truth

In an analysis of closing reflections written by departments when they submitted the results of student learning outcomes assessment, four lessons learned seem to reflect Gallaudet's assessment spirit:

1. Assessment can benefit teaching and learning.
2. Assessment is not rocket science.
3. Assessment is not a report.
4. Assessment fosters conversations about one's discipline.

In many ways I felt vindicated by these outcomes and the exit report of our MSCHE accreditation team. More people than I had anticipated had acknowledged that what we were doing could improve student learning. The naysayers were falling further and further into the background as the hands, voices, and actions of those actively demonstrating that assessment works came to the forefront.

"Aha," "Wow," and "Oh My God" Moments

As I look back on our campus experiences, I realize there were many moments of "Aha," "Wow," and "Oh my God." Sometimes I would laugh out loud—something really needed in this business—and other times I would smile inwardly. An early "Aha" experience clarified my new role as executive director of the Office of Assessment, as the job description was considered a work in progress. One department chair sent me his department's draft of learning outcomes for feedback. What I realized was that I could not give the kind of feedback the department needed because what was really needed was a conversation among department members about their discipline. Oh sure, I could send back a few definitions and comments, but the professors needed to have a conversation among themselves. I could be there to facilitate that conversation, but those in that discipline needed to own the conversation, take direction themselves, and make decisions themselves. This experience helped me realize and value the importance of my role as a facilitator of dialogue rather than an expert dispenser of answers.

What I am about to describe started out as an "Oh my God" moment, signaling a disastrous decision, but ended up becoming an "Aha" moment of awakening. In an effort to be transparent, I sent out a lot of information in hard copy and through e-mail because our assessment website was not yet up and running. One day in February I sent out a simple chart with a fancy name, "Institutional Assessment Progress Report," that used check marks to identify parts of the assessment process each department had completed. These check marks spawned a wide range of emotional responses. Some departments felt pride in learning that they were moving ahead at a fast pace and ahead of the pack. Others indignantly claimed my information was wrong. Some department chairs admitted that they needed assistance; others accused me of losing their materials. Negative reactions, and sometimes overreactions, took me by surprise. More important, they demonstrated to me that the campus community was indeed examining and monitoring our assessment efforts. I realized from this experience that the momentum for working on the assessment process was not coming from the long hours I put in. It was coming from the faculty and staff involved in the process. Without their interest and commitment to teaching and assessing student learning outcomes, nothing I could have said or done would have made a difference.

Another benefit of the "Institutional Assessment Progress Report" was that it showed the entire community our progress in moving closer to instituting an assessment culture. Establishing a university-wide comprehensive assessment process was not about any one department, but about our collective efforts to better articulate the cognitive, psychomotor, and affective abilities of the Gallaudet student and especially the Gallaudet graduate. Wow!

The use of rubrics provided a "Wow" moment for many faculty and staff: As the use of rubrics began to spread across the undergraduate programs, more of us began to realize that grades are only good for calculating grade point averages. Grades do not tell us what a student has learned. Student grades more accurately reflect an individual instructor's standards; therefore, we should exercise caution when we write students' letters of recommendation based solely on their grades. Accurately recorded student assessment data based on scoring rubrics allows us to more precisely inform a student and others about that student's abilities and enables us to maintain the integrity of the institution's degree program.

Future Work on My To-Do List

Of course, all that the university needed to do to develop a comprehensive university-wide assessment process could not be done in one year, so I kept two lists of things to do. One list contained essential actions that had to be addressed during the inaugural startup year; the other list contained important issues I would resolve in the following year or years. Here are a few issues we still need to resolve:

1. There has been too much paperwork involved in our process. Companies are rescuing those of us inundated by paper with electronic systems for maintaining assessment data. Unfortunately, in the thick of bringing the entire university to a shared understanding of assessment, there was simply no time to examine the various software packages available.

2. As long as I can remember, there has been a data access problem at Gallaudet. After 3 years of being without an Office of Institutional Research, the university reestablished one in 2008. The question still remains as to how easily faculty and staff will be able to access data or receive assistance in accessing data needed for making educational decisions. Faculty and staff cannot be expected to use data in decision making if data access is limited to a chosen few.

3. Finally, the university must resolve how all its various academic processes are integrated. Simultaneously, the university initiated within the last year and continues to implement a new general studies curriculum, a university-wide assessment process, a new Office of Academic Quality, action plans for a variety of initiatives, a university

strategic planning process that consumed one initiated by the Division of Academic Affairs, a diversity plan operating out of the president's office, a bilingual center, a proposed center for teaching and learning, a new Office of Diversity and Equity for Students, a new faculty development office, the restructuring of the Division of Academic Affairs, the appointment versus the hiring of individuals to positions in unprecedented numbers, and the search for a new president. One can imagine that even with a continual flow of informational e-mails sent to the entire community, the connections among these initiatives often seem ambiguous to the onlooker.

Transforming Tomorrow

In spite of these concurrent developments at the university, there are clear signs that transformation in each of these areas will result in a stronger Gallaudet. One theme that is consistent across campus is a constant call for assessment, evidence, and data about student learning to answer questions such as:

- How do we justify not changing courses in which the majority of students are not successful?
- Don't we want to know why graduation rates differ among the students we serve and how those rates are related to their learning?
- If evidence shows that particular groups of students are more successful than others, what actions are we taking to help those who are less successful?

The university seems to be in the earliest stages of transforming into a place where the culture of evidence holds sway with an emphasis on student learning outcomes. There are clearly times when we stumble, falling back into our old ways of making decisions about student learning on the basis of anecdotes. I hope those relapses will become fewer and eventually disappear. For right now, Gallaudet seems to be ushering in a new epoch in which assessment has become integral to a student-centered teaching and learning process focused on improving student learning and student success.

References

Angelo, T., & Cross, P. (1993). *Classroom assessment techniques.* San Francisco: Jossey-Bass.

About the Author

Eileen Matthews, a native Washingtonian, earned her B.A. in English and M.A. in comparative history from Howard University in 1970 and 1972, respectively. She started her career in education as a high school teacher in Baltimore, Maryland. Her interest in curriculum development led her to undertake doctoral studies in education at the University of Maryland and a specialization in education of the deaf at Gallaudet University. During her 25 years at Gallaudet, Ms. Matthews has served as a faculty member, department chair, associate dean of the Center for Academic Programs and Student Services, executive director of the Office of Diversity and Equity for Students, and executive director of assessment. She established the first Office of Assessment at Gallaudet and was instrumental in developing a university-wide assessment process that met the assessment standard established by Gallaudet's regional accreditation body.

7

SLOUCHING TOWARD ASSESSMENT

One Department's Journey Toward Accountability Bliss

Hardin L. Aasand, Stevens Amidon, and Debrah Huffman
Indiana University–Purdue University Fort Wayne

Indiana University-Purdue University Fort Wayne (IPFW) is a comprehensive university in Fort Wayne, Indiana, offering associate, bachelor's, and master's degree programs, as well as specialized certificate programs at the undergraduate and graduate levels. The university is accredited by The Higher Learning Commission of the North Central Association of Colleges and Schools. It has the broadest scope of programs of all institutions of higher learning in northeast Indiana, offering about 200 degrees and certificate options. IPFW has a diverse enrollment of about 13,000 students encompassing many ages, races, and nationalities. Through exemplary standards in teaching, research, and service, IPFW demonstrates a commitment to excellence and lifelong learning. IPFW provides students the opportunity for success through its academic diversity, affordability, and flexibility.

I f our title alludes, however elusively, to Yeats's "The Second Coming," it is because the road to departmental assessment can seem both dramatic and apocalyptic, especially if one's departmental "centre cannot hold" and the purpose of the assessment is called into question. The Department of English and Linguistics at Indiana University–Purdue University Fort Wayne (IPFW) is presently on this journey, slouching toward its own revelations of mission and fulfillment of purpose. To the outsider, the Department of English and Linguistics at IPFW has a set of clearly articulated learning goals for the diverse programs (concentrations, majors, and minors) housed under its roof: baccalaureate programs with concentrations or minors in literature, linguistics, creative writing, professional writing, teacher certification, and folklore and a graduate program in English and in teaching English. These goals stress the acquisition of abilities such as critical and precise writing, the demonstration of the ability to use research tools and methods, the knowledge of the evolution of English language, and appreciation of English literature. These goals are stipulated in the "Enchiridion," the governance document whose title harkens back through its Greek etymology to the liberal arts tradition: like Ariadne's thread, these goals provide direction for the faculty and for the students as they wend their way through our department.

In practice, however, the assessment of our learning outcomes is arbitrarily conducted and randomly evaluated. The "Enchiridion"—though providing the semblance of integrity to our assessment strategies—actually gives us little in the way of a clearly defined pathway or map to meeting the goals it articulates:

> Interim Assessment is based on one paper submitted by each student upon completing 15 hours toward the major. No later than the end of the semester in which the student completes the first 15 core and concentration credits, the student will select the paper from a course in the major that represents his or her best work, and will provide a brief explanation of the assignment and information about course number, title and date. The Undergraduate Studies and Assessment Committee will review these papers, evaluate student achievement consistent with the department's mission-and-goals statement, and report their findings and recommendations to the department Chair. Interim Assessment of MA and MAT candidates will be based on at least one individual conference annually with the Director

This is an interim assessment in search of an accountability measure. It lacks a coherent structure for ensuring adequate artifacts and cedes responsibility to the student. To its credit, the Undergraduate Studies Assessment Committee recognized the shortcomings in its 2007 assessment report: "Evaluation of materials submitted by students is generally satisfactory, but the department continues to be concerned that the material available for review through the voluntary assessment process is minimal." The committee is in the middle of a complete review of the curriculum to identify areas within the curriculum for curricular revision and embedded assessment.

It is arguable that this conversation might never have begun had one event not occurred: the ides of March 2006—actually March 24—and the resolution by the Educational Policy Committee of the campus to implement the baccalaureate framework and provide an overarching direction for all IPFW academic programs, and the entrance of a new English and linguistic department chair and the renewed determination of the undergraduate and graduate studies and assessment committees to reconsider their strategies of assessment and the implications for strengthening our curriculum and providing a coherent set of experiences that can be evaluated effectively and structured cohesively. This alignment of forces invited this critical examination of our program: The baccalaureate framework provided the compass, and the faculty the impetus, to embark on this journey.

The baccalaureate framework—following on the heels of the Association of American Colleges and Universities (AAC&U) report "Greater Expectations"—provided the compass points for departmental guidance. "Greater Expectations" expected colleges and universities to offer their students "a clearly articulated, collective conception" of what it means to be educated, "intentionality and coherence" in its programs, and "assessment" to measure the attainment of these values. Indeed, the AAC&U itself provided a framework of five desired educational outcomes that resonate within the baccalaureate framework created by IPFW:

- Strong analytical, communication, and information skills
- Deep understanding of and hands-on experience with the inquiry practices of disciplines that explore the natural, social, and cultural realms
- Intercultural knowledge and collaborative problem-solving skills
- A proactive sense of responsibility for individual, civic, and social choices
- Habits of mind that foster integrative thinking and the ability to transfer skills and knowledge from one setting to another (www.aacu .org/liberaleducation/le-fa04/le-fa04feature1.cfm, citing *Our Students' Best Work*, 2004, 5–6)

The IPFW Baccalaureate Framework provides a reverberating echo of these desired outcomes (see Figure 7.1). These outcomes provided our department with articulated qualities that were implicit within our programs but had become fragmented and unspoken. The department faculty knew what they were doing, and these outcomes correspond with the shared values we embrace, but we had lost our way in expressing them within our programs and had failed to offer a coherent means of assessing our success both for ourselves and for our students.

Maki (2004) observes that assessment begins with collaboration, in dialogue that builds consensus and shapes a sense of purpose. The questions generated by this dialogue are rich and vivifying: How does the department provide students with the opportunity to learn what we value? Do students

FIGURE 7.1
The IPFW Baccalaureate Framework

Outcome	*Description of Outcome*
Acquisition of knowledge	Students will demonstrate breadth of knowledge across disciplines and depth of knowledge in their chosen discipline. In order to do so, students must demonstrate the requisite information-seeking skills and technological competencies.
Application of knowledge	Students will demonstrate the ability to integrate and apply that knowledge and, in so doing, demonstrate the skills necessary for lifelong learning.
Personal and professional values	Students will demonstrate the highest levels of personal integrity and professional ethics.
A sense of community	Students will demonstrate the knowledge and skills necessary to be productive and responsible citizens and leaders in local, regional, national, and international communities. In so doing, students will demonstrate a commitment to free and open inquiry and mutual respect across multiple cultures and perspectives.
Critical thinking and problem solving	Students will demonstrate facility and adaptability in their approach to problem solving. In so doing, students will demonstrate critical thinking abilities and familiarity with quantitative and qualitative reasoning.
Communication	Students will demonstrate the written, oral, and multimedia skills necessary to communicate effectively in diverse settings.

have multiple opportunities to learn and reflect on that learning through the entire spectrum of the program's offerings? Does the department take the opportunity to assess its students meaningfully and qualitatively in order to allow for potential changes within the curriculum? Does the curriculum— literally the course of a student's academic trek—cohere and build on its varied experiences? To begin to answer these questions, the department needed to create alignments between the various programs it offers and the baccalaureate framework. This alignment required the department to examine its courses and the path those courses created: Does the program cohere and coincide with the values that IPFW promulgates for the institution as a whole? One example from our alignment document demonstrates this process (see Figure 7.2). This example demonstrates how the acquisition-of-knowledge outcome is threaded within each of our distinct programs and how it becomes a measurable activity. It was imperative for our department to produce this alignment in order for the undergraduate and graduate assessment committees to examine the curriculum as a whole and ask the following questions: What shape should our core curriculum take and how do the experiences of that core permeate the particular concentrations our students have the opportunity to engage in?

FIGURE 7.2

Alignment of Acquisition of Knowledge Component of the IPFW Baccalaureate Framework with the Departmental Outcomes

Acquisition of Knowledge	Objectives
Students will demonstrate breadth of knowledge across disciplines and depth of knowledge in their chosen discipline. In order to do so, students must demonstrate the requisite information-seeking skills and technological competencies.	English majors demonstrate knowledge of literary, historical, linguistic, and rhetorical conventions and traditions of English through critically sound oral and written expression reflective of this integration of curriculum material. *English Language Concentration:* Students demonstrate their familiarity with the fundamental rules of operation and the social connections of natural languages, especially English; the evolution and transformation of the English language; and the analytical and descriptive tools of English linguistics. *English Literature Concentration:* Students demonstrate their acquisition of essential literary skills: familiarity with a broad range of American and English literary texts through the application of a variety of critical approaches to the analysis of literary texts. *Writing Concentration:* Students demonstrate their ability to read and write clearly and persuasively in various rhetorical contexts in the production of original compositions. *Teacher Certification Concentration:* Students will demonstrate their acquisition of the fundamental skills necessary for the secondary education classroom, knowledge of American and British literary texts, fundamental rules of oral and written communication, and acquisition of pedagogical methodologies necessary for the instruction of literature and language in a secondary education environment.

The Department of English and Linguistics is structured as a complex concatenation of programs: Students are required to fulfill 15 hours of a core curriculum before focusing on either a concentration (English literature, English and communication media, English language, teacher certification, writing) or a minor (English literature, creative writing, folklore, professional writing, teaching English as a new language). The rich permutation of paths our students can undertake in shaping their programs complicates our assessment strategies because of the lack of consistent, cohesive opportunities to assess performance at midpoints or at completion, the latter being even more complicated because of the lack of a capstone experience. The road to an English major branches off in myriad directions, and it remains the goal of our assessment committees (undergraduate and graduate) to articulate and to assess each of these branches and how they stem from common expectations and shared outcomes. To that end, the writing faculty within the department have taken the lead in providing the department with both the structure and the articulation of an assessment strategy that other departmental programs can emulate.

Charting the Course: The Writing Program as a Compass

The adoption of the baccalaureate framework was a major step for the university, and for our department, but adopting these overarching goals at an institutional level highlighted some gaps in the institution's assessment system. The most obvious gap was the fact that the existing assessment process focused only on majors and certificate programs—there was no process for assessing other parts of the curriculum. General education courses and service courses (such as writing courses specifically designed for engineering and business majors) taught by the department have always outnumbered courses specifically reserved for English majors.

The work of the department's Composition Committee, which has been assessing the effectiveness of the writing program, provided a map that the department as a whole could follow. Even before the university adopted the baccalaureate framework, the Composition Committee was beginning the task of assessing these programs. The driving forces behind these efforts were not external—they grew out of a desire among the writing faculty to improve writing instruction at the university.

The general education component of our writing program consists of four courses: W129, Introductory Elementary Composition; W131, Elementary Composition I; W233, Intermediate Expository Writing; and W140, Honors Composition, which essentially compresses the work of W131 and W233 into a single one-semester honors course. About 70% of our students place directly into W131, bypassing W129. All majors in the College of Arts and Sciences and most in the College of Business must also take W233 or an equivalent advanced writing course; most majors in our professional colleges do not. In a typical school year, these courses result in more than 200 sections of writing instruction that must be assessed.

The department is fortunate to be ahead of the game regarding writing assessment. In 2006, the department's Composition Committee adopted a set of outcome statements for these courses built around four broad categories derived from a set of national guidelines adopted by the Council of Writing Program Administrators in 2000: rhetorical knowledge; critical thinking, reading, and writing; processes; and knowledge of conventions. These outcomes were not adopted without dissensus. Like many universities, we rely on a cadre of underpaid part-time instructors who teach the majority of these 200 sections. Many of us were concerned that long-time instructors, some of whom were retired high school teachers, would struggle with the requirement to "Use various technologies to address a range of audiences." We wondered if these instructors were willing to create assignments that required students to write both in an electronic format and in a traditional paper format and we wondered how we would prepare them to meet this requirement. From the first day we promulgated these outcomes statements in 2006, we were asking instructors to mold and revise their syllabi.

Through 2006 and 2007 we began the process of implementing these outcomes. The outcomes were posted and discussed by the director of writing in an e-mail to all faculty. Feedback sessions were held during monthly peer seminars for our part-time instructors. We also offered peer workshops and worked with our Center for the Enhancement of Learning and Teaching to develop workshops to improve our faculty's ability to work with electronic texts. We developed simplified versions of the outcomes statements and asked all instructors to place those desired outcomes in their syllabi.

When the university adopted its baccalaureate framework, the committee made the decision to map these writing program outcomes onto the broader university outcomes. Figure 7.3 shows the detailed outcomes for the fourth of these categories of outcomes, knowledge of conventions. The italicized passages are outcomes from the baccalaureate framework that link to these specific outcomes from the writing program.

As we moved into 2008, the work continued. We collected three student research papers from each member of our entire writing faculty for the purpose of assessing the performance of the program (as opposed to individual instructors) at achieving those outcomes. The Composition Committee also developed and approved a rubric to evaluate these papers. Finally, the director of writing wrote a grant proposal for resources to help some of our faculty

FIGURE 7.3
Category 4 Outcomes: Knowledge of Conventions

WPA (National) Outcome	W129/131 Outcome	W233 Outcome
Learn common formats for different genres of texts	Students must meet format guidelines established by their instructors. *IPFW: application of knowledge, communication*	Students must meet not only format guidelines established by their instructors but also guidelines they are likely to encounter in other discourse communities. *IPFW: acquisition and application of knowledge, communication*
Develop knowledge of genre conventions	Students must demonstrate that they can adapt such issues as stance (voice), organization, format, and development appropriate to a given genre. *IPFW: application of knowledge, communication*	In addition to meeting the requirements for W131, students must demonstrate that they understand how particular genres may function within particular discourse communities. *IPFW: acquisition and application of knowledge, communication*
Practice appropriate means of documenting one's work	Students must be able to document secondary research using at least one style (e.g., MLA or APA) and to understand how at least one other style differs. Students should be able to use a handbook to support their efforts at documentation. *IPFW: acquisition and application of knowledge, personal and professional values, communication*	In addition to meeting the requirements for W131, students must also be able to document various types of sources (e.g., print texts, electronic texts, moving images, interviews). *IPFW: acquisition and application of knowledge, personal and professional values, communication*
Control syntax, grammar, punctuation, and spelling	Students must demonstrate that they can apply the conventions described in their course handbook, when appropriate. *IPFW: sense of community, communication*	In addition to meeting the requirements for W131, students must also demonstrate that they understand the conventions of a given discourse community. *IPFW: sense of community, communication*

read and evaluate this collection of papers, and the department received a $750 award, which went toward paying 10 instructors who helped rate those papers during a summer assessment day.

The original intention of the assessment was to evaluate a sample of 150 research papers submitted in the annual portfolios by part-time and full-time writing faculty. Each faculty member was asked to submit three papers: one representative of the best work from a class, one representative of average work from a class, and one representative of weak work from a class. The interim director of writing reduced the sample to 72 papers for two reasons: (1) Some instructors submitted papers in genres other than those requested, and (2) some papers were so heavily marked that masking instructor comments to prevent undue influence on the evaluators was impossible.

In June 2008, a group of 16 individuals came together to evaluate these papers. The group consisted of the interim director of writing, who directed the process; the director of the IPFW writing center; four full-time members of the writing faculty; six limited-term lecturers; and four graduate teaching assistants. The day began with a rating session during which the evaluators practiced rating sample research papers and then discussed their evaluations. This exercise, intended to improve interrater reliability, took approximately 2 hours. The group then began the process of evaluating the papers. Each paper was read and scored by two evaluators. Each of the areas defined by the rubric was assigned a score from 1 to 4, and the evaluators were asked to assign only whole numbers. The rubric covered eight areas defined by the writing program outcomes, which meant the lowest score that could be assigned to a weak paper was 8, and the highest score assigned to a strong paper was 32. If the score assigned by the two evaluators differed by more than 5 points, the paper was read and scored again by a third evaluator. Twenty papers were evaluated a third time. This scoring process took approximately 6 hours. Figure 7.4 shows the rubric for the Category 4 outcomes.

The director of writing prepared a report with both numerical findings and analysis and recommendations based upon those findings. Although we weren't happy with the overall level of writing skills demonstrated in this assessment, we were pleased to see that those skills improved as students progressed through the writing curriculum. The report was promulgated to the Composition Committee, the chair of the Department of English and Linguistics, and the university administration, and the results were shared with all writing program faculty during our fall orientation. The Composition Committee and the director of writing began making adjustments to the program on the basis of these results. One site where these assessment efforts had an immediate impact was in our graduate course, which prepares students to teach in our writing program.

Closing the Loop: Using Assessment to Improve Faculty Development

Essentially, we use two types of vessels to propel us along a course of assessment. One is the identification, and often improvement, of existing opportunities for assessment; the other is the creation and implementation of new

FIGURE 7.4
Category 4 Outcomes Rubric

4a. Style

4.0	3.0	2.0	1.0
The prose is engaging, clear, and cohesive. Word choice is felicitous and sentences generally flow from one to another.	The prose is clear and cohesive but not as engaging as a 4 paper. Word choice is generally felicitous, but a couple of problems (poor word choice, choppy sentences, lack of sentence variety) weaken the prose.	The prose is generally clear and usually cohesive. Several significant problems weaken the prose.	The prose is unclear in more than a few places. Problems with word choice, choppy sentences, and lack of sentence variety occur often.

4b. Correctness

4.0	3.0	2.0	1.0
The prose is free of distracting errors in grammar, mechanics, and spelling.	Although the prose is free of major errors, it may contain a couple of obvious mechanical or spelling errors.	The prose contains a couple of major, sentence-level errors and more than a couple of obvious mechanical or spelling errors.	The prose contains more than a couple of major grammar errors. It may also contain more than several obvious mechanical or spelling errors.

assessment measures. In our department we have done both. We have identified existing desired departmental, institutional, and national outcomes, and we have combined those into a new diagram guiding the baccalaureate degree and the writing program. We have identified interim assessment as an existing area of assessment needing improvement and we have begun discussing the possibility of a new capstone course as a measure of student learning at the completion of the major. We have also used student essays from our general education program to create an assessment day project that was productive on multiple levels.

Not the least of the benefits gained from the assessment day was the generation of important faculty discussion about the assessment of our writing students' learning and progress. This brings us to another consideration that the writing program has identified that can help us both firmly establish the goals that drive our department and assess how well those are working: a focus on the professional development of our writing instructors. We have identified an opportunity to actually assess new and inexperienced instructors who want to teach for us: a graduate-level course on teaching writing. We have also created a way to support instructors in their continuing efforts to achieve our goals and desired outcomes in the classroom: the addition of an administration position devoted to working with (and for) the writing instructors.

Teaching Composition, a graduate-level course commonly referred to as C505, is a course designed to teach current and soon-to-be instructors how best to teach writing. Student instructors discuss readings and theoretical approaches, write reflective essays, and practice developing curricular materials. All these activities incorporate the baccalaureate framework and the departmental and writing program goals and outcomes discussed here. The course is an excellent assessment opportunity in two ways. It allows us to actually assess writing instructors, and it provides a place to establish changes that we determine we need to make to our curricula. Both allow us ways to keep our fingers on the pulse of how well we are teaching students in our general education program.

Through the C505 materials and activities, student instructors learn about rhetoric, critical thinking, reading and writing processes, and writing conventions. They read and discuss the theoretical backgrounds of the desired writing program outcomes through key pieces of composition scholarship. Certainly, one of the goals on our journey to assessment is for instructors in the department to be onboard. And a critical prerequisite to this is that they understand the outcomes, their importance, and how their conceptualization and achievement function to improve student learning. Critical work on theory that backs the learning outcomes allows them to do this. The next step, of course, is that the student instructors actually reflect the outcomes values in their pedagogies. C505 allows them to put the outcomes values into practice through the development of effective teaching materials for the writing classroom. Hence, they can see how the learning outcomes values can be developed into writing activities for their students. Furthermore, the student instructors' own activities in C505, their in-class and out-of-class work, often mirrors those practices they are encouraged to use in teaching, allowing the course to embody the learning outcomes and literally practice what it preaches. Moreover, C505 is a place where curricula and assessment *are* the subjects, which makes it an ideal venue to discuss the importance of continued methods of assessing student learning.

As the course is a prerequisite for graduate teaching assistants in the department, the goals and desired outcomes are established early on. The instructors who go through the course begin with teaching methods that reflect departmental values instead of having to try to blend those into existing, and often long-standing, practices. In other words, each time the course is offered, it's a new group of graduate instructors we have who can begin from a point of acceptance and understanding of departmental goals. So, we have instructors who build into their curricula assignments that reflect principles from the baccalaureate framework and desired outcomes from the writing program, methods of assessing student writing that are most effective for gauging progress toward those outcomes, and practices in the classroom that make the learning experience more meaningful for our students. Because the course is offered twice a year, this means that we constantly have an infusion of writing instructors who are already knowledgeable about teaching practices designed to be most effective for our students.

Moreover, C505 is used to determine if graduate students in English and linguistics are ready to teach, if they can actually do the kind of curriculum building that reflects our values. The students receive grades throughout the course that indicate how well these prospective instructors are internalizing and achieving the goals and outcomes we have established in the different outcome areas. Ultimately, the C505 instructor looks through a portfolio of work submitted by each graduate student that includes a syllabus, assignments and rubrics, classroom observations made by the C505 instructor about a graduate student's teaching, and a statement on writing instruction philosophy, all with accompanying reflection. The C505 instructor can determine if a graduate student is ready to become a teaching assistant by whether or not a student's portfolio material demonstrates the outcomes established by the writing program and the department. If a student doesn't incorporate practices that lead to the outcomes and show understanding of their importance in the reflection paper, he or she is not recommended to teach. The course maintains quality of teaching and, therefore, quality of the students' learning.

Along with being a locus for assessing the students' success in incorporating the writing program's goals and outcomes, C505 allows for identification of places where revision is needed in the curricula and implementation of those revisions. In other words, we can use the course to determine areas that need improvement and go about making those improvements. Through the careful collection and interpretation of the portfolio materials, we can better ascertain how well the learning outcomes will gain a foothold in writing classroom practice and where problems may occur. Class discussion can also bring to light possible difficulties our teachers and students may face. And the C505 students' critical writing could reflect struggles and conflicts in effective student learning that we haven't thought of. Throughout the course the instructor and students work together to explore how well the departmental and programmatic outcomes mesh with the theoretical and practical considerations of the composition field and what gaps in instruction may still exist. The course gives us a forum to discuss what is likely to be successful and problematic in the implementation of the outcomes. Through this discussion and through what we find to be effective and problematic in the actual teaching and learning of the composition courses, we can make changes to the C505 content that allow for constant improvement of our general education program.

Preparation of new instructors begins with C505, but the course cannot follow those instructors. How do we then continue what the course begins to assess? How do we know that what we have provided our graduate teaching assistants is actually working for them in their classrooms? How is it working for the students taking those classes? Where do we get the information that lets us know we need to change the curriculum of C505 to better reflect the goals we determine for the department and the writing program and better prepare our instructors?

This brings us to what we determined was a needed addition to our program: the creation of a secondary administrative position. On the basis of the recognized impact of the C505 course on teachers and consequently students of writing, the C505 instructor was made associate director of writing in charge of support and development. With a one-course release, this position allows the instructor to follow up with the graduates in the course, who are now teaching assistants. She does this in three ways: by visiting the teaching assistants' classrooms and providing observation feedback, by maintaining a dialogue with the TAs and being a supportive resource for them, and by providing workshops on topics of interest to writing instructors.

In the first semester that the graduate student begins teaching a composition course for the department, the associate director sets up with the TA a date to observe the TA in the classroom. Afterward, the associate director writes up her observations, including remarks about the TA's strengths and questions based on what she observed. Some of these questions are for clarification or more information (for example, questions about the assignment), and some are designed to provoke critical reflection in the instructor (for example, questions about why the instructor isn't doing something). A copy is given to the instructor, and the associate director sets up a time to meet with the instructor to discuss the visit. In this half-hour- to hour-long meeting, the instructor can answer questions and ask some of his own. The associate director can also address areas of greatest concern regarding what she observed and underscore what the instructor is doing well.

The associate director emphasizes that this is an opportunity to open up a conversation about pedagogy, not engage in a judgmental observation. However, it is undeniably a form of assessment. Certainly, if the associate director observed anything that contradicted the pedagogy of C505, and if the instructor were averse to addressing that problem, this information could be taken to the director of writing, who could then decide how to follow up with the instructor or whether to ask the instructor to teach again the following semester. More likely to occur is the determination to pursue further dialogue and work with the instructor to address difficulties. In this way, the associate director and C505 instructor continually reaffirm the goals and desired outcomes of the writing program.

Equally important, the associate director becomes a resource for the instructors, providing them with information that can better their teaching and their scholarship. A specialist in writing pedagogy, the associate director also acts as coach, consultant, and mentor to the TAs and to other lecturers who seek her advice or assistance. They come to her with questions about how to handle plagiarism cases, how to deal with sensitive subject matter divulged by one of their students, how to deal with belligerence or disruptiveness, and how to manage time for grading. They also rely on her for letters of recommendation and advice on how to use the classroom as a site of research. Thus not only can the associate director help improve the teaching and learning in the composition classrooms, but she can also help the graduates improve their work and their regard for the program. As such, the existence of an associate director position can be another gauge by which to assess the success of the writing program for undergraduates and the success of the graduate program.

Finally, the associate director is in charge of providing regular workshops open to all writing instructors in the department. These hour-long workshops cover such topics as grading student essays, using reading in the composition classroom, using technology, and even goals and desired outcomes for certain courses. Soliciting information from the writing instructors on what they want or need to know, the associate director plans workshops for which guest speakers are invited to present on areas of interest and provide an open forum for discussion among professors, lecturers, and teaching assistants. These are opportunities for ongoing professional development for the instructors and for the ongoing development of the department in its efforts to solve problems and fill in gaps that could affect the effective learning of students.

The information gained from work in these three areas (classroom observation, maintaining a dialogue, constructive workshops) allows the associate director to assess the effectiveness of the C505 course itself, beyond what the standard semester-end evaluations can provide. These efforts allow for continual refinement of both the C505 course curriculum and the writing program based on student instructor needs. Thus, an existing measurement opportunity and a newly created one can work hand in hand.

Reaching the Destination: A Conclusion of Sorts

We are proud of the efforts we have made within the department to more seriously approach issues of assessment and accountability, but the journey has been, and still is, a difficult one, more a stumbling or a slouching along crooked paths than a drive down the autobahn. And although we are making progress, we still face challenges. One challenge is maintaining interest—

despite the work of a core group of faculty who are committed to this process, much of our department is at best disinterested and at worst opposed to the notion of outcomes-based assessment. Apathy at the macro level might lead to disillusionment among those "carrying the water" down the path to assessment. Another challenge is institutional—changes in leadership at the college and university levels inevitably lead to different attitudes among administrators about the way assessment should be done, potentially undermining departmental progress. Finally, as assessment often leads (at least in our case) to curricular change, the slow nature of proposing, debating, and implementing such change requires us to be patient along the journey. Year after year of meetings and incremental progress makes us want to shout, like the child in the back of the car, "Are we there yet?"

We aren't there yet. But we are getting there. And frankly, we don't worry so much about the pressures and forces at work outside our department. The biggest reason is this—we are going down this path because we want our department to be a better provider of educational opportunities for our students and a more interesting and fulfilling place to do our faculty work. The assessment journey is, in itself, worth the effort it demands.

References

American Association of Colleges and Universities. (2004). *Our students' best work.* www.aacu.org/liberaleducation/le-fa04/le-fa04feature1.cfm.

Maki, P. (2004). *Assessing for learning: Building a sustainable commitment across the institution.* Sterling, VA: Stylus.

About the Authors

Hardin Aasand is professor of English and chair of the Department of English and Linguistics at Indiana University–Purdue University Fort Wayne. He is a member of the editorial team for the New Variorum *Hamlet* for the MLA and editor of *The Winter's Tale* for the Internet Shakespeare Editions. He has written essays on Shakespeare, the Jacobean court, and the editorial process for a number of volumes and journals. He also has written review essays for *Renaissance Quarterly, Seventeenth-Century News, Medievalia et Humanistica,* and the *Sixteenth-Century Journal.*

Stevens Amidon is an associate professor in the Department of English and Linguistics at Indiana University–Purdue University Fort Wayne, where he directs the writing program. He has a number of publications in the areas of organizational writing and genre theory and has served on assessment committees at the university, college, and departmental levels.

Debrah Huffman is an assistant professor in the Department of English and Linguistics at Indiana University–Purdue University Fort Wayne. She is an associate director of the writing program in charge of support and development for the lecturers and teaching assistants. Her specializations include composition pedagogy, writing across the curriculum, and rhetorical reading.

8

DESIGNING, IMPLEMENTING, AND SUSTAINING DEPARTMENT/PROGRAM REVIEW AND ASSESSMENT AT A COMMUNITY COLLEGE

Althea Smith and Susan Bayard
North Shore Community College

North Shore Community College (NSCC) is a 2-year community college located about 30 miles north of Boston, Massachusetts, offering lifelong education through credit and non-credit courses at three different campus locations—Lynn, Danvers, and Beverly. Established in 1965, now with over 135 full-time faculty members and over 300 adjunct faculty members, the college offers approximately 80 different certificate and associate degree programs in college-level academic and career education. Almost 7,000 full- and part-time students attend each year, many recruited from local high schools. After graduation, many students transfer to in-state 4-year colleges, and others major in one of the college's career programs and find a job in the workforce. Still others come to NSCC to take a few courses to improve or enhance their skills in order to find higher-paying jobs, apply for promotions within their current organizations, or try another career path. The student population is diverse; many are the first generation in their families to attend college. There is a sizable immigrant and English-as-a-second-language population. Almost 30% of the student population are members of minority groups (Latino, African/African American, Asian/Asian American).

s a community college, we believe we have a unique mission to focus on the quality of teaching, learning, and assessment. In the past decade, NSCC has made a commitment to expand the work on these interrelated issues. Guided by the dean for academic assessment, curriculum, and special programs and NSCC's Center for Teaching, Learning, and Assessment, the college began a process to change the culture in the organization to deepen and broaden the conversation about improving teaching, learning, and assessment. The purpose of this chapter is to discuss the organizational change process we used to extend the department/program review efforts at the college. We also describe the model we designed to engage faculty in the department/program review and assessment process. Each year we revise and update the model on the basis of feedback from faculty and staff. After 5 years, we still call it a work in progress (Patton & McCalman, 2000).

Our History

During the 1990s, the national landscape was one in which accountability and assessment issues in higher education were beginning to receive attention. NSCC recognized the importance of ensuring the quality of programs and student competency and, in 1993, was awarded a Title III grant titled Improving Academic Quality Through Outcomes Assessment that provided funding for faculty to develop a mission, goals, and outcomes for their department or program. In 1997 the Title III grant also provided funding for the creation of the Center for Teaching, Learning, and Assessment (CTLA), a resource for faculty with a focus on improving teaching and learning through assessment processes.

In 1999, when NSCC completed its self-study for the New England Association of Schools and Colleges, it received feedback from the evaluation team indicating a need for improvement in assessment of general education outcomes. As a result, in 1999, two committees were formed to address the deficiencies stated in the report of the evaluation team. One committee was a grassroots effort and the other was convened by the director of the CTLA.

The grassroots effort developed because faculty recognized that there was a need to create a department/program review template. The committee researched models at other colleges and developed a department/program review template to be used by departments and programs at NSCC. Twenty-four departments and programs completed department/program reviews that were facilitated by the CTLA under the guidance of the center's director. The template that was developed provided a foundation for the current department/program review and assessment process. In 2001, the position of director of the CTLA became vacant and was not filled until 2003. The

CTLA operated for a 2-year period without a director and with scarce resources to assist faculty in conducting reviews of their departments or programs. Unfortunately, as a result, no work was done on department/program review or on developing a process for assessing department/program or general education outcomes during this period.

In 2003, after 2 years without a director, NSCC made a renewed commitment to the department/program review process and assessment of general education outcomes by hiring a new director of the CTLA who actively mobilized and focused institutional efforts to integrate assessment of student learning outcomes into the campus culture. She recognized the need to finalize the template, engage faculty in the ownership of that template, and design a process that would encourage people to come together to talk about general education outcomes, workforce readiness, curriculum, assessment, pedagogy, and instruction. It was a daunting task! In support of this process, the college hired an education consultant in assessment in September 2003 to guide the NSCC in developing an assessment process that would lead to identification of patterns of strength and weakness in student achievement allowing for the revision of educational practices that improve student learning. In addition, a Title III grant was awarded to the college in the fall of 2003. It provided the initial funding to hire a professional staff member to assist faculty in the department/program review and assessment process. This was the first time inter- and intra-departmental and divisional conversations were organized and facilitated around these topics and as part of a systematic approach to improving learning and teaching.

Designing a Faculty-Driven Process for Institutional Change Planning: The Program Review and Workforce Readiness Leadership Team

Several things became evident about the college as the department/program review and assessment work proceeded: (1) Departments and programs worked *in silos* as they approached department/program review and general education outcomes; (2) department/program review needed to be linked to the assessment of general education outcomes; (3) a successful department/program review and assessment initiative on campus would require the support, in some form, of the academic leadership; (4) academic departments and career programs had different approaches as they began a self-study process; (5) this was an opportunity to reinforce and deepen the college's focus on teaching, learning, and assessment; (6) to foster permanent change, we needed to build a culture of self-reflection and collaboration across the college.

With funds from the Title III grant, the director of the CTLA established the program review and workforce readiness (PRWR) leadership team. On the basis of the work being done across the country, we believed that an institution-wide cross-sectional team comprised of faculty, staff, and administrators would best be able to accomplish this work (Eckel & Kezar, 2003). The PRWR team consisted of 19 motivated, enthusiastic, and committed faculty and staff members who diligently worked away at their charge—to recruit five departments or programs to undertake department/program review each year. At first this seemed like a straightforward and doable task, but we were a naive, unsuspecting group, not knowing at the time how much we needed to learn. For example, although the college had taken initial steps to review departments and programs with some key questions, what the college needed to do was get the whole institution involved not only in assessing the curriculum for each department and program but also in assessing the institutional general education outcomes. It also became clear that there was a need to develop and assess workforce readiness as well. The PRWR team worked for almost 3 years on developing and piloting processes for assessing student learning outcomes and a department/program review and assessment process.

For the PRWR team, the first order of business was to elect cochairs. A faculty member and the director of the CTLA volunteered and were quickly elected to serve for 2 years. Fortunately, the director of the CTLA had worked with academic leadership to arrange for the college to hire an education consultant in assessment 3 months before the PRWR leadership team formed. The consultant was instrumental in getting the process started and giving the PRWR leadership team the confidence to accomplish its goals. We devoted the first several weeks to learning the assessment vocabulary, understanding the scope of our charge, learning how other colleges had worked through the assessment mire, and developing the skills necessary to move forward. We learned about curriculum mapping, assessment of student learning outcomes, direct and indirect assessment methods, criteria and standards of judgment, rubrics, prompts, and interrater reliability. As we became more comfortable and confident, we were able to rely less and less on our consultant, so that by Year 2 the PRWR leadership team felt comfortable to go it alone.

Assessment: Important Elements of the College Culture

The PRWR leadership team quickly realized that somehow it needed to integrate the assessment of the college's general education outcomes into the department/program review process, but it took the team 3 years of discussion and sometimes heated and passionate debates to decide just how that was to happen. What the PRWR leadership team accomplished in the first

5 months was setting the groundwork for everything that would develop over the next 2 years. The PRWR leadership team began with a discussion of some key cultural issues that surrounded its work, which led to re-envisioning the entire process of department/program review and assessment. For example:

- Philosophically, the culture at NSCC supports the notion that major initiatives are most successful when developed as grassroots efforts. We recognized that it was important to get faculty to engage other faculty in the department/program review and assessment process. The PRWR leadership team was just one successful example of faculty engaging other faculty in the department/program review and assessment process.
- In discussions of faculty engagement, questions were immediately raised about workload and compensation regarding, for example, workload adjustments, stipends, course releases, and community service credit for the department/program review work. Historically, NSCC faculty have been compensated by stipend or course release for additional work. Thus, we determined how to offer course releases or stipends for faculty who would serve as review team leaders or team members. Assessing the climate at any institution regarding faculty expectations about compensation for work beyond teaching, advising, and committee work would constitute an important early conversation.
- The role of classroom research is a part of the culture at NSCC. The challenge was to create a college-wide culture of dialogue, reflection, assessment, and systematic research. This had to become an essential focus of the department/program review and assessment process. We wanted to develop a process that had a new and strong focus on inquiry into student learning.
- In discussions of the use of assessment and general education outcomes, predictably the conversation turned to the questions "Where will standard department/program outcomes take us?" and "Will faculty academic freedom be threatened?" The PRWR leadership team recognized there were at least two perspectives on campus. One perspective was that faculty can be held accountable to a standard set of outcomes with the freedom to teach students to achieve these outcomes as they choose without a threat to academic freedom. Another perspective held that instructional style and faculty choice in content are both aspects of academic freedom. We found it crucial to initiate and continue the conversation with faculty as we progressed. If you don't raise these issues, we guarantee you they will come up sooner or later.

- As we initiated this project in the fall of 2003, we were facing high faculty turnover: About 20% of the faculty had been teaching at the college for 20 years or more and were about to retire. Over the past 5 years, almost 60 new faculty members had been hired. We therefore recognized that we needed to think about what the role might be for seasoned faculty in contrast to newer faculty in department/program review and assessment. Long-term faculty bring history and knowledge of the campus culture as well as experience with teaching, learning, and assessment at the college, whereas newer faculty bring another perspective and a fresh set of eyes. Both have been informative to the development of the process. It is important to be thoughtful and intentional about how to engage all members of the academic community, if an institution wants comprehensive change.
- Language is important, especially in a faculty-driven process with perspectives from career programs and academic disciplines. For example, is the template for the self-study process a guide? A template? A document? Instructions? The CTLA thought of the template as a set of guidelines that could be tailored to meet the different needs of each department or program. However, some participants thought of the template as rigid instructions that could not be changed.

The Template: A Faculty Guide

To engage the faculty and staff to undertake department/program review each year, we needed a template to follow. This was no small task, given the range of perspectives and opinions of faculty, educational support programs, staff, and administrators. And swirling in the background were issues regarding the assessment of the general education outcomes and the role of workforce readiness. What do these words mean? Where do we get the information? Whose responsibility is it? What does the college want? What does our regional accrediting agency want? Where do we start?

By the end of Year 1, the PRWR leadership team had developed a draft definition of workforce readiness, a draft department/program review process template that incorporated the assessment of workforce readiness and the general education outcomes, a recommendation for faculty compensation, and draft rubrics and pilot processes to assess the general education outcomes for information literacy and computer literacy. Highlights of some of the changes developed in the program review template are listed in Table 8.1.

Along with our work at the college, members of the PRWR leadership team attended regional and national conferences and brought back vital information and renewed enthusiasm, which assisted the PRWR leadership team in moving forward more strategically. In addition, in the spring of

TABLE 8.1
Comparison Table of Template Content in Old
and New Department/Program Review

Topic	Old Department/ Program Review	New Department/ Program Review
Mission	X	X
Goals	X	
Outcomes		X
Standards	X	
Objectives	X	
Curriculum		X
Assessment		X
Student data		X
Faculty data		X
Student support services		X
Workforce readiness and market trends		X

that first year, the CTLA hired a staff member to assist in facilitating the department/program review process.

Implementing a Faculty-Driven Process for Institutional Change

A lot of work was accomplished by the PRWR leadership team, but we were not finished yet! With the assistance of the division deans and the dean for academic assessment, curriculum, and special programs, we needed to recruit five departments and programs to pilot the new department/program review process in the fall of 2004. The deans and faculty rallied: Six departments and programs were recruited to pilot the department/program review template and process.

The Pilot Phase

It was important to design a pilot that could test the template and the proposed processes that programs and departments would need to use. The PRWR leadership team also wanted to design a way for participants to provide input about how well the department/program review process actually worked. The vice president for academic affairs endorsed the process by agreeing to provide course releases and/or stipends for department/program review team leaders and members. A cohort of six departments and programs volunteered to pilot the template and the process beginning in the fall of 2004, using the department/program review template developed by the PRWR leadership team and an evaluation and feedback form. The six departments and programs, including their division deans, gave ongoing feedback to the PRWR leadership team throughout the year so that the team could evaluate the template and process and make appropriate revisions. The dean for academic assessment, curriculum, and special programs was kept informed about the kinds of feedback that departments and programs provided. As a result of the pilot, the template was revised and the department/program review and assessment process was increased from 1 to 2 years. Year 1 became the self-study and Year 2 was devoted to assessment of student learning outcomes.

A Cohort Professional Development Model

Because the new department/program review and assessment requirements asked faculty to respond to content and issues they had not addressed in their previous department/program reviews, the PRWR leadership team believed it was necessary to create a context for this new kind of review to explain the template and its intent as part of the creation of a new culture of inquiry; development of a common language; and, significantly, facilitation of cross-department conversations about teaching, learning, and assessment for department/program review and assessment participants. Therefore, by design, departments and programs from across the college now go through the department/program review and assessment process in cohorts. The CTLA facilitates professional development sessions for faculty regarding the elements of the self-study. The sessions are a combination of reflection, discussion, and teaching about elements of the self-study template. Topics such as revising a mission statement, developing departmental/program outcomes, creating a curriculum map, charting a sample of assessment methods, reviewing student data, and discussing workforce readiness and market trend issues are all covered. Getting the PRWR leadership team to agree on these topics, which were presented in the form of interesting questions or activities, was challenging but interesting. Can you imagine the different types of questions raised by faculty from different departments and programs?

The Process

In order to engage faculty in dialogue on teaching, learning, and assessment and deepen it over time, we developed a process based on a consultation model, with the CTLA staff members working one-on-one with faculty and staff, developing strong working relationships with the department/program review teams, and recognizing that establishing trust through teamwork, coaching, and dialogue would be the way to go.

The department/program review and assessment process began as a single-year pilot and quickly evolved into a multiyear endeavor that now integrates the assessment of student learning outcomes into the process. Although it was originally envisioned as an ongoing 2-year process, it evolved into a 3-year process facilitated by the CTLA.

Year 1 is a self-study during which departments and programs develop or update their mission statements, desired department/program outcomes, and curriculum maps, as well as review curricula, student services, and student data; examine workforce readiness issues and market trends; and develop a department or program action plan. These topics are now regularly discussed by faculty and staff in review team meetings and in department/program meetings to inform and build consensus among all members of a department or program.

In Years 2 and 3, review teams focus on assessment of student learning outcomes and closing-the-loop strategies. In the second year, the review team selects one of the desired department/program outcomes generated in the first year and develops an assignment to assess that student learning outcome. After collecting the student responses, faculty use a rubric or other standard of judgment about student performance to score student data. The scores on the rubric are tallied and reported in a table. The results are interpreted in terms of implications for teaching, learning, assessment, curriculum, advising, and the like. The goal is to generate information to continually improve the approach to teaching, learning, and assessment by the department or program. By improving the department or program, faculty close the loop of their assessment process, which basically means tying the findings of the assessment project to their action plan. For example, faculty in one program found during their assessment of a critical thinking outcome that many of their students did not write adequately. On the basis of their collaborative discussions about this finding, faculty decided to add a writing proficiency requirement for all courses beyond the introductory-level course.

In the third year, the team selects another outcome to assess and deepens its research on teaching, learning, or assessment. The work in Years 1 through 3 is facilitated by the CTLA. For each year there is a template with a series of questions to guide faculty dialogue and reflect, such as "Is there a dominant method for assessing student learning rather than variation in the methods?"

Sustaining a Faculty-Driven Process for Institutional Change

Important to the success of the department/program review and assessment process is the process itself. At NSCC we believe the dialogue about teaching, learning, and assessment is part of the professional development of all faculty and professional staff with teaching responsibilities. It engages faculty in a discussion about how to improve their departments and programs as well as improve student learning through the quality of their teaching.

College-Wide Dialogue: Professional Day

In the spring of 2005, NSCC faculty and staff attended a professional day of presentations and discussions by the CTLA and PRWR leadership team designed to include faculty and staff in the progress of the department/program review process to date. The goal was to inform faculty and staff, get feedback, and continue to build support for and interest in participating in the process. The results were exciting. The conversations were lively and engaging. Participants listened and asked thoughtful questions. The evaluations were positive and encouraging. It was the first chance for the PRWR leadership team to hear the reaction of the faculty and staff to the proposed process. The academic leadership attended and supported the event and the belief that a grassroots process was the best strategy for success.

College-Wide Review Team Presentations

In May of each year, department/program review teams present their findings at a college-wide presentation. The college president, vice presidents, deans, faculty members, administrators, and staff attend. Usually there are at least 70 in attendance over the course of the day. This annual event is a way of developing a culture of inquiry and now has an audience of present and future participants. It helps those who are going to start department/program review and assessment for the first time to understand what's involved by allowing them to hear from colleagues what they have just been through.

Feedback Processes

To make the department/program review and assessment process more efficient, relevant, and useful, faculty members and deans are periodically asked to give input about the process, the template that guides the process, and the professional development sessions that support department/program review and assessment. Here are the ways that the CTLA currently gains feedback about the process and the template.

Professional Development Feedback Forms

After each professional development session, faculty are asked to identify three aspects of the session they found helpful and one that needs to be improved. Responses to these questions affirm that we in the CTLA are achieving our goal by helping colleagues through the process. In addition, faculty feedback increases buy-in and involvement.

Annual Feedback on Process and Content

At the end of the department/program review and assessment process, each department/program review team is given an assessment form. This form asks faculty for feedback on the questions in the template, such as whether there are redundancies, ambiguities, omissions, and the like. They are also asked similar questions about the professional development sessions. In addition, the form asks for general comments about the process and/or specific suggestions for other revisions.

Benchmarking

In 2008, the college again hired the assessment consultant to evaluate the department/program review and assessment process and template. Her feedback was instrumental in guiding us to make revisions and providing a framework toward developing possible next steps.

Faculty/Staff Focus Group on Template and Process

In March 2009, the CTLA hosted a forum for faculty and staff members who had undertaken department/program review and assessment over the past 5 years to gather feedback about the department/program review and assessment process and template. Faculty had specific and creative suggestions about how to improve the process and template. Suggestions were made to continue to deepen the conversation in department/program meetings and to develop alternative processes for departments and programs for engaging in dialogue about improving teaching, learning, and assessment.

Results of Feedback

As a result of the feedback garnered, the CTLA, the CTLA advisory committee, and the academic deans will utilize a transparent process to redesign and modify the department/program review and assessment process. These revisions will address issues such as flexibility in the process; the differing needs of academic departments and career programs; and means of broadening participation, deepening the level of assessment, understanding the difference between qualitative and quantitative assessment, incorporating non-instructional areas, and integrating the process into the college's governance structure. An initial redesign will then be piloted with multiple venues for feedback and continual refinement.

Key Aspects of the Department/Program Review and Assessment Process at NSCC

As we listened to our consultant, researched other colleges, attended conferences, and compared ourselves to sister schools in the state, we observed some key components of a process and template. When designing a department/program review and assessment process, consider which elements of your college culture to translate into the process. For NSCC, these are the elements of the culture considered by the PRWR leadership team:

- The department/program review and assessment process is faculty driven. Historically, faculty engagement has been an important part of any successful change initiative at our college.
- Each department/program review team consists of a team leader and at least three team members who may be full-time or adjunct faculty or professional staff with teaching responsibilities. Most successful initiatives at the college are accomplished through collaboration in teams.
- A focus on reflection and dialogue is integrated throughout the process. The college community values discussion, the sharing of ideas and opinions, and critical thinking.
- All participants in the process are encouraged to offer feedback throughout the process. Templates and the process are always a work in progress. At the end of each professional development session and at the end of each year, faculty members give written feedback to the CTLA to improve the process and the templates. Gathering information, conducting research for planning, and decision making have been a common starting point for any new initiative on campus.
- Assessment of the institutional general education outcomes is folded into the process: each department or program writes desired departmental or programmatic student learning outcomes that reinforce the institutional general education outcomes. Accountability has increasingly become a core value at the college.
- In May, all review teams present their findings at an all-college presentation. Present are the president, vice presidents, deans, faculty members, administrators, and staff. Communication and collegiality are common components of the culture of the college.
- After the department/program review teams have completed Years 1 and 2, they present their findings, discuss their action plans, and make requests for budgetary items based on findings from the self-study or the assessment project with the vice president for academic affairs; the dean for academic assessment, curriculum, and special programs; their division dean; and the director of the CTLA. The college's planning and budgeting take into account these results. We have found this to be a critically important aspect of the process. The faculty and staff value the support from academic leadership.

Next Steps: Strategic Conversations

Over the past 5 years, throughout the department/program review and assessment process, faculty and staff have raised numerous issues and engaged in conversations about curriculum changes, course competencies, responsibilities for achieving desired general education outcomes, and the meaning of workforce readiness to academic disciplines at a community college. The new cohort model as the basis for professional development has stimulated people to ask new kinds of questions about their departments and programs and about the institution. Thus we have learned that in building a culture of department/program review and assessment, it is important to engage the academic leadership, including the vice presidents, deans, faculty, and staff, in ongoing conversations about the issues that surface through department/program review and assessment. Each year we learn there are bigger concerns about teaching and learning that emerge through this process and that may map new directions for our institution, such as campus-wide assessment of general education outcomes. Here are some of the questions raised by colleagues or by the process:

1. What are the appropriate measures of success for a community college? Number of graduates? Number of credits that students take? Number of applicants who graduate? What about the number of students who complete a certificate?
2. Who is responsible for achieving general education outcomes? Liberal arts departments? Career programs? Both? How?
3. Who is responsible for preparing students for work? Career programs? Liberal arts departments? Both? How?
4. When students don't listen, study, or learn, what are the causes that we can address? Student motivation? Study habits? Instruction? Pedagogy?
5. What is the appropriate role of advisory boards or external perspectives (e.g., sister schools, faculty peer review) in developing curricula in career programs and departments? How can we use them most effectively?
6. As individual faculty add variety to their classroom teaching and assessment methods, what is the role of the departments and programs in determining the best methods to use to achieve general education outcomes?
7. What is a learning-centered college? What is the difference between *learner centered* and *learning centered*? Which is NSCC?

What Difference Has Department/Program Review and Assessment Made in Assessing Student Learning?

At the end of each year of department/program review and assessment, each team is asked to identify specific action steps they plan to implement or have actually implemented on the basis of the findings from the department/program review and assessment process. Overall we have witnessed numerous new practices that have emerged as a result of this collaborative process. Specifically, some faculty now:

- Review and clarify grading criteria in course syllabi or assignment rubrics
- Distribute a scoring rubric to students before they start assignments
- Confer with the tutoring center staff to better address student academic needs
- Use student journals

Some departments or programs have:

- Recommended the institution of a Writing Across the Curriculum course to improve student writing skills
- Required a speech class for all students
- Hosted faculty retreats to discuss issues related to teaching, learning, and assessment
- Developed a more focused student recruitment plan
- Developed an advisory board

Lessons Learned

As the old saying goes, hindsight is 20/20. If we had known the lessons we learned before we started the planning and implementation of this process, it would have been much easier. These lessons range from insights about the college culture, to the journey that faculty take in this process, to the importance of building in ongoing feedback from faculty and staff. These are all crucial to establishing a "learning organization" and keeping the organizational change alive (Senge, 2006).

- Start where the faculty are in the dialogue about student learning outcomes. Ask them questions. Engage faculty in conversation.
- Focus the process not solely on the products requested; conversations, questions, and the actions taken to gather more information or to make improvements are all good success indicators of department/program review and assessment. Some faculty wonder, "How do I

teach without lecturing or what do I do if the students are not moti-vated?" Others ask, "What do other faculty do to assess learning other than midterm and final exams?" Engage them around those issues that are important to them. Bring resources to bear to execute change, including support services to improve teaching and learning.

- The process is iterative, incremental, multilevel, and long term. There are no quick fixes here!

- Never confuse the purpose of the department/program review and assessment process with faculty evaluation. It is a reflective self-study process of department/program evaluation that leads to increased department/program effectiveness. The purpose is continual improvement in teaching, learning, and assessment for the individual departments and programs. Currently it is designed to assist faculty in improving teaching, learning, and assessment, although it has other institutional benefits.

- Plan and continually use a vetting process for brainstorming, asking questions, gathering data, and planning next steps, whether in teams, in departments/programs, across campus, or among executive staff, to improve the template and process.

- Give the process away. Don't try to control, limit, or restrict discussion, criticism, alternatives, or diversions.

- Ask for and use ongoing feedback from faculty, staff, and administrators, as well as peer institutions and colleagues at conferences regarding improvement of the process, goals, and next steps.

References

Eckel, P. D., & Kezar, A. (2003). *Taking the reins: Institutional transformation in higher education.* Westport, CT: American Council on Education and Praeger.

Patton, R. A., & McCalman, J. (2000). *Change management: A guide to effective implementation.* Thousand Oaks, CA: Sage.

Senge, P. (2006). *The fifth discipline: The art and practice of the learning organization.* New York: Doubleday/Currency.

About the Authors

Althea Smith holds a doctorate in psychology with an emphasis on leadership and organizational development. She has been an educator, consultant, facilitator and administrator for various change initiatives in colleges and universities throughout the Unites States. For more than 15 years she has designed, facilitated, monitored, and evaluated change projects, from diversity initiatives and institutional climate and culture change, to developing collaborative high-performance work teams, to designing college first-year programs and measuring institutional effectiveness. Formerly on the Staff of North Shore College's Center for Teaching, Learning, and Assessment, she is now the Director of Assessment, Teaching and Learning at Mt. Ida College, Massachusetts.

Susan Bayard has been the director of the Center for Teaching, Learning, and Assessment at North Shore Community College since 2003. Her responsibilities include supervising the academic department/program review and assessment process, supervising the service learning program, and coordinating professional development activities for faculty. Before coming to NSCC, Mrs. Bayard taught at Boston University, Wheelock College, and Salem State College. She also owned and managed a learning center that provided educational consulting in curriculum development and performance assessment as well as tutoring in all school subjects. Mrs. Bayard has an M.A. in curriculum and instruction from the University of California, Berkeley, and a certificate of advanced graduate study in science education from Boston University.

9

DISCOVERING OUR WAY

Defining and Implementing an Integrated Culture of Assessment

Mia Alexander-Snow and Christine Robinson
Seminole State College of Florida

Seminole State College of Florida (SSC), formerly Seminole Community College, located outside of Orlando, Florida, and led by Dr. Earl Weldon, opened its doors in 1966 with 700 students. In 1996, Dr. E. Ann McGee took the reins. During her tenure, SSC (n.d.-1) articulated its mission "to serve the community by offering a learning-centered, high-quality educational institution that anticipates and meets its needs with a comprehensive range of programs and services." SSC (n.d.-2) embraces the vision of becoming "renowned, first and foremost, for its enduring commitment to learning, and focus on individual student success" by building and sustaining a "future-focused," "student-centered," and "community-connected" learning environment. Today, SSC is a largely open-access midsized comprehensive community college serving approximately 30,642 students from diverse ethnic and socioeconomic backgrounds. SSC offers an A.A. in 38 different pre-major areas to students who transfer to 4-year institutions, 36 A.S. programs, 39 college-credit certificates, and 17 vocational-credit certificates to students who are interested in entering the workforce, and a variety of other opportunities for those interested in improving their skills and knowledge or pursuing personal interests.

Seminole State College's inroads to campus-wide assessment came at a time when one internal force and two external mandates required the institution to address long-held misconceptions about assessment, the role of faculty and other professionals at the institution, and the use of assessment. In fall 2005, the college set out a 2005–2010 strategic plan that provided an initial source of motivation to assess our students' learning. It articulated a college objective "to undertake continuous assessment of learner needs, expectations, satisfaction, and achievement." In 2007 an external motivation took shape when a Florida statewide assessment task force mandated that all community colleges adopt five general education student learning outcomes (communication, critical thinking, scientific and quantitative reasoning, information literacy, and global-sociocultural responsibility) and measure each by 2013. In spring 2008, we were also preparing for our interim report for our regional accreditation, the Southern Association of Colleges and Schools (SACS). Successful assessment compliance requires the college to satisfy two areas:

1. Institutional effectiveness: "The institution identifies expected outcomes for its educational programs *(including student learning outcomes for educational program)* and its administrative and educational support services; assesses whether it achieves these outcomes; and provides evidence of improvement based on analysis of those results."
2. College-level competencies: "The institution identifies college-level competencies within the general education core and provides evidence that graduates have attained those competencies."

Within this context, this chapter captures the strategic processes that SSC initially built in response to these forces. Specifically, our case study traces the history of an institution that began its institution-wide efforts on the basis of both internal and external demands, which now, in retrospect, we view as having prompted us to engage the community in effective assessment. Specifically, we document how these demands drove our initial process but then how administrators, faculty, and other professionals developed and implemented our assessment process by opening up lines of communication across the institution to establish campus-wide buy-in—from establishing a common vocabulary to identifying methods of assessment that would provide us useful results to act upon. We hope that reading about the SSC way provides you with an understanding of how you can best lead your institution to discover its way in defining and implementing a culture of assessment even within the context of mandates.

Serendipity played its hand in bringing the authors of this chapter together to work on SSC's assessment. Four years earlier, Drs. Robinson and Alexander-Snow, who were in graduate school together, ran into each other at a conference. At that time, they discovered that they lived a few miles apart and were both administrators whose responsibilities included assessment. At that time, Dr. Alexander-Snow was the assistant director of assessment at a 4-year institution in Florida. Dr. Robinson had just been assigned the position of the dean responsible for leading Seminole State College's institutional assessment efforts and supporting its implementation. Throughout the assessment process, Dr. Robinson shared her ideas and expressed concerns with and sought advice from Dr. Alexander-Snow. By virtue of their assessment knowledge, experiences, and responsibilities, a bond was formed.

Developing a College-Wide Structure and Organizing a Plan

In summer 2005, the president of SSC reorganized senior management, appointing new vice presidents and reshuffling midlevel managers. The vice president of planning, technology, and institutional effectiveness was named the vice president of educational programs. This left a void in leadership in relation to planning, assessment, and accreditation. The institution filled this void by creating the Office of Planning, Assessment, and Quality Improvement. This office was designed to provide institutional leadership in (1) assessment and the evaluation of key college operations and activities, (2) coordination of accreditation activities, (3) development and disclosure of internal performance indicators and results, and (4) implementation of the college's strategic plan. Personnel with background and experience in these areas were reassigned to this new office, and Dr. Robinson was appointed to the newly created position of dean of assessment, planning, and quality assurance.

Unfortunately, the creation of a new office did not mean a changed attitude toward or renewed commitment to planning, assessment, and accreditation. The dean quickly learned that although she was ready for and excited about assessment, many faculty and staff at SSC were not. She found very little support from the faculty and lukewarm support from campus leaders—student services and administrative units and academic deans. Only for the decennial accreditation process had the college community leadership taken the initiative to address issues of assessment. The student support services and administrative units were too consumed with meeting the daily operating needs of the students and college, and deans and department chairs often complained that the assessment activities were taxing to an extremely overworked and underpaid faculty. The faculty appreciated their autonomy in the classroom and felt that the new impetus in outcomes-based assessment threatened that autonomy. They questioned any external authority, fearful that having outsiders with the power to evaluate performance would translate into faculty evaluation. Resistance to assessment mirrored how change had been historically addressed: Faculty historically had full purview of curricular issues—new course development, program offerings, and classroom and program assessment; and the college administration had full responsibility for anything the faculty did not want, primarily any administrative tasks that supported faculty work—accreditation activities and facilitation of institutional assessment initiatives. There existed clear tensions between administration and faculty, although they were working toward a common goal—the intellectual, moral, and ethical development of students.

Frustrated by the community's resistance to measuring student learning outcomes, the dean reached out to local institutions that had developed a regional and national reputation for successfully implementing plans for student learning outcomes. She spoke with directors and vice presidents of assessment at community colleges and 4-year baccalaureate colleges and universities. In particular, she sought assistance from the Office of Operational Excellence and Assessment Support at the University of Central Florida, an institution that had been engaged in working toward institutional effectiveness for more than 10 years and had successfully undergone SACS reaffirmation. Learning from these models, she identified the initial importance of involving key institutional constituents in the assessment process; thus, after a year, the dean of assessment, planning, and quality improvement developed and established a structure for the assessment of student learning outcomes that involved key constituent groups. A quality instruction (QI) task force was formed to review and revamp the college's current student learning outcomes to assess general education. The dean issued a college-wide invitation and targeted emails to faculty to join the task force. The task force would eventually consist of 10 faculty members from mathematics, biological science, networking and office administration, and accounting; and 7 administrators from curriculum, student services, library and learning resources, computer technology services, and the honors institute. The initial charge of the QI task force was to create a student learning outcomes assessment plan and time line in alignment with SSC's general education. That is, the task force was responsible only for the planning that needed to occur until a standing committee was established. For the next 2 years, the QI task force worked diligently on a college-wide assessment strategy. The dean chaired the task force meetings and provided guidance and assistance when requested or needed.

Without hesitation, the task force members engaged in planning activities. The motivation to accomplish this task was fueled by the fact that the president expected regular updates about the team's progress. Members initially developed a chart with a time line and list of key players to identify what party was responsible for an activity and when the activity needed to begin and end. Necessary activities were listed on sticky notes so that they could be moved around on the chart to ensure proper sequencing, timing, and assignment. The committee framed its work by identifying key questions related to the assigned activities and a list of key persons involved in completing these activities. Among the questions discussed were the following:

1. By what date should all outcomes be measured?
2. What activities must be accomplished in the design, implementation, measurement, and analysis processes?
3. By whom and how often should assessment efforts be communicated?
4. How should activities be assigned (i.e., by division, position, level, etc.)?
5. To whom should particular assessment activities be assigned?
6. When should assessment activities occur?
7. How long should it take to measure one outcome?

Concurrently, while the QI task force was completing its student learning outcomes assessment strategy, the Florida Community College's Council on Instructional Affairs approved the following general education student learning outcomes (GE-SLOs) for all Florida community colleges:

- Communication: Effective reading, writing, speaking, and listening
- Critical thinking: Reflection, analysis, synthesis, and application
- Scientific and quantitative reasoning: Understand and apply mathematical and scientific principles and methods
- Information literacy: Find, evaluation, organize, and use information
- Global-sociocultural responsibility: Participate actively as informed and responsible citizens in social, cultural, global, and environmental matters

Each of the 28 community college presidents agreed to adopt these GE-SLOs for his or her institution. In addition to adopting the GE-SLOs, each of the Florida community colleges was asked and agreed to measure all five of the statewide GE-SLOs by 2013. Seminole State College's administrative leadership and QI task force embraced the GE-SLOs because they actually supported SSC's strategic plan to enhance the quality of instruction and learner support servives; would provide additional data for their SACS report; and would garner more SSC support and collaboration, particularly for faculty working on the QI task force. The QI task force took the statewide GE-SLOs and integrated them into the newly developed campus-wide assessment strategy.

Following the decision to integrate the new GE-SLOs into assessment plans, the dean also educated the task force about assessment of general education by distributing other institutions' assessment materials and resources and asked members to conduct their own research on relevant materials and resources. One suggested resource was a community college website (http://valenciacc.edu/slo) that tracked and posted information about student learning outcomes and assessment measures used in all Florida community colleges. Another resource was a book titled *General Education Assessment for Improvement: Guidance for Academic Departments and Committees* by James O. Nichols and Karen W. Nichols (2001). Research became a great place to start in developing a foundation for a basic understanding of assessment and student learning outcomes.

To develop a college-wide integrated assessment strategy, the dean and the task force members engaged in community outreach. The task force immediately sought out leaders from the arts and sciences division, such as the dean and department chairs from mathematics and English, and, whenever possible, made its assessment work known across the institution. Specifically, task force members asked to be scheduled to speak at division and department meetings about the details of the assessment process. They also invited professionals from non-academic areas of the college, such as assessment and testing, the library, counseling and advising, and institutional research, to participate in committee meetings and provide feedback about the role each played in supporting the measurement of student learning outcomes. Contributions from these professionals helped to build an assessment process that put students at the center of this commitment. As the task force completed its planning activities with contributions from other professionals on campus, members made presentations to the campus-wide community, requesting feedback and recommendations about who should be involved in identifying and measuring student learning outcomes and about the timing of the process.

They made sure that they reported back to the task force with new recommendations that emerged from those in the community at large. Within several months, the task force could see that it had made progress in moving the college toward a culture of assessment. Specifically, the Seminole community displayed greater support of the task force efforts as faculty and administration began to engage in conversation about the statewide general education outcomes. In addition, community members were starting to understand the importance of assessment and its potential contribution to improving student learning and development at the college, program, and classroom levels. Emerging, then, was an understanding that assessment involved the entire community: Everyone had important roles in the design and implementation of the assessment strategy. Within 3 months of the task force's outreach efforts, a draft of the general education assessment cycle was completed, presented to, and approved by the executive team of the college.

Opening the Lines of Communication

Organizing the structural process simply required the task force to establish the *what* and *when*. Defining *how* and *who* presented challenges. Three months after adopting the five GE-SLOs proposed by the state, the QI task force continued its work to determine how to better define the five general education outcomes in terms of specific behaviors, using clear and explicit language, so that they were measurable—that is, what knowledge, skills, abilities, and attitudes students should gain from the academic programs for each of the outcomes. The task force members soon discovered that team members lacked the knowledge to identify measurable competencies. To this end, the chair of the committee and a few task force members engaged in extensive research and reviewed several other colleges' definitions of the five outcomes. For 6 months, task force members discussed and drafted competencies corresponding to the five general education outcomes.

Upon completing a draft of the competencies, the QI task force was committed to finding an acceptable and implementable way to communicate them across the institution and obtain feedback from the community. The task force shared its work with department chairs and faculty, who were asked to discuss their thoughts during department chair meetings and then share their input and feedback with the task force. Feedback and suggestions were provided at the end of spring 2008. Some of the feedback related to language; other feedback related to the ability to measure a competency. Much discussion, for example, centered on the global-sociocultural responsibility competencies: how best to measure these student learning outcomes and how to hold departments accountable for integrating them into their curricula. A final version of all the competencies was adopted 6 months later (see the appendix at the end of this chapter).

In addition, the QI task force was charged to develop a curriculum-mapping tool. Upon completion of a draft of the competencies, the dean designed a tool to map general education outcomes to a course. Specifically, the map was designed to document the degree to which a course emphasizes one or more general education learning competencies and to document the method used in a course to assess a competency. In fall 2008, the curriculum mapping process began for a number of the college's courses. Faculty used their master syllabi to complete the forms. Once all the course mappings were completed for a program, the results would be used to identify gaps in the curriculum. In going through the assessment process, faculty determined that master syllabi were woefully outdated and thus could not be used to identify the general education competencies. As a result of this recognition, faculty members worked to adjust and update master syllabi so that they reflected course objectives, core competencies, and measures. In addition, in this updating process, faculty achieved consistency across the same course taught by different faculty or instructors; thus, for example, all Introduction to Psychology courses being taught would cover the same material in relationship to course objectives and student learning outcomes. To create instructional consistency in terms of content, all faculty now use updated master syllabi as a foundation in the development of individual course syllabi; and new faculty members, and especially adjuncts, receive these master syllabi as they develop their courses.

Making Decisions About Competencies

An equally challenging responsibility for the task force was implementing the appropriate assessment tools to assess the competencies. The task force debated whether tools such as standardized tests should be developed internally or externally. Given the budget cuts and issues surrounding convenience, time, reliability, and validity, the task force determined that purchasing an established and previously tested tool would be more advantageous than developing a tool internally. Here the task force relied on the research conducted by the dean. The dean of assessment reviewed several tools based upon research from other colleges and a paper titled "A Culture of Evidence: Critical Features of Assessments for Postsecondary Student Learning" (Millett, Stickler, Payne, & Dwyer, 2007). A matrix of the pros and cons of each tool was designed. The task force was asked to review the tools identified in the matrix and provide input about the use of each tool in terms of its suitability for community college students and utilization by other community colleges, as well as the usefulness of results for faculty. Once a tool was identified, the dean discussed the proposed recommendation with the appropriate department chair and then asked that chair to review the tool and provide departmental responses to the task force. To help determine which tool was best, the chairs asked the task force if the proposed standardized exams could be administered during one class period, if the exams were diagnostic in nature, and what other community colleges had experienced in using the exams.

The Measure of Academic Proficiency and Progress (MAPP), developed by the Educational Testing Service, was selected to assess the critical thinking, quantitative reasoning, and communication competencies of at least 50 graduates in spring 2009. Starting in summer 2008, the dean worked with the Assessment and Testing Office to set up the testing process and also worked with institutional research to identify courses with potential spring 2009 graduates. Once a list of courses was identified, the dean worked with academic deans, department chairs, and faculty to narrow the list. In April 2009, upon identification of a final list, the dean developed and sent invitations to students to sit for the exam, identified financial incentives for students to participate, and helped organize the test-taking process with the Assessment and Testing Office. Half of the number of SSC graduates who needed to conduct comparative analyses on the MAPP were tested. As a result, the dean identified summer 2009 graduates who might sit for the exam.

In addition to assessing general education outcomes, one of the college's focus areas for 2008–2009 was improving student success in college prep courses. Assessment of the students enrolled in these courses would provide helpful data about both our communication and quantitative reasoning student learning outcomes, supporting the state mandate and accreditation requirements. The dean proposed the idea of measuring value added rather than solely end-of-program outcomes. To accomplish the goal of measuring learning gains, the team members agreed that the same instrument used to test students before they take a college prep course needed to be used to test students enrolled in a final college prep course toward the end of class. Community colleges often require students without an SAT or ACT score to take ACCUPLACER, a standardized exam developed by the College Board to provide academic advisors and counselors with useful information about a student's academic skills in math, English, and reading. This exam is used to place students in either college prep or college credit courses. Given that a majority of the college prep students at SSC take the ACCUPLACER, the task force's idea was to conduct a pilot test using the ACCUPLACER among college prep students in their final college prep course. On the basis of a couple of one-on-ones about the purpose of this test and about how the institution could use results to gauge value-added learning with faculty who teach sections of Basic Algebra and Fundamentals of Writing II, two faculty members agreed to engage in this pilot study. Analysis of these results and their relationship to other student assessment data, such as state exit exam scores and final course grades, were also discussed with these faculty members to help them recognize how useful college prep courses are, as revealed by students' incoming and outgoing ACCUPLACER scores. The dean and director of institutional research stated that the next steps in the process would be to understand if there was a relationship between ACCUPLACER results and courses grades and ACCUPLACER results and grades in subsequent English and mathematics courses. Each participating faculty member provided students' final exam and state exit exam scores. The dean, director, and faculty members analyzed the results and determined that in some cases a relationship existed between the ACCUPLACER results and students' performance in the courses. However, it was determined that further study was necessary to see if this relationship continued to occur for some students and to see what other kinds of factors explained students' results.

Case Study Summary

Our initial motivation for campus involvement in assessment came from one internal and two external sources. In fall 2005, the establishment and acceptance of the college's 2005–2010 strategic plan identified enhancing the quality of instruction as a priority. Dean Robinson was assigned to address this issue, using college-wide personnel and resources; thus, the QI task force was born. Externally, pressure from our statewide task force and agreement from all community college presidents to adopt and measure five desired general education student learning outcomes and an impending SACS visit also motivated us to integrate assessment into institutional life. Even within this context, however, we learned that to integrate assessment into institutional life, administrative leadership needed to change the campus community's perception of the assessment process so that it would no longer be seen as an inconvenient, meaningless, and sometimes costly exercise to a purposeful, significant experience. Our dean's initial structural and organizational changes became the backbone of our institutional commitment to assessment, thus positioning us for committed action. However, real cultural change was reflected in the assessment efforts and successes of the QI task force composed of representatives from across campus. By charging the task force with the primary responsibility for creating the assessment process, the administrative leadership began to dislodge the long-held belief that assessment is an administrative responsibility. The task force representation and execution of activities fostered a renewed spirit of commitment, collaboration, and cooperation among community members, all of which were important for promoting cultural change.

Significantly, the dean was well received and respected by faculty and academic and support services personnel alike. Without respect and honesty, she and the task force would not have been able to facilitate conversations so that all key stakeholders were heard and valued throughout the assessment strategy process. Her ability to explain the value of defining and assessing student learning outcomes/competencies across all constituent groups made her central to the task force's success and effectiveness. It is critical for faculty and other professionals to be involved in all levels of the assessment design and implementation process and provide input into a process they will themselves engage in.

One of the most engaging issues that task force and community members wrestled with was defining the skills, knowledge, and abilities that all SSC students should possess upon graduation. The statewide GE-SLOs provided the platform for the discussion. Yet the college had to articulate the competencies in measurable terms and agree upon an assessment measure—one of the most challenging tasks for any department, program, or unit, particularly at the college level. Articulation of these competencies and identification of assessment methods required the critical involvement of faculty and other professionals. We quickly learned that assessment has multiple meanings, depending on whether a member is an instructional or non-instructional employee within the organizational structure. Yet a common language and understanding of assessment came out of the engaged collaborative efforts of the task force and community members facilitated by the dean. Furthermore, to have sustained assessment, it was vital that we established a common understanding of what would be assessed and how assessment methods would be integrated across the college. The most effective and efficient means of obtaining faculty engagement was through the curriculum mapping process. The process clarified for them how the core values, concepts, and skills that students were expected to possess upon graduation related to their courses. Also, during the curriculum mapping activity, faculty recognized the need to update master syllabi to include relevant desired learning outcomes supported by their courses and to identify how these outcomes were measured. Faculty saw the mapping tool and process as useful because they directly related to course instruction. Had SSC engaged in curriculum mapping prior to faculty participation in the GE-SLO process, the mapping process would have streamlined their discussions about assessment measures as well as discussions about how to assess for differences in skill levels across disciplines.

Seminole State College learned that in order to get buy-in and use of assessment results, faculty and other professionals must participate in or provide feedback about the implementation of the process. For example, soliciting faculty members' help in determining GE-SLOs was critical. In addition, discussing how assessment results showed that faculty added value to students' knowledge, as well as how results allowed for identification of patterns of student performance that faculty could aim to improve through pedagogical or curricular changes, was crucial to the success of the assessment process. Assessment success is built on engaging faculty as active participants in the process—an essential principle we hope will provide the foundation for sustaining our assessment activities.

The task force's charge to create the assessment strategy reflected a transparent collaborative process. The participation of both academic and student support service areas ensured that campus-wide assessment could become integrated into the everyday practices of teaching and learning and could provide the foundation necessary for sustainability, so that no one department, program, or unit would be solely responsible for documenting student learning and development. It is vital that all affected stakeholders support and be actively involved in planning and implementing the assessment process: Each involved party plays a distinct and meaningful part. Without the involvement of all parties, the institution may well lose its full educational mission and purposes.

Ideally, colleges and universities would like to be able to say that the culture of assessment reflects bottom-up leadership; however, the reality for SSC was that our culture arose primarily from external forces: our state mandate and regional accreditation. Campuses that find themselves under an externally imposed mandate or promulgation may find it particularly difficult to develop an integrated culture of assessment that reflects a collaborative process; however, we found that it can be done.

References

Millett, C., Stickler, L., Payne, D., & Dwyer, C. (2007). *A culture of evidence: Critical features of assessments for postsecondary student learning.* Princeton, NJ: Educational Testing Services.

Nichols, J. O. and Nichols, K. W. (2001). *General education assessment for improvement: Guidance for academic departments and committees.* University of California, San Diego: Agathon Press.

Seminole State College. (n.d.-1). *Mission statement.* Retrieved from www.seminolestate.edu/aboutscc/vision.htm

Seminole State College. (n.d.-2). *Vision statement.* Retrieved from www.seminolestate.edu/aboutscc/vision.htm

About the Authors

Mia Alexander-Snow is assistant professor of higher education and policy studies at the University of Central Florida in Orlando. Prior to Dr. Alexander-Snow's present position, she served as the assistant director of assessment in the Office of Operational Excellence and Assessment Support at the University of Central Florida, where she assisted academic and administrative units in university-wide assessment initiatives (institutional effectiveness, departmental performance review, and program review) designed to promote quality assurance and institutional improvement. She earned her Ph.D. in education and human development from Vanderbilt University, M.Ed. in college student personnel services from Peabody College, and B.A. in English from the College of William and Mary. Dr. Alexander-Snow's teaching and research focus on organizational culture, with an emphasis on assessment and evaluation of student learning and program development.

Christine Robinson is the dean of planning, assessment and quality improvement at Seminole State College. Currently, she provides leadership and direction for institutional strategic and annual planning, enrollment management, student learning outcomes, and program review. She acts as the college's accreditation liaison and is responsible for ensuring that accreditation requirements are incorporated into the institutional planning and evaluation processes, familiarizing employees with accreditation policies and procedures, and coordinating the efforts for reaccreditation. Dr. Robinson earned her Ed.D. in curriculum and instructional leadership from Vanderbilt University, M.B.A. from Indiana University in Bloomington, and B.S. in mathematics from Purdue University.

APPENDIX
Seminole State College's GE-SLOs

1. **Communication**: Effective reading, writing, speaking, listening

Core Competencies:
A student who is competent in communication can:
- Comprehend and interpret various types of written information
- Communicate thoughts, ideas, opinions, information, and messages in writing
- Compose and create documents with correct grammar, spelling, and punctuation, as well as appropriate language, style, and format
- Construct and deliver a clear, well-organized verbal presentation
- Participate effectively in conversations, discussions, and group activities by speaking clearly and asking questions relevant to the topic
- Receive, attend to, interpret, and respond appropriately to verbal and nonverbal messages
- Recognize all differences and utilize effective methods for cross-cultural communication

2. **Critical Thinking**: Observation, analysis, synthesis, application

Core Competencies:
A student who is competent in critical thinking can:
- Identify a problem or argument and ask appropriate questions
- Gather and analyze data relevant to a problem
- Consider diverse perspectives and alternative points of view when generating and assessing solutions to a problem
- Anticipate and evaluate consequences and revise the thinking process
- Select well-reasoned solutions to problems and use sound evidence to justify positions
- Apply knowledge to new situations and larger contexts in an effort to adapt it to other circumstances
- Develop solutions to new situations and more complex problems through the application of newly acquired knowledge

3. **Scientific and Quantitative Reasoning**: Understand and apply mathematical and scientific principles and methods in appropriate situations

Core Competencies:
Quantitative
A student who is competent in quantitative reasoning can:
- Identify and extract relevant data from given mathematical situations
- Interpret mathematical models such as graphs, tables and schematics and draw inferences from them
- Use graphical, symbolic, and numerical methods to analyze, organize, and interpret data
- Organize data, identify a process to solve a problem, and determine if the results make sense (or if the results are reasonable)
- Understand consumer related mathematical concepts

Scientific
A student who is competent in scientific reasoning can:
- Appropriately apply scientific principles in problem solving and decision making by organizing, analyzing, and interpreting data appropriately

- Use appropriate basic scientific equipment, vocabulary, methods, and safety precautions (when applicable)
- Describe the changing nature of and the interaction among science, technology, and society
- Generate an empirically evidenced and logical argument
- Distinguish a scientific argument from a non-scientific argument
- Reason by deduction, induction, and analogy
- Distinguish between causal and correlational relationships
- Recognize methods of inquiry that lead to scientific knowledge

4. Information literacy: Find, evaluate, organize, and use information
Core Competencies:
A student who is competent in information literacy can:
- Locate and use appropriate and relevant information from print and electronic sources to satisfy informational needs
- Identify, analyze, and evaluate information for relevancy, accuracy, authority, bias, currency, and coverage
- Synthesize collected ideas and materials into original work in appropriate formats
- Use information ethically and legally
- Use appropriate technology to manage information, solve problems, communicate, develop products, and provide services

5. Global-sociocultural responsibility: Prepare students to participate actively as informed and responsible citizens in social, cultural, global, and environmental matters
Core Competencies:
A student who is competent in global sociocultural responsibility can:
- Identify scientific principles underlying human influence upon the earth and its inhabitants
- Recognize current social and political issues in his or her own community
- Demonstrate knowledge of diverse cultures, including global and historical perspectives
- Demonstrate an understanding of and appreciation for human diversities and commonalities
- Recognize the impact of biases, assumptions, and prejudices in interactions
- Realize the political, cultural, and economic impact of global interdependence
- Understand how the natural world affects our daily lives and in turn is affected by our activities

OUTCOMES ASSESSMENT, THE PUBLIC RESEARCH UNIVERSITY, AND THE HUMANITIES

Laura J. Rosenthal
University of Maryland, College Park

The University of Maryland, College Park, is a Carnegie doctoral/research university with 37,000 students, approximately 26,500 of whom are under-graduates. It is the flagship state university of Maryland, consisting of 13 schools and colleges. Each college has its own structure for assessment, but a representative from each of the schools and colleges participates on a university-wide assessment committee chaired by the dean of undergraduate studies. The College of Arts and Humanities has 17 departments that range from relatively small ones like the dance department, with fewer than 10 faculty members, to large ones like the English department, with over 60. All the departments teach writing, research, a body of knowledge, and thinking in their discipline, but some, such as the studio art and theater departments, have strong creative practice components as well.

In the spring of 2009, the associate dean of arts and humanities and I changed the name of our ARHU (Arts and Humanities) Assessment Committee to the Committee on Student Learning. The membership of the committee has remained the same and the name change did not represent any major shift in responsibilities. It did, however, represent an evolution in our thinking about this project, which I trace in this chapter. In the relatively brief time that this committee has been operating, we have gradually moved from the enormous task of organizing and learning to report assessment practices in ARHU departments to exploring, albeit in sometimes rudimentary ways, how well we think students are learning. At first it was difficult to get to the more interesting questions. Although some colleges at the University of Maryland, such as the College of Education, had long been engaged in outcomes assessment as a routine part of their work, the systematic implementation of learning outcomes assessment across the university came rather suddenly in 2004 in response, at least in part, to a new emphasis on assessment from our accrediting agency (the Middle States Commission on Higher Education). Most faculty members remained blissfully ignorant at this point in the process. Many brought into it in the first round did not exactly welcome it with open arms. This, I believe, was mainly because it seemed like one more task to add to an ever-growing list, but also because it seemed connected with President George W. Bush's No Child Left Behind legislation. It seemed punitive and bureaucratic, a top-down system rather than one built from the grassroots of educational prac-tice on campus. We knew our students were learning, so why create more paperwork to address a non-problem? My department chair, however, assigned to me the project of developing an assessment plan for our depart-ment in my capacity as the director of undergraduate studies.

Although somewhat overwhelmed by the prospect, I was not entirely unfamiliar with learning outcomes. Before I became involved with assess-ment at the University of Maryland, I had participated in a "virtual listen-ing"—something like an online conference—sponsored by the Teagle Foundation, which first introduced me to some of the fundamental issues. At that point those issues seemed entirely abstract to me; nevertheless, the conference gave me some helpful familiarity with what was at stake. I also participated in a week-long summer workshop on assessment sponsored by the university's College of Education as part of a project to improve align-ment between student training in education and in their content areas. Whereas the Teagle conference had introduced me to some of the larger philosophical issues around assessment, the College of Education workshop explored some particular strategies in detail. Both were helpful, but I did not leave either with a clear understanding of the value of assessment. It still remained mysterious and a little suspect. How would the information be used? Would assessment become part of tenure and promotion files? Salary reviews? The assessment project threatened to be at best a waste of time, and at worst a pseudo-scientific erosion of academic freedom.

Effective Strategies and Processes to Address Challenges at a Large State Research University

Bureaucratization

The particular challenge at a large state research university such as Maryland, I believe, has been in reconciling the massive bureaucratic task necessary to ensure accountability with the very local and specific ways outcomes assessment has the potential to improve programs, courses, and classroom experiences. In this chapter, then, I want to explore my own idiosyncratic pathway through outcomes assessment and my attempts to move between bureaucratic accountability and classroom experience, and a few points in between, a movement that lies behind the change from chairing an assessment committee to chairing a committee devoted to student learning. As I have continued to work on outcomes assessment by first devising assessment strategies for my own department (English) and then chairing the ARHU committee at Maryland, I have become more optimistic about the potential value of the process, even if some of my initial skepticism remains. This skepticism, however, has been valuable, forcing me to think in more concrete ways about what I do in the classroom. In working with a range of faculty members in different liberal arts disciplines, I have also discovered that my own points of resistance were far from unique. In particular, these include perplexity over the apparent redundancy of assessment after grading, concern that outcomes assessment misdirects precious institutional resources and could be used in damaging ways, and the nagging possibility that some things can't be measured. I have found a fair amount of consistency in the points of conflict in the range of venues at which I have engaged this issue: at my home institution, in many informal discussions with colleagues at different institutions, and at the Modern Languages Association, first in a delegate assembly discussion on outcomes assessment that I organized in 2006, and the following year in a panel presentation intended as a follow-up to the previous year's discussion. (Both of these events were very lively and well attended.) Similar points were raised at the Teagle online conference and at the College of Education workshop and continue to crop up in opinion pieces on the subject in places like the *Chronicle of Higher Education* and *Inside Higher Education.*

What most instructors I have talked to who are engaged in assessment projects will agree on is that there can be no one-size-fits-all model: Projects need to be specific to the institution, the department, and the discipline. Large state universities cannot simply adopt the strategies that have been used with such great success at liberal arts colleges; even within similar kinds of institutions, local conditions make a difference. In his recent book *The Last Professors,* Frank Donahue (2008) argues that public research universities tend to suffer from a particular kind of confusion over their identity and their mission. Faculty research productivity receives considerable emphasis—in some ways, as Donahue argues, even *more* emphasis than at elite private research institutions, which have greater access to traditional forms of prestige. This competition for prestige lies in tension with the traditional obligation of public institutions to open up professional and personal possibilities for populations that might otherwise have limited opportunities.

This tension that Donahue (2008) identifies has implications for outcomes assessment. First, faculty members at these institutions are pulled in several different directions. Although most care deeply about their teaching, public research institutions tend to reserve most of their (increasingly limited) rewards for research productivity. Accustomed to feeling like stones squeezed for more and more blood, faculty members are unlikely to see advantages in their own investment in outcomes assessment. Second, the increasing bureaucratization of state universities, as Donahue describes, often leaves faculty generally detached from broader institutional goals. They are, perhaps, more likely than colleagues at liberal arts colleges to greet outcomes assessment as a new form of micromanagement rather than as a genuine effort to improve learning. Indeed, some administrators at these institutions may themselves see assessment as a new opportunity for micromanagement, a possibility that would clearly undermine any positive commitment to the improvement of learning. Third, faculty members at public research universities are accustomed to having a great deal of autonomy in their teaching; outcomes assessment, by contrast, demands a level of collaboration that might be more familiar to instructors at other kinds of institutions. Finally, the sheer size of some public research institutions makes any conversation about institutional goals and values particularly challenging.

These tensions became visible to me at my own institution: faculty members had a range of other obligations; they felt, as individuals, a fairly minimal connection to accreditation; most did not immediately see outcomes assessment as connected to better teaching. The institutional strategy, mainly put in place by Donna Hamilton, the dean of undergraduate studies, was first to build the organizational scaffolding and work from there. The advantages of this model were that it made possible the sorting out of a huge amount of information and also made clear the lines of responsibility. It took advantage of existing structures already in place. The disadvantage was that faculty members and administrators found themselves charged with a project they knew little about and that challenged their sense of autonomy. To address this, Dean Hamilton organized workshops and speakers (some of which I found invaluable). Given that the newly systematic assessment project came from higher levels and even outside the university, and not from the faculty themselves, my colleagues on the university committee and I all spent a fair amount of time negotiating points of confusion and resistance. (I should add here that I'm not sure there would have been any other way to get an outcomes assessment process in place in a timely manner in such a large institution.)

Before moving on the specific discussions that these issues generated, I want to mention the forms of process that I found most productive. In chairing the ARHU committee, I got used to the fact that a certain amount of time during the meeting would be devoted to faculty discussing their objections. Because the administrative scaffolding was already in place, these weren't generally discussions about whether or not we should move forward on the project, as that was a given. Elizabeth Loizeaux, the associate dean with whom I worked, often made the important point that departments need to take control of their own assessment projects, as it is better for them to come from the people who understand the discipline. This made sense to most faculty members. Nevertheless, I found that it was helpful to spend a certain amount of time just letting people discuss their various philosophical objections and quandaries. These discussions helped committee members get to know each other better and bond (or perhaps commiserate) over our shared task. At a Teagle-Spencer assessment conference that I attended in the fall of 2008, Derek Bok made the simple but resonant point that most faculty members are highly invested in student learning. When faculty objected to assessment in these meetings, they were not revealing a lack of investment in student learning; instead, they were working through a possibility that flew in the face of much training and experience: that student learning can be a shared responsibility, that teaching can be a collaborative project, that information from assessment can be used to improve learning. Most faculty were accustomed to having their teaching measured by students (through evaluation), but not to measuring the extent to which the programs in their departments were themselves effective. As faculty cycled in and out of administrative jobs in their own departments, personnel on the committee changed. Given the size of our college (17 departments or programs, most with several different degree programs and different components), I regularly scheduled two meetings for each session so that everyone would be able to get to one. As a result, the makeup of each meeting constantly changed, and we would go through many of the same issues at the beginning of each semester. What started to happen after awhile, though, was that more experienced faculty members would engage the less experienced ones and soon they were talking to each other in productive ways.

I learned from this the value of repetition and the importance of patience in setting up assessment. Given a good administrative structure and the truth of Bok's basic insight that instructors want their students to learn, good assessment procedures can develop even at gigantic state universities. The first time through, the sheer management of information was overwhelming. But as we started to get that aspect a little more under control, and especially with the added help of a graduate assistant, it became possible to focus on the more interesting questions: What were these results telling us? What should we now do with this information? In short, I think that perhaps in the context of a large research institution, you have to focus first on the structures and chains of responsibility before the work itself becomes revealing or meaningful.

Grades

At these meetings, the issue of using grades came up nearly every time. Although in the College of Arts and Humanities we generally discourage programs from using grades, I have learned from serving on the university committee that disciplines vary in their approach to this and there are some cases in which the use of grades seems appropriate. The College of Education, for example, relies on grades to assess learning in content areas. In the ARHU committee, however, we decided that grades would probably not give us much information about our programs. To take an example from my own department, under our current major, students need to take four courses at the 400 (highest undergraduate) level. These courses are supposed to be distinguished from 300-level courses by the inclusion of a research component. In practice, however, instructors emphasize different things in their classes, and some might spend less time on research and more on close reading. Depending on which courses an undergraduate has chosen, he or she *could*, for example, complete the English major with very high grades but with limited research skills. Looking at grades, then, would not necessarily indicate that the learning goal had been met. And, of course, standards can vary considerably from instructor to instructor. But more important than their inconsistency, grades don't reveal much about the program as a whole. The move from the individual class to the program was, I think, the conceptual leap behind many of these discussions: Faculty tend to think about their teaching in highly individualistic ways, but outcomes assessment ideally trains its attention on an entire program and thus asks faculty to consider what they are *collectively* teaching their students.

Shifting from student success revealed by grades to program effectiveness revealed through more holistic forms of assessment has prompted some departments in our college to rethink their programs. For example, our theater department revised its major as a result of discussions that emerged from an assessment project led by the department's associate chair, Heather Nathans. The theater major at the University of Maryland has three major components: history, performance, and design. The first time the department went through the outcomes assessment process, each area was fairly satisfied that students were ultimately integrating these components. The students, essentially, were doing fine. But by meeting as a group about assessment results, looking at student evaluations, and taking into consideration some issues that had emerged in advising sessions, faculty realized that students would often take upper-level courses before completing preliminary course work in all three foundational areas. The aspiring actor, for example, might postpone his theater history course; the aspiring designer might leave her Introduction to Performance course until later. After much discussion, the faculty concluded that, given the other university requirement that students had to fulfill, they were spreading out the foundational material over too many courses. By condensing the number of required foundational courses from six to four, they have enabled all students to get some exposure to each area before they move to higher levels of course work. Faculty could not have solved this problem by looking at grades, which did not reveal any significant shortcomings. At the same time, however, students were not consistently moving to the upper-level courses with the full range of exposure to these different aspects of the discipline whose integration defines this particular program. The more holistic approach suggested a way to improve the program.

In devising other measures besides grades, most departments developed rubrics and have been using them to assess samples of work from various classes. This strategy will generate a set of scores that allow departments to compare success in various areas. In our ARHU meetings, however, one faculty member from the philosophy department, who probably understood quantitative methods better than others in the room, objected that most of what we were doing was not legitimate from a quantitative point of view. He judged that it would probably be possible to conduct a legitimate quantitative study and it might even be interesting, but that it would take up far more time than any faculty member would be able to devote to it. Although few of us in ARHU have much expertise in quantitative methods, we also ran into this problem at a much simpler level in trying to assess small programs. What kind of quantitative legitimacy, for example, could the assessment of a doctoral program that graduates one or two students each year possibly have? After much discussion of this issue, we realized that the objection was valid. There are, of course, legitimate large-scale quantitative studies of learning outcomes being undertaken by trained experts in the field. This, however, was not what we were doing; instead, we were asking professors from various academic and artistic fields who have little or no training in quantitative methods to look at their own programs. The answer that emerged for us was not the conclusion that no assessment was possible (tempting to some as that may have been) but that we should think about what strategies *were* legitimate. It seemed to us in the end that outcomes assessment was as much an art as a science, and that *qualitative* approaches might tell us more than quantitative ones. My conclusion (at this writing, at least) is that the kind of faculty-run assessment we are doing must emphasize qualitative approaches, and that quantitative results from individual programs are useful for prompting internal discussions, but not as any legitimate basis for comparison. In other words, the hypothetical finding that, say, 70% of students in the American studies program reached Goal 1 and 80% of students in the history department reached Goal 1 provides no useful or legitimate point of comparison. This is an important realization because to set up outcomes assessment for the purposes of comparison across departments or schools on a campus would demand a kind of standardization that would defeat the purpose of improving student learning (thus our change from a committee on *assessment* to a committee on *student learning*). Even the documentation from Middle States suggests that the accreditors are looking for a process rather than a set of results (*Characteristics of Excellence in Higher Education*, 2006).

Limited Resources

Another issue that consistently comes up in these meetings is concern over whether or not outcomes assessment is the most effective use of limited resources. This objection has a couple of components. Resources are tight everywhere, so how much time and money should be spent on this project? In a practical sense, this is often a purely theoretical question, as the demand for accountability often comes from the accrediting agencies. Universities have little choice but to seek accreditation, and faculty are better off taking hold of the process. Nevertheless, to the extent that we are engaged in not just responding to educational objectives but shaping them as well, it remains reasonable to think about whether or not outcomes assessment projects make the best use of limited time and resources.

It probably needs to be conceded that there would be other ways to improve learning on campus. For example, as many of my colleagues would point out, the best way to improve learning in higher education would be to hire more full-time faculty, enabling departments to offer smaller classes and to address the current imbalance in the ratio of adjunct instructors to tenured/tenure-track instructors. Although in my discipline, there have always been classes taught by faculty off the tenure track, a recent report by the Modern Language Association has shown that the ratio of classes taught by tenured/tenure-track instructors to those taught by adjunct faculty has significantly shifted in the wrong direction (Bartholomae, Kaplan, Laurence, Lauter, Morris, & Steward, 2008). Although individual adjunct instructors often do a wonderful job, their lack of job security gives students less access to their time; and the full-time faculty members, with their decreasing numbers, end up performing more service work than ever. Without a doubt, the increasing reliance on contingent faculty undermines student learning more profoundly than any lack of attention to goals and outcomes could do.

We addressed this issue in a couple of different ways. At the most fundamental level, there is no point denying the force of this point. Possibly, though, outcomes assessment could become an ally for critics of this trend by investigating the educational impact of the increasing reliance on instructors off the tenure track. Furthermore, outcomes assessment brings attention to the aspect of university life most damaged by this trend. It is also pointless to deny that outcomes assessment adds to the work of currently overburdened faculty members. For this reason, we have tried to find ways for departments to organize their assessment processes around structures that they already have in place. For example, doctoral programs usually have a qualifying exam and a defense of the dissertation. Several ARHU departments have taken these events as opportunities for outcomes assessment by devising a survey for faculty to complete after them. Some also have a survey for the student. Because the committee is already convened and an in-depth discussion of the student's work has taken place, faculty can take a few extra minutes to discuss or think individually about whether or not the student's progress has corresponded to the goals of the program. Most of our doctoral programs are fairly small, so it will probably take awhile to see any meaningful patterns. Nevertheless, I recall an interesting yet jarring experience of my own in filling out one of these forms after a master's project defense. The student had worked very hard, undertaking considerable research and completing several drafts. Upon filling out the assessment form, however, I was forced to recognize that there were areas in which her project fell short. In particular, although she covered considerable ground, she really hadn't sufficiently managed to place the project in the larger context of critical debates about her topic. I had seen this come up in other M.A. defenses, and from then on I made sure that I integrated this aspect of the discipline into my introductory graduate courses rather than leaving it for the seminars that students would take later in the program.

Although many programs, then, found opportunities for outcomes assessment in structures they had already set up, in some cases departments were in fact already practicing a form of outcomes assessment and only needed to describe their process in a way that made sense to people outside their discipline. In our studio art department, for example, each year ends with a juried exhibition at which every faculty member evaluates the portfolio of every student. Now, many departments are simply too big for that kind of assessment. Studio art, however, was already engaged in an effective and thorough assessment process and only needed to translate practice into expressions that fit the forms that the university had developed. Faculty evaluation of these exhibitions turned out to be a good assessment practice not just because it involved something that the department was already doing anyway but because it assessed something that they knew they cared about, which emerged as another key issue in assessment strategies. The theater department had adhered to a similar principal: Its faculty felt that it was worth the trouble to revise their major in light of assessment information because the program specifically defined itself as an integrated one. There are programs at other institutions oriented, for example, specifically toward performance, but this program wanted all its students to graduate with the ability to see the connections between and among several different aspects of theater.

The classics department also took advantage of a structure they already had in place, although they had to add a step to find out what they wanted to know. Faculty collected several batches of final exams and had the department secretary remove the grades from them. Then they sat down with the exams to see if there was any pattern in the kinds of mistakes that students were making. This was not prompted by a rash of failures or inadequate exams; instead, they wanted to see if there was any way they could improve student learning. Professor Greg Staley, who led this process, reported that the committee had only briefly chatted at the beginning of the process and then each member looked at the exams on his or her own. When they reconvened, they found that they had all reached the same conclusions. Students seemed to be able to figure out the structure of Latin sentences and showed knowledge of grammar but were particularly weak in their mastery of vocabulary. The department is currently trying to figure out how to address this problem. The textbook they use, Staley notes, does not have a good system for learning vocabulary, although it has strengths in other areas. One possibility might be to change the textbook; another might be to give more vocabulary quizzes. So although they have not yet decided how to address this issue, at least at this point they have developed a good sense of where their undergraduate program could benefit from improvement—and they developed this without adding an inordinate amount of work.

Immeasurablity

I have left the third and most challenging objection to the end: What if some kinds of learning simply cannot be measured? This skepticism is perhaps more likely to come from some departments than others. Instructors who teach foreign language acquisition have been, in my experience, comfortable with certain kinds of measurement, as have directors of composition programs. Others, however, feel that what they teach simply can't be measured. Sometimes these issues were fairly practical. In our women's studies department, for example, students can take a wide range of courses that focus on women and gender to count toward their major. They may, then, end up with courses in history, English, Italian, and dance as part of their completion of the women's studies major. Although in a large department like English we can sample papers from an upper-level class with the assumption that most of these students are English majors, women's studies majors can be found all over the college. Women's studies couldn't do what some of the larger departments were doing; they do, however, have a single advisor who talks to all the majors. Women's studies majors couldn't easily be tracked through classrooms, but, alternatively, the advisor could collect papers from all the majors and turn them in to the faculty committee.

The challenge of immeasurability, however, goes deeper than the practical challenges faced by interdisciplinary departments. To illustrate this point,

I will turn to the assessment projects whose beginning stages I am most familiar with: that of my own department. How does one measure what an English major should learn? The graduate program goals were easier to define because students needed to reach a certain level of professionalism. They should show mastery of a particular field, the ability to conduct research, and the ability to distinguish their arguments from the arguments of others, among other things. At first we proposed that they needed to write "publishable" essays, but that was too vague. They need to be able to write essays (and longer pieces) based on primary sources that say something important that hasn't yet been noticed or analyzed in quite the same way. They need to contribute to the field. Faculty members in English departments hold widely divergent views of what constitutes the best scholarship; nevertheless, I have seen relatively little disagreement over whether a student has done well enough to pass a qualifying exam or sufficiently revised the dissertation. Figuring out how to measure these abilities was not all that hard either, as many mechanisms for doing so were already in place. Students take an exam (in our department, an oral exam) to determine whether or not they have mastered a field; they write and defend a dissertation to show their ability to contribute original thought to a particular field. In my department, we simply added an extra step to both of these occasions, and now faculty fill out a very brief rubric evaluating whether or not students have reached certain goals.

The undergraduate program, however, has proved more vulnerable to the challenge of immeasurability. Graduate students are being trained for certain professional activities at which they will need to succeed when they become professors themselves. Of course, many graduate students do not become professors, but this doesn't change the way graduate programs should be run. Without the assumption that students will eventually enter the field they are training for, graduate programs would be entirely different. Undergraduate English majors, however, are not designed with the assumption that students are training to enter the field, and only a small fraction are headed for graduate study in literature. We did eventually come up with a system that has offered some good insight and pretty closely resembles others that I have seen; however, taking a close look at my discipline at times revealed its instability. This issue was not entirely new to me: The year before the University of Maryland began systematic outcomes assessment, I had been asked by the department chair to revise and update the major. When this task of revising the major came to me, I had not thought systematically about what an English major should learn. The more high-profile discussions in my field have tended to be about which written works students should be reading, with some advocating the study of a more traditional canon and others pushing the discipline toward a wider range of perspectives. Within departments, this discussion becomes further complicated by the multiple fields often housed in English departments, such as rhetoric, creative writing, and cultural studies, which do not necessarily focus on literary texts.

The revised major that emerged from these discussions is such a composite of intense faculty discussion, looming financial constraints, and outright plagiarism of other institutions' majors that I can't really claim it as a personal vision or expression of insight about what the study of English should be. However, I believe that I understand the revised major and the motives behind it a little better in retrospect and through the lens of engagement with outcomes assessment. Two previous majors are relevant here: In a much earlier version of the major, students took a series of courses on "masterworks"; this and other requirements organized the major around a traditional canon. As the discipline changed, the English major changed as well: In the major adopted in the 1990s, students took a core distribution of courses but then beyond that chose a concentration from a range of both traditional and emergent fields, such as women's writing, postcolonial writing, and the literature of the African diaspora. A new course was added to introduce students to critical issues and methods in the discipline. The revised-again 2002 major opened up even more choices for students and allowed for courses that crossed the boundaries of both new and traditional fields. The major no longer required the concentrations, but it made more of a distinction between the lower-level and upper-level courses, with particular skills expected at each level. In short, then, the emphasis of the major has shifted over the years from a mastery of a particular set of literary works to greater flexibility in the object of study yet more delineation of skills. The first major was based on the mastery of a canon; the 1990s major was based on familiarity with fields, allowing for more contextualized approaches and requiring an introductory course in critical methods. Without the concentrations and with greater distinction made between course levels, the 2002 major looks more like a pyramid, with students first studying a broad range of periods and genres, but later having the chance to pursue a particular interest in greater depth.

At the time of the 2002 revision of the major, motivated at least in part by financial exigencies, no one in my department was discussing outcomes. Looking back, though, it seems like this was one direction we were moving in, and that an awareness of outcomes assessment projects could have helped in this process. When we later needed to come up with a series of goals for our department assessment plan, we mostly looked at skills rather than mastery of content. By the end of their years as English majors, students should be able to think critically, write a critical essay, conduct research in the field, cite sources properly, persuasively analyze a piece of writing, and show an appreciation for literature. We had initially had another: "Students will acquire a broad foundation of literary knowledge and an awareness of the diversity of written expression and authorial perspective." We had intended to measure this by looking at course selection patterns and had decided that if students took a range of courses and if at least 75% of them received a C or better on the final exam, then we were meeting this goal. At a certain point, though, we realized that although we were very much committed to students graduating with both breadth of knowledge and awareness of diversity, the strategy we were planning would not actually measure either of those things. We didn't see an efficient way to measure those goals, which felt a little disappointing, but found ways to measure four others:

1. Students will be able to analyze critically a literary text.
2. Students will be able to write persuasively.
3. Students will be able to conduct research in English studies.
4. Students will gain an appreciation for the importance of writing, past and present, in society; for the complexity of literature; and for the variety of perspectives that written expressions represent.

We measure the first three by sampling papers from appropriate classes. The last one is perhaps the trickiest, but we are measuring this by adding a few questions to a senior survey that the department has long conducted anyway. As noted earlier, all this inevitably involves subjective judgments from those conducting the assessment, but this doesn't invalidate the process. Mostly, I think it means that results have the greatest value for internal use—for departments learning more about how their students could be learning better rather than for the purposes of any meaningful comparison.

Benefits to the Institution

In spite of the hazards, the bureaucracy, and the frustration, then, outcomes assessment has the potential to benefit the large public research institution if it can avoid becoming one more pile of forms or one more form of micromanagement. In some ways, assessment offers potentially the *most* significant benefits to these institutions, as they don't always make enough room for reflection on teaching and learning or reward faculty accomplishment in this area. The stakes are significant: These institutions have a particular form of obligation to the public that should involve not just credentialing but genuinely educating. As Christopher Newfield (2008) has recently argued, "the genius of public education has been high quality on a mass scale—the equivalent of a senior thesis for everybody. The genius is *mass* quality. The means is achieving *independent inquiry for all*" (p. 191). To the extent that outcomes assessment can help us figure out how to do this, it is worth the trouble.

References

Bartholomae, D., Kaplan, D., Laurence, Lauter, P., Morris, A., & Steward, D. (2008). *Education in the balance: A report on the academic workforce in English.* Report of the ADS Ad Hoc Committee on Staffing, Modern Languages Association and the Association of Departments of English. Retrieved from www .mla.org/pdf/workforce_rpt02.pdf

Bok, D. (2008). *Advancing student learning.* Paper delivered at the Teagle-Spencer Conference on How Can Student Learning Best Be Advanced? Achieving Systematic Improvement in Liberal Education, Durham, NC. Retrieved from www .teaglefoundation.org/learning/conference.aspx

Donahue, F. (2008). *The last professors: The corporate university and the fate of the humanities.* New York: Fordham University Press.

Middle States Commission on Higher Education. (2006). *Characteristics of excellence in higher education.* Retrieved from www.msche.org/publications/CHX06_Aug08 REVMarch09.pdf

Newfield, C. (2008). *Unmaking the public university: The forty-year assault on the middle class.* Cambridge, MA: Harvard University Press.

About the Author

Laura Rosenthal is professor of English and chairs the Student Learning Committee for the College of Arts and Humanities at the University of Maryland, College Park. When not doing assessment, she specializes in Restoration and 18th-century British literature and is the author, most recently, of *Infamous Commerce: Prostitution in Eighteenth-Century British Literature and Culture* (Cornell University Press, 2006) and editor of *Nightwalkers: Prostitute Narratives from the Eighteenth Century* (Broadview, 2008). She is currently working on a project on 18th-century cosmopolitanism in theater and print culture.

II

TURF BATTLES, SUBCULTURES, AND PROCEDURAL TECHNICALITIES

Multiple Pathways Toward Assessment
at the University of Southern Maine

Ann C. Dean and Susan McWilliams
University of Southern Maine

The University of Southern Maine (USM) is a comprehensive metropolitan public university, one of the seven campuses of the University of Maine system. The university provides a range of liberal arts and sciences and professional programs responsive to students diverse in age, background, and experience, many of whom are part-time, employed, and/or commuter students, as well as first-generation college students. USM offers baccalaureate, masters, and Ph.D. programs. USM's schools and colleges are the College of Arts and Sciences, the School of Business; the School of Applied Science, Engineering, and Technology; the College of Nursing and Health Professions; the College of Education and Human Development; Lewiston-Auburn College; the School of Law; and the Edmund S. Muskie School of Public Service. Although it is a midsize university (10,478 students enrolled for the fall 2006 semester), USM offers some of the features of both the small liberal arts college and the larger research university. Classes are relatively small (average class size is 22 and the student-to-faculty ratio is 16:1), and opportunities for students to work with faculty engaged in recognized research and scholarship are plentiful.

The authors, Susan McWilliams and Ann Dean, have been involved in assessment at USM in differing ways. Susan McWilliams, assistant provost of undergraduate programs, has been involved in USM's curriculum reform since 2001. In 2003 she moved from the faculty to a professional staff position specifically charged with assisting with the redesign of USM's core curriculum. Her involvement with assessment grows out of her work in helping faculty design a new curriculum based on clearly defined desired learning outcomes. Ann Dean is associate professor of English and director of college writing. Ann has been a member of the General Education Council since 2000. As administrator of the writing program, she has participated in developing course work, assignments, writing assessments, and writing desired outcomes for general education. The Faculty Senate gave the university's "writing person" lifetime tenure on the General Education Council, and assessment seemed to be the most effective way of incorporating attention to writing into the committee's work.

Our Context

The context for assessment at USM is a long process of general education reform beginning in the 1980s. We held a yearlong program of faculty research and discussion to enhance faculty awareness of the performance of the core. This work revealed that the general education curriculum had strayed far from its original intent. The curriculum lacked adequate institutional structure, ownership, and funding. There was no regular assessment of the program; it seriously lacked coherence.

In these conversations, the word *assessment* was widely used, and participants imagined that assessment would be part of the eventual curriculum. At first, however, conversations went no further than giving people the opportunity to get their lips around the word, and to begin to think about who might gather what information, where it might be stored, and how expensive the process might be. This part of the process was exploratory and diffuse; we did not know what the committee structure might be, how the different campuses and programs in the university would relate to revised general education, how the curriculum revision process related to faculty governance, or anything about what a new curriculum might look like. In this context, assessment became another item on a list of vague future possibilities.[1]

Discussions that year led to the creation of a proposal for a new institutional structure, the General Education Council, to support reform of general education at USM. The council then created two documents, "The

---

1. This and subsequent curricular reform efforts at USM have been generously supported by grants from the Davis Educational Foundation. The foundation was established by Stanton and Elizabeth Davis after Mr. Davis's retirement as chairman of Shaw's Supermarkets, Inc.

Vision, Goals, and Outcomes" (VGO) and the "Guidelines and Criteria for General Education at USM." These documents, and the General Education Council itself, provided the framework and oversight for the design of multiple curricular pathways by faculty groups (the USM core, Lewiston-Auburn College's common core, and the USM honors program).

The work of revising the general education curriculum was supported by senior administration. The provost created two new positions, an associate and assistant provost of undergraduate programs, and dedicated a small gift fund to support the work. The process benefited greatly from the support and expertise of an associate vice president of academic affairs and the director of academic assessment and their ability to communicate their knowledge to novices.

USM's process of curriculum redesign and assessment has also been influenced by external forces—a pending New England Association of Schools and Colleges (NEASC) accreditation in 2011 and state university–level calls for accountability. Although the impetus for curricular reform grew out of homegrown concerns about the effectiveness of the old distribution requirements, the work also has been tied frequently to the pending accreditation. Specifically, a move from inputs to outcomes has been repeatedly cited as a crucial step in moving toward meeting accreditation standards. Similarly, when concerns were raised about the possibility of increasing the number of required general education credits, supporters of the curriculum revision would site NEASC standards regarding distribution of student credit hours across general education, the major, and electives. Thus, although external accreditation concerns may not be the primary focus of curricular reform at USM, at times they loom large.

Three Steps Sideways, One Step Around: Nonlinear Change

USM's experience with the beginning stages of assessment (defining goals and desired outcomes, educating ourselves about assessment practice) provides some insights into curricular reform and assessment as organizational change. Like those Awbrey (2005) describes, our process has moved irregularly and recursively. As some participants in the curriculum revision process got more involved and knowledgeable, a differential began to emerge between people who could confidently use specialized assessment language, refer to programs at other institutions, and imagine alternative possibilities and those who could not. In the first group, many, though not all, were administrators; in the second, many, though not all, were faculty. Meetings meandered as we misunderstood each other; attempted to teach and learn new ideas; and worried over the budgets, classroom space, teaching power, and faculty commitment implied by the various new models we encountered or imagined. Assessment appeared and disappeared from view along with other related concepts such as desired learning outcomes, student engagement, learning communities, and interdisciplinarity.

At the same time, some university programs were carrying out their own homegrown assessment projects. The university's first-year composition course had been overhauled by the English department back in 1997. Because all full-time faculty in English regularly teach composition, this was a complex and contested process. A charismatic composition director helped the department craft a lengthy course description, which, without using the word *outcomes*, laid out the theoretical and practical approaches the department would take to the course, and the results that students and faculty could expect to see. The curriculum, a rigorous introduction to academic discourse through critical reading and sequenced writing assignments, required a difficult and labor-intensive transition for the full- and part-time faculty who teach the course but resulted in improved student writing and a consensus in the department about the value of the course description and approach.

When Ann took over as composition director in the fall of 2000, this departmental consensus was in place. By relying on it, the College Writing Committee was able to carry out an assessment process. We called it a course review to avoid the associations of managerial exploitation that assessment language tends to bring up for English faculty. For each section taught, we collected a syllabus, a set of assignment questions, and one paper that struck the instructor as characteristic. We asked for B−/C+ papers. Readers from the committee (three full time and two part time) read materials and used a simple yes-or-no checklist to match up the elements of the course description to the materials from each section. Ann counted up the various categories and prepared a report for the department. Results were encouraging: More than 90% of the sections were demonstrably delivering the course, and the results, described in the department's document. Because first-year composition is so difficult and labor intensive to teach, faculty were cheered to have this result, which helped assuage the nagging fear that a large number of people were really letting things slide and not working as hard as others.

Meanwhile, USM's professional schools encountered assessment differently. Their accreditation by national bodies required fairly extensive engagement in assessment long before the rest of the institution. While the English department carried out a homegrown process fairly far under the radar, each of the professional schools created large data-rich, photocopying-heavy assessments and produced reports as big as telephone books. As general education curricula began to emerge from committees and come before the Faculty Senate and departments, faculty experience in developing desired course outcomes, assessing those outcomes, and assessing whole programs fed into the process in several ways:

1. Individuals provided professional expertise. Professors of education and policy, for instance, helped us understand how to craft workable documents.
2. First-year composition provided a model for committees developing courses in terms of its development process, its desired outcomes, and its teaching practice.
3. Faculty in professional schools brought their experience with reporting to accrediting bodies to bear.

The nonlinear nature of our change process facilitates the achievement of some worthy goals and hinders that of others. For example, one positive outcome of the process is the capacity to map three different curricular paths in relation to each other and in relation to the vision, goals, and desired outcomes. This capacity reflects the needs and realities of a multi-campus commuter university. On the other hand, tensions have emerged among the three curricula in terms of human and financial resources that reflect old institutional divisions and practices. These tensions and divisions have been fanned by the process of Faculty Senate approval of the three curricular pathways.

Furthermore, our focus on the fundamental relationship among vision, goals, and more specific desired outcomes has slowed down our clear articulation of the mechanics of assessment plans for the individual pathways and makes decisions about our university-wide assessment plans even more complex. Even for faculty invested in carrying it out, the work has posed overwhelming challenges. Both of us have sat in meetings where the first order of business was literally for the people present to try to figure out what the committee was and why they were present. Am I representing my department or my school? Is this a subcommittee of the Faculty Senate or a group convened by the provost? Are we discussing general education *courses* at our main campus, or general education as a *phenomenon* in the university as a whole? The smaller curricular pathways, specifically Lewiston-Auburn College and the honors program, have had an easier time articulating an assessment vision and plan, and engaging their small faculties in the design and early stages of implementation.

In contrast, the largest of the three curricula, the new USM core, will serve the vast majority of our nearly 10,000 undergraduates and will be taught by faculty in our largest colleges. The detailed and ambitious assessment plan for the USM core was, in fact, written largely by a single staff person (one of the authors of this chapter) in the privacy of her office. It was approved by the General Education Council with minimal comment, and it was accepted as part of the larger curriculum proposal by the Faculty Senate. Some senators raised concerns about feasibility. Others raised questions about academic freedom and expressed concerns about the possible interference of assessment processes with the process of evaluation for promotion and tenure. One influential senator responded to these concerns with the comment that the plan was merely about "program evaluation," not professional review. This characterization seemed to defuse governance concerns about assessment for the time being. However, a process of curricular reform that respects and engages faculty oversight and governance creates the possibility that change itself can be slowed down or even halted when faculty oversight and governance bodies object to the particular forms that change takes. We do not yet know how ongoing assessment will be viewed by these important groups.

It is worth noting that even though the detailed assessment plans of the three curricular pathways have not inspired much formal response, the articulation of the vision, goals, and desired outcomes and the desired learning outcomes for the courses in the new USM core certainly have. Specifically, the Faculty Senate in 2008 charged both the General Education Council and the Core Curriculum Committee with the task of "simplifying, shortening, and clarifying" the desired learning outcomes for general education as a whole and for the large curricular pathway. Indeed, the Faculty Senate called for the revision of the desired core curriculum outcomes in the same motion by which they approved the curriculum. The process of revision is discussed further later in this chapter.

Our Current State

In many respects, our assessment process is quite advanced. Because we devoted so much time and energy at the outset to articulating vision, goals, and desired outcomes for our new curricula, we are well situated to begin formulating a plan for how to determine whether we are meeting these goals and achieving these outcomes. In other respects, our assessment process is still in its infancy. We have collected relatively limited data on new courses, and most of these data are indirect. We have all sorts of information: We have been participating in the National Survey of Student Engagement since 2002, and we have reams of student course evaluations, grades, and student work in various files. But we still know very, very little about our students outside what we know from our own interactions with them and discussions with our colleagues.

We don't say this to be negative about our processes, our students, or our colleagues. But we do want to emphasize the complexity and expense involved in gathering, interpreting, and acting on information about how students learn. Faculty have not been particularly engaged in using the data from the National Survey of Student Engagement, which appears to them to be statistically suspicious, extracurricular, and structured around administrators' rather than faculty's values (for a full discussion of such issues, see Slevin, 2001). Student work and student course evaluations are interpreted within frequently repeated high-stakes processes that loom so large in the experience of faculty that other interpretive possibilities are often blocked out of conversations. In the absence of significant investment in faculty development, alternative interpretations of this data will not appear.

We have, however, identified significant information about *faculty* learning. In order to engage in assessment, as is well known, professors need to move from an input mode to an outcomes mode. This shift requires the same sorts of processes and experiences as other learning—exposure to new ideas and information, repeated experiences of attempting to integrate the new ideas and information into existing models, experiments, conversations, a context, and opportunities to perform and articulate new understandings. At USM, these processes and experiences have taken place within the structures of formal and informal faculty governance. The following account of the tedious and arduous process of taking new general education outcomes to the Faculty Senate serves as an illustration of this point that faculty can and do learn from and through deliberative parliamentary processes designed for other purposes.

Learning From Subcultures and Procedural Technicalities

Discussion of general education reform was, from the first, permeated by concerns for turf. "What about the philosophy department?" people asked at the beginning. "What if we write something that takes away all their gen ed courses?" Later, others pointed out that the draft outcomes did not use the word *history* anywhere, and that a prominent reference to students as "producers and consumers" put the economics department in a central position of defining our students. Although this approach was irritating to people who wanted to consider students' best interests first, it did engage more faculty, in a more sustained way, with the desired outcomes themselves. In fact, moving the outcomes from draft stage to a formal curricular proposal before the Faculty Senate involved intensive outreach by faculty leaders of the Curriculum Planning Committee to departments and individual faculty, recording concerns and objections, and taking these back to the planning committee. Members of the planning committee would themselves object to the objections of their colleagues outside the committee, expressing frustration with concerns for turf, and reflecting their different levels of engagement with and knowledge of the process of curricular reform.

One pattern observable from this process was that engagement by faculty outside the planning committee with the curriculum design became more and more intense as it became more apparent that some form of curricular change was going to happen. On the one hand, this meant increased faculty participation in designing and teaching pilot courses. On the other hand, it meant intensified scrutiny and criticism of the curriculum plan. This scrutiny reached its peak when the proposal for the new USM core came before the Faculty Senate in 2008. As senators and others considered the curriculum proposal itself, they returned to a more careful look at the vision, goals, and desired outcomes that the curriculum was designed to achieve. In some instances, objections to desired course-level learning outcomes brought them back to the broader desired general education outcomes articulated in the Vision, Goals, and Outcomes (VGO), which had escaped close attention when the VGO was originally approved. Theoretical statements about learning drew more intense attention when they were translated into more concrete statements about what students would be able to do (and, by implication, what kinds of learning opportunities courses would need to provide and what kinds of teaching faculty would be engaged in).

The Faculty Senate's call for a revision of the desired learning outcomes was based on the perception that the language of the outcomes was unwieldy, vague, and overly prescriptive. Revision of two major outcomes documents began in fall 2008. In the case of the VGO, the council based its revision work largely on the charge to "simplify, clarify, and shorten," but with some important institutional memory of earlier reactions by faculty to the document. In the case of the desired learning outcomes for courses in the new USM core, the Core Curriculum Committee followed this charge as well but also benefited from direct and more immediate feedback from faculty who had designed and piloted new courses or were in the process of doing so. Although unsystematic, this feedback provided critical guidance to the committee as it made decisions about just how to "simplify, clarify, and shorten." The assessment loops described here hardly adhere to proper assessment methodology. Revision of the desired outcomes commenced on the basis of unsystematic data and in the absence of any direct data about student learning. Despite this, the process has nonetheless yielded good insights and important changes. The language of the outcomes is measurably improved by the standards the senate put in place (clarity, simplicity, brevity). This suggests that however flawed the process, if it is actually engaged in, it can produce important, unanticipated results. In this case, debates over wording increased the number of faculty engaged with the desired outcomes in one way or another and increased acceptance of those outcomes by a larger number of faculty. We can now say that we are not at the point of debating whether we will have desired learning outcomes; we are talking about which outcomes we will have. This is significant progress.

This kind of imperfect assessment loop does not replace more systematic data on what students are actually learning. But until we have actually implemented a new curriculum (and have something to collect data on), these approximations of assessment can still bear fruit. They also highlight the tension between proper assessment methodologies and the challenges of getting things done.

When the senate discussed the desired outcomes in 2008, they charged the relevant committees to "shorten, simplify, and clarify" the outcomes. New people more suspicious of the previous work were elected to key committees, and everyone returned to the difficult issues of whether *global* is the same as *multicultural* or *diverse*, whether *holistic* refers to a form of medicine or has some broader meaning, whether history is a humanistic field of study or a social science, and whether students' affective experiences are the concern of university faculty and, if so, how. Committees and subcommittees reworked documents word by word, in some cases repeating discussions for the second or third or fourth time, and in other cases departing entirely from the previous process. It would be difficult to overstate the tedium, especially for the two of us, who had been having some of these conversations for more than 5 years. But the documents changed in ways that allowed more faculty to engage with and support the curriculum (and its eventual assessment).

One example of these changes is the way references to personal health disappeared from the outcomes document. The original document included a goal that students would be able to "demonstrate ethical action to maintain their own health and contribute to the social, environmental, and economic welfare of local and global communities." Two desired outcomes (among others) included under this goal were that students would be able to "recognize and practice a healthy lifestyle" and would have knowledge of "health and healthy practices."

From the first unveiling of draft versions of the document, this goal and these outcomes stirred up strong responses. Faculty reactions ranged from disbelief ("Do you really expect me to teach this?") to dismay ("There is no way I'm going to lecture students on why they shouldn't come to class with a hangover or why smoking isn't good for them. That's not my job and it's not what a university education is about."). Years later, as the General Education Council sat down to revise the VGO in response to the Faculty Senate's charge, these reactions still reverberated. As the council deliberated, some members expressed concerns about abandoning something that the document's drafters had, at some point, seen as a desirable goal. Others echoed those early concerns about the true purpose and proper purview of a liberal arts education and cautioned that if the goal were left as stated, it would never be achieved anyway, because faculty would simply refuse to play. In the end, all references to health were eliminated from this goal and its associated desired outcomes.

As another committee began to revise the desired outcomes for a new curriculum, it too experienced reverberations from past critiques of the curriculum and from more recent feedback from faculty designing and teaching pilot courses. One issue this feedback focused on was the sheer number of desired learning outcomes for each course. Faculty (both committee members and others) expressed concerns about becoming overwhelmed by the charge to achieve too many outcomes, and about courses created by statute (required outcomes) rather than through a more organic process of faculty creativity. As the language of individual outcomes was simplified and clarified, the question of whether the achievement of certain desired outcomes should be made optional emerged repeatedly. Some resisted this notion forcefully, arguing that if outcomes were made optional, they should not be articulated at all. Others argued that we should trust our colleagues to make reasonable choices from a range of desirable outcomes. Still others argued that we should wait for the results of assessment (Which? Whose? When?) to demonstrate whether making outcomes optional means they aren't achieved. In the end, the committee arrived at a compromise. They selected a subset of desired outcomes for each course that is required, and the remaining outcomes for each course are left up to faculty choice. Thus, each course template is headed with a statement in the form of "Each course should accomplish Outcomes *x* and *x* or more of the other outcomes." We have yet to fully conceptualize the assessment implications of this compromise. At the very least, making some desired outcomes optional makes tracking their achievement through assessment a more challenging task.

In April 2009, the General Education Council returned a new "Vision, Goals, and Outcomes for General Education at USM" to the Faculty Senate. At the same time, the Core Curriculum Committee, responsible for the course-level outcomes of the new USM core curriculum, submitted to the senate their revisions of desired outcomes for five of the courses in the new curriculum. These documents have been fought over, picked at, edited, and reedited. Groups have voted on the documents line by line and as a whole. The documents have been posted on a general education website and then taken down again. Parliamentary processes developed to ensure representation and to balance factions have been used to imagine what our students could experience, learn, and become. And the documents are better.

We make that last statement somewhat to our surprise. Though at many points in the process one or the other of us wondered if it was going to be possible to sit through one more meeting, and though many of the people involved in the process distrust the motives of many of the other people involved in the process, and although we were using processes developed for quite different purposes, we both think that the vision, goals, and desired outcomes and the revised outcomes for courses in the USM core are actually shorter, simpler, and clearer than they were. We can move forward now.

And what will moving forward look like? Probably more of the same. As of this writing, the General Education Council continues to discuss how to align assessment of the three curricula (all of them at different stages of implementation) while respecting their autonomy and their differences. The Core Curriculum Committee will continue to revise the desired learning outcomes for the rest of the courses in the curriculum consistent with the Faculty Senate charge to shorten, simplify, and clarify. The entire institution will begin the labor-intensive task of gathering, sorting, and digesting evidence to write a roughly 100-page report for accreditation. That certainly means that committee work will only increase. Fifty sections of a new freshman seminar, the Entry Year Experience, will be run in fall 2009, and consensus on how to meaningfully assess student learning in Entry Year Experience courses has still not been reached. In sum, curricular reform as organizational change will continue and it is likely that the processes by which that change occurs and the forms that change takes will continue to surprise.

References

Awbrey, S. M. (2005). General education reform as institutional change: Integrating cultural and structural change. *Journal of General Education, 54*(1), 1–21.

Slevin, J. F. (2001). Engaging intellectual work: The faculty's role in assessment. *College English, 63*(3), 288–305.

About the Authors

Susan McWilliams joined the faculty of USM's sociology department in 1995. She received her Ph.D. from the University of Washington in 1997. Her participation in USM's general education reform began in 2001 when she was invited to participate in the early discussions of curriculum and assessment referred to in this chapter. In 2004 Dr. McWilliams moved to the position of assistant provost for undergraduate programs, where her primary responsibility is to provide administrative support to the individual faculty and faculty groups centrally involved in USM's curricular revision and assessment processes.

Ann C. Dean is associate professor of English and coordinator of college writing at the University of Southern Maine. She received her Ph.D. in English from Rutgers University in 2000. She is the author of *The Talk of the Town: Figurative Publics in Eighteenth-Century England* (Bucknell University Press, 2007), and coeditor of *Teaching Literature: A Handbook* (Palgrave, 2003). As a writing program administrator, she has worked with assessment of general education, of first-year writing courses, and of multi-campus writing initiatives.

ENGAGING FACULTY IN THE ASSESSMENT PROCESS AT THE UNIVERSITY OF WEST FLORIDA

Eman M. El-Sheikh, Justice Mbizo, Claudia J. Stanny,
George L. Stewart, Melanie A. Sutton, Laura J. White,
and Michelle Hale Williams
University of West Florida

The University of West Florida (UWF) is a relatively young institution, founded in 1967 as an upper-level institution enrolling juniors, seniors, and graduate students. The university became a full 4-year undergraduate institution and admitted its first class of freshmen in 1983. A significant number of undergraduate students transfer to UWF after beginning their studies elsewhere; nearly 50% of students who graduate with a bachelor's degree from UWF matriculate with an A.A. The university admitted the first cohort of graduate students in an Ed.D. program in 1996. The university currently enrolls approximately 11,200 students. This enrollment allows for relatively small class sizes (the average class enrollment is 25 students). The student population is drawn largely from Florida (89% of students are Florida residents, and 11% are non–Florida residents), although the student population includes students from all 50 states and 92 countries. Approximately 23% of UWF students identify themselves as members of a cultural/ethnic minority group.

We became engaged in assessment at UWF through our contributions to institutional efforts to establish a culture of assessment. The assessment initiative at UWF was instigated by two major forces that converged in 2003. First, the university was engaged in a self-study in preparation for a reaffirmation-of-accreditation site visit by the regional accrediting body (the Southern Association of Colleges and Schools). In addition, the board of governors of the state of Florida established a mandate to create and adopt academic learning compacts for undergraduate degree programs. Academic learning compacts describe desired student learning outcomes for each program and the methods that departments use to assess student learning. This mandate includes the expectation that departments routinely collect assessment evidence and use that data for continual improvement of student learning and their programs. Most of the authors began their assessment work in the role of assessment liaisons to a department chair. We developed our expertise by learning about assessment practices and assisting with the development of program-level student learning outcomes for the department's academic learning compact and the assessment of student learning for undergraduate programs, departmental contributions to the general education curriculum, and the assessment of student learning in graduate programs. Those of us from the School of Allied Health and Life Sciences (Mbizo, Stewart, and Sutton) experienced assessment through the additional lens of disciplinary accreditation during our preparations to use ongoing assessment work to document compliance with accreditation standards established by the Council on Education for Public Health for the newly established master of public health (MPH) program. Eman El-Sheikh and Claudia Stanny became more deeply engaged with assessment work in their efforts to develop institution-wide faculty skills in assessment through their faculty development roles at the Center for University Teaching, Learning, and Assessment.

Establishing a culture of assessment is a winding road. Accreditation needs and mandates from the state of Florida were addressed against the backdrop of discussions originating with the Spellings Commission on the Future of Higher Education. External pressures serve as motivators ("We have to get this done!") but they also inspire resistance ("What business do these outsiders have telling us how to do our work—we're professionals, we should be trusted!"). Moreover, initial organizational efforts were interrupted when the campus was forced to close for 3 weeks following a direct hit from Hurricane Ivan in 2004. Attention was necessarily redirected toward the removal of over 2,000 toppled trees and repair of storm-damaged buildings on campus as well as personal recovery efforts to the homes of faculty, staff, and students. As we were catching our breath the following year, the university received a second, although less devastating, direct hit from Hurricane Dennis. Nevertheless, faculty and staff pulled together and the cohesion that supported us with personal and institutional efforts toward hurricane recovery also fueled efforts to meet deadlines related to assessment of student learning. Administrators leading the effort to create a culture of assessment realized that the university could not create an entire system overnight, especially in light of these other pressing demands on time and resources. The university adopted a deliberate strategy of implementing assessment practices in a slow but methodical manner that enabled faculty to acquire the skills needed to do this work well without feeling overwhelmed.

Assessment of General Education

Within the College of Arts and Sciences, individual departments have taken responsibility for assessing student learning outcomes in four domains (critical thinking, communication, integrity/values, and project management) by embedding assessments in courses that the departments offer as part of the general education curriculum. The Department of Government chose to assess student learning in two domains: critical thinking and integrity/values. Information literacy learning outcomes, which are included in the critical thinking domain, are assessed in the course titled Introduction to Comparative Politics. Civic engagement learning outcomes, which are included in the integrity/values domain, are assessed in Introduction to American Politics. Both courses are offered every semester. Students may select these courses from a menu of courses that fulfill specific lower-division requirements in the general education curriculum. These courses have some of the highest student traffic in terms of departmental enrollment and attract a diverse group of students from a variety of academic majors.

Data are collected in both courses every semester. Course instructors determine the most appropriate techniques to assess student learning in each skill domain. The information literacy assessment is based on a module of 10 graded exercises that build skills over the course of the semester and culminates in a research paper in which students demonstrate these skills. Civic engagement skills are assessed through an exercise in which students write an editorial piece for publication in a news outlet and write an informed letter on a matter of public policy to a congressperson. Performance on these assignments is used to provide a basis for assigning assessment ratings on a scale ranging from high- to low-level skill demonstration.

Ensuring that assessment data are used for course improvements remains a challenge. However, a number of positive changes have resulted from the assessment process. The process of creating skill-building activities and assignments to serve as embedded assessments seems to drive higher grading standards on key assignments in which information literacy and civic engagement skills are an important component. In other words, had the same assignment been given in a course in which these skills had not been explicitly developed, the instructor might have reluctantly been more lenient with grades, making allowances for the lack of student preparation while focusing on the evaluation of content learning outcomes. For instance, students are expected to pose a strong research question and thesis, describe an analytical structure designed to answer the research question, and demonstrate superior scholarly source utilization and citation and the ethical use of intellectual property in research papers that incorporate information literacy. Papers failing to exhibit these characteristics receive low grades. Similarly, the course in which civic engagement is assessed had not previously included a practical exercise that required civic engagement, even though this topic is central to the course discussion of the democratic political process. The course now includes a civic engagement module that teaches students to craft an editorial position on a contemporary issue, using knowledge gained about these issues over the semester. Students also learn strategies for bringing an issue to the attention of a public official in a way that gains reception and possibly produces results. The instructor now uses a practical assignment to assess student learning, whereas this concept had previously been evaluated only as content in an exam. In summary, instructors now apply greater levels of scrutiny to student learning outcomes when these skills are emphasized as part of assignments included in the course.

Assessment of Undergraduate Degree Programs in Computer Science

The Department of Computer Science experienced several challenges and obstacles to the development of its assessment plan that were encountered in many other departments across the university: the need to integrate institutional and state requirements, minimal knowledge of assessment practices within the department, and faculty resistance. These challenges were addressed through the use of a phased approach to assessment. The department focused first on developing learning outcomes and assessment methods for undergraduate programs, followed by the assessment of graduate programs. General education learning outcomes and assessment methods were implemented in the final phase when the Department of Computer Science began to offer its first course in the general education curriculum. This phased approach kept the assessment process manageable.

As part of the first phase of undergraduate assessment, the department developed program learning outcomes documented in the departmental academic learning compact with faculty participation. Initial assessment efforts focused on learning outcomes in the domains of critical thinking and project management, because these outcomes were considered to be critical to students' success in the undergraduate computer science program. The department identified courses in which learning outcomes could be assessed and developed embedded assessments for these outcomes that were included in several senior-level courses. Assessment efforts included the creation of rubrics and worksheets for collecting assessment data. This approach minimized effort, provided feedback to students, and kept data collection consistent across courses. Assessment results were beneficial when the department evaluated its existing programs and planned the creation of future programs. Early assessment evidence revealed similarities between existing undergraduate programs and provided a rationale for subsequent curricular revisions that were implemented in new programs.

Several recommendations and best practices emerged from the undergraduate assessment process in computer science. When one is implementing assessment at the departmental level, it is useful to develop an effective plan before starting and to monitor the plan regularly.

- Think about the questions you really want to answer about your program or your students' learning.
- Determine the types of assessment methods and measures (e.g., embedded assessments, exit exams, student portfolios) that will work best for your program.
- Develop your assessment plan as necessary to refine the learning outcomes, assessment processes, and measurement methods. Most important: Keep the assessment process simple.
- Use a phased process and identify a subset of outcomes to assess in each phase.
- Identify or develop rubrics that will provide meaningful and easy-to-use assessment data. Involve faculty in all stages of the process.
- Keep faculty informed about all aspects of assessment (requirements of internal and external audiences, deadlines, potential benefits to department, scholarly potential).
- Create opportunities for regular feedback from faculty on the appropriateness of current desired student learning outcomes and rubrics used for assessment.
- Schedule regular meetings for faculty to discuss assessment results and determine how the results will be used.
- Remember to close the loop: How can the department use assessment results to improve student learning or update its programs? How can the results and feedback from faculty be used to refine the assessment plan and process?

360-Degree Assessment to Improve Faculty and Student Engagement in Online Programs

The School of Allied Health and Life Sciences used assessment in the design, implementation, and maintenance stages of launching online courses for the creation of an online MPH program and the self-study undertaken to prepare that program for accreditation (Council on Education for Public Health, 2005). The school used characteristics of the 360-degree feedback model to create a multisource approach to assessment (Armstrong, Blake, & Piotrowski, 2000; Sachdeva, 2005; Swain et al., 2004). This model emphasizes faculty engagement as the driving force to create high-quality courses in which students respond with similar levels of engagement.

Through the use of a variant of the 20-item Client-Centered Care Organizational Assessment instrument (Center for Health Care Training, 2000), the self-assessment process motivated the school to set the following organization priorities:

- Develop university/school communication systems, policies, and protocols to support effective learner-centeredness training
- Increase efficiency of training services through periodic examination of faculty/adjunct flow studies compared to course evaluations and student complaints
- Develop intervention protocols to address training bottlenecks and student complaints

The school implemented peer-to-peer networking to provide formal and informal confidential and comprehensive peer-based assessment of course design and implementation decisions to promote these priorities. Examples of these initiatives follow.

- Traditional didactic training in course management features was supplemented with roundtable discussions driven by needs assessment (faculty posing questions), discussion of potential solutions to problems provided by peer faculty, and peer/staff demonstrations of student-tested, engagement-reinforcing strategies or use of innovative communication tools (Gercenshtein, Fogelman, & Yaphe, 2002).
- The director of the school and lead peer faculty implemented and tested new instructional strategies in their courses with the expectation that they would then provide ongoing and follow-up peer-to-peer training on best practices (Weber & Joshi, 2000).
- Subgroups of peers were cross-enrolled in similar courses to facilitate additional peer-to-peer discussions and mentoring opportunities (Watson & Groh, 2001).
- Avenues for voluntary but formal and confidential peer-based interventions were created to provide a comprehensive assessment of course design and implementation decisions to correct subpar levels of student engagement.

Finally, the school established mechanisms for using solicited and unsolicited feedback from students about their level of engagement. A sense of community is an important contributor to effective learning and student engagement and can be more difficult to establish in online courses than in face-to-face courses (Rovai, 2002). The online environment provides many mechanisms for increasing engagement. One of the innovative communication tools included in faculty training was the virtual world Second Life. Class participation in a virtual scavenger hunt for course-related information through the use of Second Life was offered as an extra credit activity in selected courses. In fall 2007, approximately 30% of the students enrolled in courses with the virtual scavenger hunt assignment used Second Life to complete the activity. Approximately 50% of these students experienced technical difficulties related to installation or initial problematic navigational issues. Among students who were able to install Second Life successfully and explore the virtual world for course-related content, course feedback regarding Second Life was extremely positive. Students reported that the experience of locating, visiting, and describing multiple virtual sites enhanced or reinforced their learning of course topics.

As a result of peer-to-peer training, faculty with initial subpar student evaluations showed sustained engagement over time and noted improved course evaluations, increased student engagement, and overall improvement in course quality when their courses were revised and offered in subsequent terms. The success of the 360-degree approach thus far is based on a willingness to offer multiple types of blended process-oriented and product-oriented training interventions and strategies in addition to moving from a hierarchical organization to a team-oriented organizational structure that has worked well in other domains emphasizing technology or change adoption without loss of quality and public accountability (Hoogveld, Pass, & Jochems, 2005; Leung, 2002; Weber & Joshi, 2000).

Individual Professional Growth

Michelle Williams's work with assessment emerged from earlier work on information literacy. The reference librarian assigned to political science faculty invited Williams to attend a summer workshop on information literacy at which about 10 subject-specialist librarians responsible for disciplines within the College of Arts and Sciences were paired with one professor from the academic area corresponding to their subject expertise. Library faculty worked with teaching faculty to construct information literacy applications and assignments for the various academic disciplines. Based on work that emerged from this workshop, the Department of Government decided to assess information literacy as one aspect of its contribution to the assessment of the critical thinking domain in the plan to assess the general education curriculum. Williams described how her approach to teaching writing skills has changed as a result of the information literacy and assessment work as follows:

> I now spend some time early in the semester talking about the paper project with emphasis on the grading criteria. I explain how the exercises build toward the paper project and that by taking the exercises seriously, students are improving their chance of achieving a higher grade on the culminating project for the course. I have found that their desire to learn improves the impact of my module and ultimately has enabled me to see greater learning as an outcome through my assessment tool.

Similarly, Eman El-Sheikh's engagement in assessment evolved out of her interest in improving computer science education. In her role as the department assessment liaison, El-Sheikh developed assessment plans for her department, kept colleagues up to date on the evolving assessment requirements at UWF, and helped faculty incorporate embedded assessments into their courses. She served as the instructional strategies and assessment fellow at the Center for University Teaching, Learning, and Assessment, where she consulted with faculty to develop useful and sustainable assessments of student learning and planned workshops and mini-conferences on innovative teaching strategies and assessment of student learning before being appointed as the Associate Dean for the College of Arts and Sciences. El-Sheikh's faculty development experience enabled her to expand her scholarship activities to include teaching, learning, and assessment.

Institutional Progress on Assessment

The learning curve for assessment can be steep. A few departments were familiar with assessment practices because of long-standing expectations for assessment from discipline-based accrediting bodies. However, for faculty in many departments, the language of assessment was completely new. UWF now has assessment practices in place in all departments for undergraduate and graduate programs and procedures for assessment of the general education curriculum. As might be expected in a developing culture of assessment, the quality of assessment methods across departments varies. Some departments have found that early assessment data may have gaps or not address the questions posed, thereby limiting their use. Initial efforts at measuring student learning frequently fail to provide information that is as useful as faculty would like. These departments are now thinking about refining their rubrics or developing new measures to improve the quality of generated data. Other departments are beginning to see tangible benefits of assessment and report implementing changes to their curricula leading to improved student learning. Both processes fuel continued improvements in subsequent assessment efforts and increased commitment to a culture of assessment.

Work is underway to recognize and reward faculty for their assessment efforts. Faculty have discovered that they can publish their findings as scholarship on teaching and learning. A joint task force of the Faculty Senate and the Office of the Provost developed new guidelines for tenure and promotion. Publications in the scholarship of teaching and learning and other evidence of meaningful engagement in the assessment of student learning are now given explicit recognition as important elements for the documentation of excellence in teaching in tenure and promotion evaluation. Implementation of these guidelines is now underway through the revision of individual departmental bylaws that incorporate these new criteria. In addition, recognition of quality work in the assessment of student learning outcomes is being woven into the fabric of routine evaluation of departments (Stanny, El-Sheikh, Ellenberg, & Halonen, in press).

Summary and Lessons Learned

Assessment practices at UWF evolved to address the demands associated with two external mandates in one overarching program of assessment. Jane Halonen, dean of the College of Arts and Sciences, wisely promoted the idea of using these mandates as an opportunity to showcase aspects of education at UWF that distinguish it from other institutions in the region. As a result, UWF chose to develop academic learning compacts that define student learning outcomes for the three domains of student learning mandated by the Board of Governors (content, communication, and critical thinking) and include two additional domains (integrity/values and project management) that are valued by the university community. UWF takes pride in the quality of student-faculty interaction made possible by its relatively small size. The project management domain highlights distinctive opportunities for students to acquire specific learning skills when they engage in collaborative work with faculty and complete significant projects as part of their course work at UWF.

Getting the assessment process rolling at UWF has not been without its challenges. Many faculty members are unfamiliar with assessment terminology, methods, and requirements for accreditation. In addition, many faculty members feel overcommitted and are reluctant to add assessment tasks to their busy agendas. This challenge can be overcome when the assessment process is kept simple. Computer science faculty focused initial assessment efforts on student learning in the core capstone courses, so that maximum benefit could be derived from the inclusion of embedded assessments in only a few courses. An annual meeting at which faculty in the department collectively review the assessment data and decide on curricular revisions helps keep all faculty involved in the assessment process and evidence-based decision making without requiring a lot of effort on everyone's part. We believe that the best way to motivate others to join the assessment revolution is to continue to present and discuss the benefits of assessment, whether in improving teaching practices and curriculum or in pursuing publication and funding related to the scholarship of teaching and learning.

Assessment can quickly become overwhelming. Rather than trying to assess everything, focus on answering questions that are important to faculty. Don't try to collect masses of data. Focus on specific points in the curriculum where the data collected will provide the most useful information and target the most important elements of the curriculum. Use a phased implementation process rather than trying to initiate undergraduate, graduate, and general education assessment at the same time. The lessons learned from early phases of implementation will make implementation of successive phases easier. Create shared responsibility for assessment and keep the assessment process open. Faculty are more likely to contribute to assessment efforts if they have a sense of ownership of the plans and practices that emerge. Open discussions lead to a better understanding of the opportunities for improvement within an academic program among faculty and increase support for implementing strategies that address these issues.

The School of Allied Health and Life Sciences implemented a learner-centered faculty training program as part of the development of a fully online MPH program. Faculty who participate in these training activities experienced improved course evaluations, increased student engagement, and improvement in course quality in subsequent offerings. A multi-perspective 360-degree feedback model appears to be effective in improving faculty engagement in assessment initiatives. If assessment can be accomplished without disenfranchising faculty or adjuncts, these activities enhance the quality of courses and programs.

Whatever the skill or learning being assessed, faculty development is important. Development activities might include training in the articulation of student learning outcomes, development of credible direct measures of student learning, practice with new strategies for instruction, and creation of learning activities that promote achievement of student learning outcomes. Faculty benefit when they collaborate with an expert in the content or skill domain and when they are provided with appropriate instructional resources that support the achievement of desired student learning outcomes.

We have learned and grown through our engagement with the assessment process. We have learned the value of collaborative learning, as when faculty work with reference librarians to develop course activities to promote information literacy or when peers assist one another in the development of learning outcomes. Curriculum development in an online environment presents unique challenges to faculty to develop pedagogies that engage students. The assessment process is proving to be a useful tool by which faculty can evaluate the benefits of new instructional strategies in both online and face-to-face environments. Departments need to keep their assessment procedures simple enough to allow time to process the meaning of their assessment findings and implement meaningful changes to the curriculum and instructional strategies. We are learning to ensure the sustainability of meaningful assessment by weaving this work into the fabric of everyday faculty work and recognizing the value of this work in the tenure and promotion process. Faculty are beginning to experience professional benefits associated with effective assessment practices. These benefits include the publication of their work and conference presentations in the scholarship of teaching and learning, funding opportunities and grants related to curriculum enhancement (especially in science, technology, engineering, and mathematics), and improved student engagement and learning.

References

Armstrong, T., Blake, S. Y., & Piotrowski, C. (2000). *The application of a 360-degree feedback managerial development program in higher education: The Florida model.* Retrieved from http://findarticles.com/p/articles/mi_qa3673/is_200007/ai_n8893800

Center for Health Care Training. (2000, March). *Client-centered care organizational assessment: How well does your agency provide client-centered services?* Retrieved from www.centerforhealthtraining.org/download/agency_assess.pdf

Council on Education for Public Health. (2005). *Accreditation criteria public health programs.* Washington, DC: Author. Retrieved from www.ceph.org/files/public/PHP-Criteria-2005.SO5.pdf

Gercenshtein, L., Fogelman, Y., & Yaphe, J. (2002). Increasing the satisfaction of general practitioners with continuing medical education programs: A method for quality improvement through increasing teacher-learner interaction. *BMC Family Practice, 3,* 15.

Hoogveld, A., Pass, F., & Jochems, W. (2005). Training higher education teachers for instructional design of competency-based education: Product-oriented vs. process-oriented worked examples. *Teaching and Teacher Education, 21*(3), 287–297.

Leung, W. (2002). Competency based medical training: Review. *British Medical Journal, 325,* 693–695.

Rovai, A. (2002). Building sense of community at a distance. *International Review of Research in Open and Distance Learning, 3*(1), 1–16.

Sachdeva, A. K. (2005). The new paradigm of continuing education in surgery. *Archives of Surgery, 140,* 264–269.

Stanny, C., El-Sheikh, E., Ellenberg, G., & Halonen, J. (in press). First things first: Attending to assessment issues. In D. S. Dunn, M. A. McCarthy, S. Baker, &

J. S. Halonen (Eds.), *Using quality benchmarks for assessing and developing undergraduate programs*. San Francisco: Jossey-Bass.

Swain, G. R., Schubot, D. B., Thomas, V., Baker, B. K., Foldy, S. L., Greaves, W. W., & Monteagudo, M. (2004). Three hundred sixty degree feedback: Program implementation in a local health department. *Journal of Public Health Management and Practice, 10*(3), 266–271.

Watson, G. H., & Groh, S. E. (2001). Faculty mentoring faculty: The Institute for Transforming Undergraduate Education. In B. J. Duch, S. E. Groh, & D. E. Allen (Eds.), *The power of problem-based learning: A practical "how-to" for teaching undergraduate courses in any discipline* (pp. 13–26). Sterling, VA: Stylus.

Weber, W., & Joshi, M. S. (2000). Effecting and leading change in health care organizations. *The Joint Commission Journal on Quality Improvement, 26*(7), 388–399.

About the Authors

Authors are identified in alphabetical order. All authors contributed equally to this chapter.

Eman M. El-Sheikh is the Associate Dean of the College of Arts and Sciences at the University of West Florida. Previously she served as the administrative fellow for the college and as the instructional strategies and assessment fellow for UWF's Center for University Teaching, Learning, and Assessment. Dr. El-Sheikh earned her Ph.D. and M.S. in computer science from Michigan State University and her B.S. in computer science from the American University in Cairo. As a fellow, she planned and facilitated events for the development of faculty skills in teaching, learning, and assessment, including five mini-conferences, and helped launch the UWF Teaching Partners Program to promote the development and exchange of successful and novel teaching practices and facilitate peer reviews of teaching. Her research interests include artificial intelligence–based techniques and tools for education, including intelligent tutoring systems and adaptive learning tools, computer science education, and assessment.

Justice Mbizo is a lecturer in public health within the School of Allied Health and Life Sciences at the University of West Florida. Dr. Mbizo has presented talks on the use of digital technology (Second Life) to increase student engagement and conducted research. He is involved in the implementation of an online M.P.H. program. Dr. Mbizo has presented on different public health topics at the American Public Health Association Annual Scientific Meetings and published several works.

Claudia J. Stanny is the director of the Center for University Teaching, Learning, and Assessment at the University of West Florida, co-director of the Quality Enhancement Plan, and an associate professor in psychology.

She has facilitated workshops and conference sessions on teaching, faculty development, and assessment of student learning. Her published research in psychology focuses on applied aspects of memory and cognition and the teaching of psychology. Her work appears in *Memory,* the *Journal of Experimental Psychology: Human Learning & Memory,* the *American Journal of Psychology, Ethics & Behavior,* and the *Journal of General Psychology,* among other peer-reviewed journals.

George L. Stewart is chair of biology and director of the M.P.H. program and the School of Allied Health and Life Sciences at the University of West Florida. He has developed two online programs and worked closely with faculty to establish models for assessment of student learning in both programs. Dr. Stewart has published over 75 peer-reviewed journal articles, chapters, and review articles on parasitology and infectious disease.

Melanie A. Sutton is the co-director of the certificate in medical informatics program at the University of West Florida and an associate professor in the School of Allied Health and Life Sciences. Dr. Sutton teaches courses in medical terminology, bioinformatics, health information systems, medical informatics, and computer applications in public health. Her research interests and publications span these areas, as well as computer vision, robotics, digital mammography, and web-based instruction and assessment. She has facilitated the eJam online faculty/adjunct training series at UWF since 2005. Her publications appear in the *International Journal on E-Learning, Image and Vision Computing,* and *Pattern Recognition.*

Laura J. White served on active duty in the U.S. Navy for 21 years. She has taught at the University of West Florida for 16 years. She is currently an assistant professor and the software engineering program director in the Department of Computer Science. Dr. White earned a B.S. (1984) in computer engineering from the University of New Mexico, an M.S. (1989) in computer science from the Naval Postgraduate School, and a Ph.D. (2006) in instructional design for online learning from Capella University. Her research interests primarily include online collaboration and learning, software engineering, and global software teams.

Michelle Hale Williams is associate professor of political science at the University of West Florida. Her research interests include far right parties, political party systems, political institutions, European politics, nationalism and ethnic politics, and scholarship of teaching and learning with an emphasis on information literacy. Her book *The Impact of Radical Right-Wing Parties in West European Democracies* (Palgrave) was published in 2006. Her published work also appears in *Party Politics, German Politics, PS: Political Science and Politics,* and the *Journal of Political Science Education.*

13

EVIDENCE OF LEARNING

Melissa Pedone and Allison Sloan
Valencia Community College

Valencia Community College is a large multi-campus institution in central Florida that has an annual enrollment of over 40,000 students each year. Valencia serves a culturally diverse community: Over 50% of our student population comes from non-Caucasian racial/ethnic groups. Valencia offers a wide variety of associate in arts, associate in science, and associate in applied science degree programs and in 2005 was ranked first among the nation's community colleges in the number of associate degrees awarded. The common threads tying our many curricular programs together are our student core competencies. These competencies are the college-wide learning outcomes articulated for graduates of all Valencia degree programs.

At our college, like most educational institutions, the faculty has ownership of the curriculum. It makes sense that college faculty have this important role. Our affinity for our disciplines and our desire to share the intricacies and complexities of the subjects we love are what draw most of us to higher education. It is only natural that faculty would be the ones to defend the integrity of our disciplines and determine what and how we teach. Over time, curricular conversations among our Valencia colleagues began to shift from what we are teaching to what students are learning. Our curricular focus on teaching objectives evolved into a desire to articulate what we want students in our disciplines to understand, apply, or be able to perform. Once Valencia made the determination to become a learning-centered institution, it did not take long for the realization to set in that planning for learning is not the same as knowing what students have learned. We quickly realized that the assessment of student learning would be an important part of our curriculum development and revision processes.

Hence, it was our roles as owners, defenders, and developers of our curriculum that engaged us in the assessment efforts of our institution. The effort described here began with the end in mind. What learning outcomes would we expect for all Valencia students?

Developing College-Wide Learning Outcomes

Significant revision of Valencia's college-wide learning outcomes began with a series of roundtable discussions more than a dozen years ago. Conversations involving faculty, staff, and administration revealed a desire to move away from a traditional discipline-based list of desired outcomes toward core outcomes that could unify the curriculum across disciplines, programs, and campuses. The following four student core competencies that describe the desired learning outcomes for Valencia graduates were developed:

1. Think: Think clearly, critically, and creatively; analyze, synthesize, integrate, and evaluate in many domains of human inquiry
2. Value: Make reasoned judgments and responsible commitments
3. Communicate: Communicate with different audiences, using varied means
4. Act: Act purposefully, effectively, and responsibly

These four core competencies—think, value, communicate, and act (TVCA)—are interdisciplinary and provide a curricular foundation for all of Valencia's degree programs. After more than a decade of implementation, the competencies have remained largely unchanged, although work clarifying learning indicators, criteria for evaluation, and assessment processes is ongoing in many programs.

The development and implementation of TVCA at Valencia has largely been a grassroots effort. With administrative support, the work of integrating TVCA throughout the depth and breadth of the institution has mainly been accomplished by individual faculty members working within their departments and programs. Administrative support for this work came primarily in the form of faculty development opportunities and compensation for the additional time and effort taken by faculty members to move the work forward. Thus, it makes sense that our model for assessing student learning of TVCA as an institution began with individual faculty members assessing the competencies with means and measures they designed for their individual classes. Although these varied methods provided valuable information on student growth and development in TVCA in specific courses, the diverse nature of the assessment methods was problematic. The different tools, techniques, and personnel involved did not allow for data collection and analysis on the scale necessary for us to draw conclusions and make recommendations to entire institutional programs. For this to be accomplished, our institution moved into a new phase of assessing student learning of TVCA. The focus of the work shifted from evaluating students in individual courses to creating processes that are capable of producing evidence of learning from entire programs and throughout the institution. Like our earliest efforts to assess TVCA, the work continues to be led by our faculty members, who demand that assessment processes remain grounded in the evaluation of actual student work.

Establishing the Learning Evidence Team

A number of internal and external forces spurred our institution to establish a team of faculty, staff, and administration to add a new dimension to the ongoing assessment work at the college. Valencia's ongoing strategic planning process had produced our strategic learning plan to guide the institution's development over the next several years. Specific goals within the strategic learning plan needed faculty involvement and new assessment procedures to inform decisions and measure progress. Also, over a decade of work to infuse TVCA throughout our curriculum and culture had resulted in significant progress. For instance, all full- and part-time faculty members had varied and ongoing opportunities to participate (on a voluntary basis) in faculty development workshops that allowed participants to infuse their lessons with learning strategies and classroom assessment techniques that align with TVCA from the inception of the student learning outcome to the lesson plan and the assessment of student learning for improving the process. The majority of faculty members at the institution had several years of experience working with TVCA within their individual classrooms. The institution now stood ready to take the next logical step; the interdisciplinary assessment of TVCA on an institutional level across all types of programs with standard assessment criteria and instruments. Our external accrediting agency, the Southern Association of Colleges and Schools, also confirmed the need for Valencia to engage in institutional assessment of TVCA to meet their criteria for institutional effectiveness. In response to internal desires and external requirements, Valencia established the Learning Evidence Team (LET) to foster a culture of evidence-based assessment to improve learning at Valencia.

The plan for the LET to collaborate on assessments across campuses and disciplines began with an invitation sent by the chief learning officer, Valencia's executive academic vice president, inviting all full-time faculty members to join the LET. Fourteen faculty volunteers from different campuses and disciplines were selected to participate along with three academic deans and one representative from the chief learning officer's staff. In addition, five professional staff members were added later as the need to collaborate directly with various divisions within the institution was discovered. For example, we found it beneficial to add representatives from our institutional research and staff development offices.

It is important to note that the LET was not initially charged with specifically assessing TVCA. Instead, the LET was given the very open-ended task of clarifying for the institution what was meant by *evidence of learning* and what specific types of learning should be measured. The open-ended charge was assigned intentionally to promote a collaborative process that would develop organically within the institution and reflect our true institutional learning goals. In hindsight it may seem obvious that the team would seek evidence of learning for TVCA, but the process leading to that decision was much more involved and complicated than one might expect.

As a large task force made up of faculty and administrators from a wide variety of disciplines, LET members all had their own ideas on important assessment questions to answer. The list of potential types of learning to measure and learning evidence to collect became very long, very quickly. In an effort to inform our decision making, the LET sponsored an institutional scan of assessment tools and processes currently in use at the college. The assessment inventory produced by the scan was lengthy and diverse, but common threads did run through both the items in the assessment inventory and the list of learning evidence ideas generated by members of the LET. Our student core competencies, TVCA, were visible throughout both lists, which testified to the depth and breadth the core competencies had reached within the institution. Interestingly, before this information was collected, some members of the team were not convinced that TVCA was integrated so fully into the curriculum across campuses, disciplines, or degrees. After months of research and debate, it became clear to all LET members that TVCA would become the focus of our institutional assessment efforts. Ultimately, the evidence-based decision-making process used to bring us to this consensus was well worth the time, effort, and expense that it took. The LET, once a loosely joined group with a variety of assessment goals, had become a united team focused on developing assessment processes to find evidence of student learning for our institution's most significant learning outcomes.

Laying a Foundation for Assessment

From the beginning of the project, it was clear that we had to make an effort to engage the diverse members of the newly formed LET in activities which would build common understandings and group purpose. We began with a

Myers-Briggs Type Indicator team report to help us understand the dynamics within the LET and reveal group strengths and weaknesses. The Myers-Briggs analysis resulted in a set of principles and procedures for productive work sessions, which we used to guide our work and to stay focused on the team's goals. For example, we learned that one Myers-Briggs type was not represented in our group, so the group made a conscious effort to regularly consider the missing perspective. Multiple shared readings by members of the LET also helped to build common understandings and inform our progress. Several of these readings are listed at the end of this chapter. Throughout the first year of our work, we also invited nationally recognized consultants, including Patricia Derbyshire, Susan Hatfield, Peggy Maki, Gloria Rogers, and Randy Swing, to share their expertise and comment on our progress.

We found that a common source of campus confusion was the use of the same assessment vocabulary by different individuals to mean different things, so the development of a common assessment language was of paramount importance. We felt it was essential to the authenticity of our work to create our glossary from definitions already used by our institution, so we began with internal documents such as a glossary used in our faculty development program for tenure-track faculty. We added terminology from our shared readings and consultant work to create an institutional assessment glossary. Building a shared language and expertise is time consuming and sometimes frustrating and requires patience by those on the LET and those expecting results from the LET, but its importance cannot be overstated.

The first several months of LET work involved team building, research, professional development, and the completion of the institutional assessment scan and glossary. As the LET continued to lay the foundation for our assessment work, we saw the need for a set of principles and purposes of assessment to guide our efforts. Our institutional planning documents, which included the strategic learning plan and our institutional values, vision, and mission statements, were key pieces to include in all our early planning and foundation work. We were also heavily influenced by the American Association of Higher Education's principles of assessment. The LET articulated 11 principles of assessment at Valencia Community College:

1. Assessment of learning at Valencia Community College reflects our mission, vision, and values.
2. Assessment is most effective when it is based on learning that is integrated and multifaceted. For this reason, assessments should address learning at all levels and reveal change over time.
3. The focus of assessment at Valencia Community College is not limited to courses but also includes a wide range of experiences that influence student learning.

4. Assessment should be based on clear, explicit outcomes that are widely published.
5. Assessment should be grounded in the standards of the scholarship of teaching and learning.
6. Assessment works best when it is ongoing rather than episodic.
7. Assessment is most effective when it is collaborative, involving students, administrators, staff, faculty, and community members in shared responsibility.
8. Assessment results should be communicated openly, honestly, and publicly in order to cultivate trust among all stakeholders.
9. Assessment of specific learning outcomes should illuminate student progress toward TVCA, utilize varied modes, and attend to experiences that lead up to learning outcomes.
10. Assessment of TVCA is central to Valencia's assessment plan.
11. Assessment should play a central role in decision making at Valencia by providing valuable information for improving learning and stimulating discussion in order to enhance the quality of education at Valencia.

In addition to these principles of assessment, the LET clarified the purposes of our assessment work. This clarification was important to focus our goals as well as allay possible fears that our assessment work would be used as a form of negative evaluation of faculty individuals within the institution. We determined that the primary purpose of our assessment work at Valencia is to improve student learning. Furthermore, comprehensive assessment supports renewal of the curriculum so that learning happens as we intend. Assessment provides useful, well-grounded information to stimulate discussion and support goal setting and sound decision making. The effective use of assessment findings empowers meaningful change and provides opportunities to celebrate success. The purpose of our assessment work at Valencia is not to evaluate individual faculty members, regulate individual course implementation or pedagogy, or prescribe assessment processes but to improve learning in individual classrooms by individual faculty members focused on individual students' learning.

Communication and coordination within any large institution are a challenge. We developed strategies to share our progress as a team with the broader institution. We recruited key staff members from student services, administration, and our professional development office to join the LET and strengthen our connection to their offices. A website was created to easily disseminate our work products to all levels of the college. We also created a monthly newsletter, *Assessment Update,* with examples from the classroom and brainteasers to stimulate readers' critical thinking and communication skills. Although we published our own newsletter, we were careful also to publish regular updates in the institution's already existing newsletter to take advantage of that established reader base. We sought out external expertise when needed to assist in our communication efforts. Our students in graphic design competed to create an LET logo that gave all the materials generated by our team a cohesive look. Our Marketing and Media Relations Office created marketing posters, which hung in all classrooms, libraries, and computer centers across all campuses, to stimulate conversations between faculty and students at the ground level about the core competencies.

It became clear that the academic deans within our institution would play a critical role in the success of our efforts. The deans formulate annual departmental assessment plans and have direct access to and heavy influence on both the faculty members and assessment activities within their departments. If we were to be successful, we would have to have the cooperation of the deans. In what could be viewed as a public relations effort, we periodically visited meetings of our deans' council to update them on our activities and build connections between our assessment goals and their departmental assessment plans. We deliberately chose to target our efforts, at least in the beginning, with those deans who wanted to work with us to our mutual benefit.

Formulating a Plan

As the first year of our work progressed, we began to formulate a multiyear plan for the institutional assessment of TVCA. We recognized that it would take a significant amount of time to clarify criteria and create assessment instruments that would be appropriate to use across disciplines and programs. We further recognized that establishing reliability, validity, trust, and ownership for those instruments would be a challenge for our large institution. Our team did not have the resources to tackle all four of our core competencies together, so a 4-year plan to cycle through each of the competencies individually emerged. In choosing our starting point, we wanted to build on a position of strength rather than the unknown or unclear. Thus, we strategically chose to first assess the competency that we believed had the broadest understanding, acceptance, and use throughout the institution. Our first year of implementation, which was actually our second year of existence as a team, focused on our think competency. We marketed this project throughout our institution as the Year of Think.

It is often true that what appears simple on the surface becomes more complex as one digs deeper. Assessing student thinking at Valencia may on the surface sound relatively simple. Many commercial instruments for measuring critical thinking or problem solving exist. We could have chosen to purchase a commercial instrument, given it to a random sample of students, and analyzed the results. However, this plan would have satisfied neither the LET nor the faculty at large. Our think core competency was well established at Valencia, and a decade of use had generated a set of learning indicators defining our institution's expectations for student thinking. We did investigate several commercial critical thinking assessment instruments, but none of them adequately conceptualized the construct of critical thinking in the same way as our existing think indicators. Adopting an instrument that did not measure thinking as established at Valencia would be equivalent to abandoning years of faculty work developing the think indicators and integrating those indicators into their instructional and assessment practices. We found this path of reasoning unacceptable.

Another issue we found with standardized assessment instruments is that many faculty and students we communicated with viewed them as separate from the classroom learning experience. Although some standardized assessments are given to students anonymously or outside class as ungraded assignments, it is often a challenge to get students to take this form of assessment seriously if they are not receiving a grade or other recognition of their performance. Furthermore, faculty view administering standardized assessments to students as an inconvenience—a loss of instructional time. Results are sometimes confusing to interpret and do not provide specific feedback to individual faculty members about changes they can make in their instructional practices to improve results.

Our faculty's concerns with standardized critical thinking assessments led the LET to conclude that we must develop our own assessment instruments for the evaluation of student thinking. Standardized measures may ultimately play a role in assessing student thinking at Valencia, but their exclusive use would not suffice. Faculty members in particular demanded that any assessment process we designed meet two conditions. First, we must make use of the existing think indicators. Second, the process must be grounded in the evaluation of actual student work. Grounding our measurements in this way provides meaningful feedback to faculty members on the strengths and weaknesses of students completing their assignments. This type of feedback is far more personal and powerful than standardized test results when it comes to informing instructional change.

Through an extensive process of reviewing literature and consulting with leaders in the field of the institutional assessment of college-wide learning outcomes, the LET developed a plan to use internally developed rubrics to assess Valencia's think competency. Two rubrics, both based on the college-wide think indicators, were developed with different purposes. First, an analytic rubric was developed for individual faculty members to use in their classes to evaluate their students' mastery of the think competency and provide specific feedback to individual students on their strengths and weaknesses in the five different indicators for this competency. The analytic think rubric presents the think indicators and levels of achievement in a matrix form, which allows for the individual assessment of each indicator (see Figure 13.1). It is the intent of the LET that faculty from across the disciplines use the analytic think rubric to assess their students individually, and that the results be shared and discussed with their students to provide both formative and summative feedback on the students' abilities to think. The five indicators, or criteria, listed on the analytic rubric are all intended to measure students' abilities to think as defined by Valencia's student core competencies. The LET also developed a student self-assessment based on this rubric that is available online. Students take the survey anonymously and receive feedback with strategies to improve their thinking based on their results. This was part of a comprehensive strategy to raise student awareness of the think core competency.

Second, a holistic rubric was developed for the institution to use as a tool to assess the think competency outside individual classrooms and across departments and programs in order to get an annual snapshot of a program or the institution as a whole. Figure 13.2 is the most recent version of the holistic think rubric. Unlike the analytic rubric, the holistic think rubric presents the think indicators and levels of achievement in a form that does not allow each indicator to be assessed separately. Instead, a single judgment is made for the entire piece of student work based on how well that work demonstrates the indicators collectively. The LET intends for the holistic think rubric to be used as a summative measure for department, program, and even institutional assessment of students' mastery of the think competency.

The LET knew the importance of getting input from faculty throughout the process of the development of these instruments. To be successful in our assessment efforts, we needed to build confidence and trust in the instruments among faculty and administration. Both rubrics are based upon the existing think indicators, which were developed by many groups of faculty, staff, and administrators over many years to define how Valencia graduates would demonstrate their mastery of the think competency. A work team of several interdisciplinary faculty members drafted the first version of the analytic rubric from the original think indicators. During this process, the team discussed what each criterion and level of achievement on the rubric meant to different disciplines. The draft analytic rubric was then shared with faculty, administration, and the governing councils of the college through a series of meetings and workshops. Next, interdisciplinary faculty volunteers were asked to create discipline-specific "think" assignments for their students to see if the rubric could measure the think competency for those assignments. This process revealed areas of ambiguity in the rubric criteria. Revisions were made to the rubric to address concerns and needs for clarification.

FIGURE 13.1

Rubric for the Analytical Assessment of Critical Thinking Across the Curriculum

Think Indicators	*Levels of Achievement*			
	Beginning	*Developing*	*Competent*	*Accomplished*
Analyzing information: Data, ideas, or concepts	**Inaccurate** Copies information (data, ideas, or concepts) often inaccurately or incompletely, or omits relevant information	**Correct** Reports information (data, ideas, or concepts) with minor inaccuracies, irrelevancies, or omissions	**Accurate** Presents information (data, ideas, or concepts) accurately and appropriately in familiar contexts	**Precise** Interprets information (data, ideas, or concepts) accurately, appropriately and in depth in new contexts
Applying formulas, procedures, principles, or themes	**Inappropriate** Labels formulas, procedures, principles, or themes inappropriately or inaccurately, or omits them	**Appropriate** Uses appropriate formulas, procedures, principles, or themes with minor inaccuracies	**Relevant** Applies formulas, procedures, principles, or themes appropriately and accurately in familiar contexts	**Insightful** Employs formulas, procedures, principles, or themes accurately, appropriately, or creatively in new contexts
Presenting multiple solutions, positions or perspectives	**Singular** Names a single solution, position, or perspective, often inaccurately, or fails to present a solution, position or perspective	**Dualistic** Identifies simple solutions, over-simplified positions, or perspectives with minor inaccuracies	**Multiplistic** Describes two or more solutions, positions, or perspectives accurately	**Balanced** Explains—accurately and thoroughly—multiple solutions, positions, or perspectives that balance opposing points of view
Drawing well-supported conclusions	**Illogical** Attempts a conclusion or solution that is inconsistent with evidence presented, that is illogical, or that omits a conclusion or solution altogether	**Reasonable** Offers an abbreviated conclusion or simple solution that is mostly consistent with evidence presented, with minor inconsistencies or omissions	**Logical** Organizes a conclusion or solution that is complete, logical, and consistent with evidence presented	**Perceptive** Creates a detailed conclusion or complex solution that is well supported, logically consistent, complete, and often unique
Synthesizing ideas into a coherent whole	**Fragmented** Lists ideas or expresses solutions in a fragmentary manner, without a clear or coherent order	**Consistent** Arranges ideas or solutions into a simple pattern	**Coherent** Connects ideas or develops solutions in a clear and coherent order	**Unified** Integrates ideas or develops solutions that are exceptionally clear, coherent, and cohesive

© Valencia Community College

FIGURE 13.2
Rubric for the Holistic Assessment of Critical Thinking Across the Curriculum

4 Accomplished   (precise, insightful, balanced, perceptive, and unified)
Does all or almost all of the following:
- Interprets information (data, ideas, or concepts) accurately, appropriately, and in depth in new contexts
- Employs formulas, procedures, principles, or themes accurately, appropriately, or creatively in new contexts
- Explains—accurately and thoroughly—multiple solutions, positions, or perspectives that balance opposing points of view
- Creates a detailed conclusion or complex solution that is complete, well supported, logically consistent, and often unique
- Integrates ideas or develops solutions that are exceptionally clear, coherent, and cohesive

3 Competent   (accurate, relevant, multiplistic, logical, coherent)
Does many or most of the following:
- Presents information (data, ideas, or concepts) accurately and appropriately in familiar contexts
- Applies formulas, procedures, principles, or themes accurately and appropriately in familiar contexts
- Describes two or more solutions, positions, or perspectives accurately
- Organizes a conclusion or solution that is complete, logical, and consistent with evidence presented
- Connects ideas or develops solutions in a clear and coherent order

2 Developing   (correct, appropriate, dualistic, reasonable, consistent)
Does many or most of the following:
- Reports information (data, ideas, or concepts) in familiar contexts with minor inaccuracies, irrelevancies, or omissions
- Uses appropriate formulas, procedures, principles, or themes in familiar contexts with only minor inaccuracies
- Identifies simple solutions, oversimplified positions, or perspectives with only minor inaccuracies
- Offers an abbreviated conclusion or simple solution that is mostly consistent with the evidence presented, with minor inconsistencies or omissions
- Arranges ideas or solutions into a simple pattern

FIGURE 13.2 (Continued)

---

1 Beginning   (inaccurate, inappropriate, singular, illogical, fragmented)
Does all or almost all of the following:

- Copies information (data, ideas, or concepts) often inaccurately or incompletely, or omits relevant information
- Labels formulas, procedures, principles, or themes inaccurately or inappropriately, or omits them
- Names a single solution, position, or perspective, often inaccurately, or fails to present a solution, position, or perspective
- Attempts a conclusion or solution that is inconsistent with evidence presented, that is illogical, or that omits a conclusion or solution altogether
- Lists ideas or expresses solutions in a fragmentary manner, without a clear or coherent order

---

© Valencia Community College

Once the analytic rubric reached the point where no more significant revisions were requested, the criteria from the analytic rubric were crafted into the overall levels of achievement on the holistic rubric. The holistic rubric went through a similar process of sharing and feedback as the analytic rubric. An exact count of all those who inspected and used both of the rubrics in the Year of Think is impossible, but the number is easily in excess of 100.

More than 30 faculty members from varied disciplines were recruited to generate student work appropriate for use in our assessment project. These faculty members, who were paid a stipend for participation, provided hundreds of student learning artifacts and associated data to assist us in our work. Faculty and staff development plays a critically important role in the success of any large-scale assessment project. Our faculty participants went through a series of workshops orienting them to the rubrics and to craft assignments that would provide opportunities for students to demonstrate competency in the general think criteria and still be appropriate for use in their individual classes. Several of the faculty participants also went through holistic scoring training so they could become part of the interdisciplinary team that holistically scored student work. Eventually these people will form a core of faculty members trained to holistically score student work across all our student core competencies.

Lessons Learned

Early in this project, we realized that our first phase of implementation would reveal more about process than about product. Certainly we wanted to draw conclusions about student thinking at Valencia, and some conclusions were possible. However, we recognized the more valuable results from our first attempt would be revelations about the strengths and weaknesses of our assessment instruments and the management of our processes. These lessons would allow us to make recommendations for the future. Thus, we sought meaningful conclusions from the think competency project in three areas: student thinking, faculty development, and assessment processes.

Our primary purpose for assessment at Valencia is to improve student learning. Hence, we were keenly interested in any conclusions about student thinking that could inform instructional practice. We collected over 400 student learning artifacts from faculty participants in our Year of Think project, although some of the artifacts had to be excluded from analysis because of various issues such as missing information. Each of the artifacts used in our analysis was given a class grade and scored with the analytic rubric by the classroom instructor. Analysis of the analytic rubric scores across multiple disciplines revealed that students scored highest in their ability to analyze information, data, ideas, and concepts. Students' weakest scoring criterion was the ability to draw well-supported conclusions. This type of information can easily be reflected back to faculty members, who can use it to close the feedback loop and improve student thinking. Faculty members may also use the think analytic rubric in their own classes to grade assignments and benchmark their students' progress at the classroom level with a program or the entire institution. Because this feedback is specific to actual class work, faculty members can easily alter assignments or instruction to target areas of weakness demonstrated by their students. It is vitally important that these individual assessments never be used to evaluate faculty performance, whether positively or negatively. To do so would completely undermine faculty trust and participation in assessment work. It would be appropriate to use the student artifacts anonymously for a program or institutional aggregate measure of how students think to set goals and inform change on a broader scale.

We were also interested in any patterns or trends in student thinking that we could find. A sample of 137 of our student learning artifacts was scored holistically by an interdisciplinary team of faculty. Class averages ranged from 1.38 to 2.70 on a scale of 1–4. These scores indicate that the classes ranged from beginning to competent on our think levels. The progression of scores correlated to advancement in course level from college preparatory to traditional freshman- and sophomore-level coursework. Although the positive correlation between course level and holistic think score cannot establish a cause-and-effect relationship between instruction and improved student thinking, it does serve as one measure demonstrating student thinking at different levels within the institution.

Insight into the development of our faculty project participants is useful for planning faculty development activities in future iterations of our assessment work. Our conclusions in this area are based primarily on observation and self-reporting by faculty participants. Although there was a broad general understanding of the think competency within the institution, it was clear at the start of our project that faculty members did not have a uniform understanding of the think indicators as represented on the two rubrics. Workshop time devoted to discussion of the indicators and levels of achievement combined with practice scoring diverse student learning artifacts significantly improved understanding. In a post-project survey given to Year of Think project participants, faculty who went through the project shared that they felt a much deeper understanding of the criteria used in the assessment of the think competency than they had before the project began. Activities orienting faculty members to assessment instruments and providing extensive practice with those instruments will be a critical part of future assessment work.

At the start of the Year of Think project, each faculty participant was asked to select an existing class assignment to work with that he or she felt demonstrated the think competency. In exercises that compared those assignments to the rubric indicators, faculty collectively revealed that they were most concerned about students demonstrating the ability to present multiple solutions, positions, or perspectives in the assignments. Interestingly, it was a different indicator in the end that seemed to present the most difficulty for faculty members to evaluate. When scoring their students' work with the analytic rubric, faculty sometimes did not apply the indicator "applying formulas, procedures, principles, or themes." Not surprisingly, faculty teaching quantitative courses such as mathematics, science, and business did not have the same difficulty evaluating this indicator as did some of the faculty teaching communications and humanities courses. Supporting faculty participants from non-quantitative disciplines in tailoring assignments to help students better demonstrate this indicator, as well as better evaluating it, will be a focus of faculty development for the think competency in the future.

To help us draw conclusions about our assessment processes, a thorough reliability and validity analysis was conducted for both the analytic and holistic rubrics at the end of our project. Although many faculty and staff are not particularly interested in the technicalities of this type of analysis, it is important for at least two reasons. First, the knowledge that the analysis was completed in a thoughtful manner builds confidence and trust among those who will make use of the assessment instruments and results. Our analysis was made available via our website for any interested parties to consider. Second, the analysis reveals areas of strength and weakness, providing a foundation for recommendations for future assessment work. Here are some of the recommendations our analysis revealed:

1. It is essential to the reliability and validity of the assessment process that future instruments for the assessment of TVCA receive the same thorough attention to their development and adoption as the think rubrics. This process has already begun for our next core competency, communicate.
2. A more in-depth faculty development experience in holistic scoring with the evaluation criteria and range-finding practice should significantly improve our interdisciplinary holistic scoring processes, specifically our interrater reliability.
3. Some of the student work we received from faculty could not be scored holistically by our interdisciplinary team. The reasons that the work was excluded must be clearly explained to faculty participants in future assessment projects so they understand what types of student work can, and cannot, be scored holistically.
4. It is vitally important that planning for data needs be conducted prior to the start of the assessment projects and that all relevant data be collected during the implementation of the project. This should include data needed to establish reliability and validity as well as to draw desired conclusions about student learning.
5. Weaknesses in our validity analysis arose from a lack of additional measures of thinking ability to correlate with our own rubric scores. This is a weakness we hope to remedy in future iterations of the assessment of the think competency and our other core competencies. Ultimately, our understanding of student learning of TVCA will be informed by multiple measures and processes.

Reflections

At the close of the Year of Think project, we took time to reflect on our work and gain some perspective on the experience. The LET had been in existence for 2 years and we were proud of the progress we had made. In that time, we laid a foundation to build an institutional culture of assessment and completed the first cycle of an assessment process that we hoped would become an integral and expanding part of institutional life at Valencia. Our assessment instruments and foundation documents, including the think rubrics, principles and purpose statements, assessment glossary, and plan for transformative assessment, were finding broader audiences and new applications at the institution. We had established the basic structure of a process to measure student achievement of our college-wide learning outcomes that could both inform instructional practice and meet external accreditation needs.

Of course, no significant project is without significant obstacles. Identification and procurement of adequate resources in the form of personnel, time, money, and expertise was a constant struggle for our team. Collaboration was vital in building strategic partnerships that shared resources and moved assessment work forward to provide information that was advantageous in improving multiple departments or programs. We also found there was a significant learning curve for new members to overcome when they cycled into our group to replace departing team members. This is a challenge for any team that, like the LET, has a considerable history and shared expertise, and we have yet to adequately address this issue. Changes in institutional leadership may also have the potential to alter long-term assessment plans. New administrators may have new ideas and priorities. External accountability and reporting requirements are also susceptible to change and, sometimes, political whim. Strong faculty leadership working in cooperation with administration can keep assessment efforts focused on measures that engage faculty, inform instructional practice, and meet administrative and external accountability needs.

These issues and obstacles raise concerns for the long-term sustainability of our assessment work that we will have to address. In recognition of the challenges we will face in the future, the LET is planning for some changes that will enable us to better manage our assessment projects and build strong partnerships. The LET will expand its membership by adding faculty members to work teams focused on specific assessment goals. The original core LET team will serve as a steering committee guiding the work. The new teams will develop assessment instruments for their specific competency, as we did for Think, with the understanding that multiple measures are ultimately necessary to create a complete picture of student learning for each competency. We will collaborate with the institution's professional development support personnel to integrate our faculty development needs into their annual program offerings to share resources and presenter expertise. We will also continue to work with deans and division leaders to find ways to incorporate our plans for the assessment of TVCA into their departmental goals in ways that are mutually beneficial.

No doubt our efforts to find evidence of student learning will continue to evolve as we learn more about assessment tools and processes at our institution. We will also be influenced by changes in administrative goals and external requirements. Regardless of the form that future assessment methods may take, the faculty leadership of the LET has dedicated itself to a course of action that respects the role of the individual faculty member as the key element in institutional transformation. Improvement in institutional effectiveness on a broad scale is only possible through the cumulative effects of small but well-informed changes made by many individuals. Our assessment processes will keep the feedback loop close to faculty and their instructional practices by remaining grounded in the evaluation of actual student work.

Suggested Readings

American Association for Higher Education.1992. *9 principles of good practice for assessing student learning.* Retrieved from www.buffalostate.edu/offices/assessment/aahe.htm

Angelo, T. A. (1999, May). Doing assessment as if learning matters most. *AAHE Bulletin, 51*(9), 3–6.

Brown, G., Ehrmann, S., & Suter, V. (2003, Summer). *Transformation and assessment: A conceptual framework.* Pre-conference materials for NLII Focus Session.

Leskes, A. (2002). Beyond confusion: An assessment glossary. *AAC&U Peer Review, 4*(2–3). Retrieved from http://ctl.stanford.edu/Tomprof/postings/448.html

Maki, P. L. (2002, January/February). Developing an assessment plan to learn about student learning. *Journal of Academic Librarianship, 28,* 8–13.

Maki, P. L. (2004). *Assessing for learning: Building a sustainable commitment across the institution.* Sterling, VA: Stylus.

About the Authors

Melissa Pedone was formerly a professor of mathematics at Valencia Community College and recently accepted an administrative position with Valencia's math department. She received her B.S. and M.S. in mathematics education and her Ed.D. in curriculum and instruction, all from the University of Central Florida. She has been teaching mathematics for 20 years at the secondary and postsecondary levels. She is very involved in learning assessment projects at her institution and has been recognized for expertise in the classroom, involvement with student organizations, and curriculum development.

Allison Sloan has been teaching at Valencia Community College for 11 years as a professor of mathematics, with an emphasis on statistics. She graduated from the University of Central Florida with a master's in statistical computing. She discovered a love for the humanities while auditing a course in interdisciplinary studies and is currently completing a master's in liberal studies at Rollins College in order to teach humanities and incorporate a more holistic understanding of the relationship among math, science, and the humanities into her mathematics courses. Since joining the Learning Evidence Team, she devotes time to conducting workshops for faculty development, including facilitating a summer-long faculty development program, and conducts workshops with an emphasis on action research for faculty.

14

SEEING THE LIGHT, FEELING THE HEAT

Patricia A. Thomas, Jeanne Mullaney,
and Deborah Grossman-Garber
Rhode Island College, Community College of Rhode Island,
and University of Rhode Island

Rhode Island College, a comprehensive public institution, is composed of five schools: the Faculty of Arts and Sciences, represented by 14 departments; the School of Nursing; the Feinstein School of Education and Human Development; the School of Social Work; and the School of Management. In 2008–2009, the total enrollment of the college was 9,085, with 7,601 undergraduate and 1,484 graduate students. Of these, about 80% were commuter students. There were 5,649 full-time students and 1,526 degrees awarded between July 1, 2007, and June 30, 2008.

The Community College of Rhode Island offers over 80 degree and certificate programs, of which 60 are associate degree programs in a large variety of disciplines. In fall 2006, there were 16,373 students enrolled at our four campuses, and in spring 2007, 1,145 associate degrees, 113 certificates, and 62 diplomas were awarded.

The University of Rhode Island is the only public research-intensive university in Rhode Island. It maintains strong land, sea, and urban grant education, research, and outreach programs designed to enrich the lives of its students and the community. As a medium-size institution comprised of eight degree-granting colleges and four distinct campuses, the university enrolls approximately 13,500 undergraduate and 2,600 graduate students. It maintains a full-time tenure-track teaching faculty of approximately 600. Students may choose from over 100 undergraduate degree programs and 58 graduate programs.

Some people change their ways when they see the light, others when they feel the heat.

—Caroline Schoeder

Rhode Island's public system of higher education consists of the Community College of Rhode Island (CCRI), Rhode Island College (RIC), and the University of Rhode Island (URI). Together, the institutions serve approximately 45,000 students, more than three quarters of whom are citizens of Rhode Island. All three schools are accredited by the New England Association of Schools and Colleges (NEASC), which began stipulating the need for assessment of student learning in the mid-1990s, but without imposing significant consequences for non-adherence. Most, if not all, faculty and administrators in Rhode Island assumed that the assessment agenda would quietly go away, so they did not comply, with the exception of those in accredited professional programs. Over the next decade, other regional accreditors and schools in the country pressed ahead with an ever-more robust assessment agenda. Following several years of public discussion, the NEASC significantly revamped its standards in 2006, requiring much more thorough assessment of student learning and institutional efficacy. Anticipating more stringent regional accreditation standards and recognizing the essential validity of routine assessment of student learning, the Rhode Island Board of Governors for Higher Education intervened in 2004 to mandate that the institutionalization of outcomes assessment at the three schools take place as soon as possible and no later than fall 2008. The schools were free to organize their work plans as long as they resulted in clearly stated, measureable student outcomes and appropriate assessments for each degree program. Consequently, the pace and depth of change increased.

This chapter addresses the factors and representative steps that are leading to robust and enduring assessment-driven institutional changes in the Rhode Island system of higher education. Given the substantial cultural shifts that are required for a successful outcomes assessment process, we examine such changes against a prominent theory of the stages associated with behavioral change.

The transtheoretical model of change in health psychology, developed by researchers at URI, is intended to explain or predict a person's ability to change (American Psychological Association, 2003). The model, which can also be applied to organizational change, can be used to understand the stages in adopting assessment. The model is intended to help people change their behavior. It portrays change in human behavior as a process that evolves over time in a predictable way. There are 5 stages: pre-contemplation, not intending to change, contemplation, preparation, and action and mainte- nance. The key to promoting change—in our case, faculty practices—was to determine where individuals or groups were in relation to the assessment process and then provide support leading to successful change.

Although assessment requires organizational change and the support of the administration, we believed—and still believe—that assessment of what and how our students are learning remains a faculty responsibility and is accomplished best when faculty driven. Consequently, we believed it was necessary to change the practices, and sometimes the beliefs, of each individ- ual faculty member across our institutions. Prochaska's model of change (APA, 2003) reflects some of the major stages we observed in our respective faculties during the last 5 years as represented in Table 14.1.

Table 14.1 provides a starting point for applying the transtheoretical model of change to the shifting cultures of the three institutions, but the events and strategies prompting movement through the different stages var- ied. At RIC, the appointment of an assessment coordinator as an assistant to the vice president for academic affairs for assessment conveyed the signifi- cance of the need for assessment to the deans, who encouraged open and regular communication with the coordinator. This consciousness raising is likely to have been the impetus for movement of the faculty, particularly department chairs, from the pre-contemplation stage, when the individual is not currently considering change to the contemplation stage. The contem- plation stage, which, when applied to changing health behaviors, may last 6 months, extended over two semesters for most faculty in most departments as programs provided by the assessment coordinator clarified the value of assessing student learning.

TABLE 14.1
Prochaska's Stages of Change and the Three Public Institutions of Higher Education in Rhode Island

Stage of Change	URI, RIC, and CCRI
Pre-contemplation	NEASC standards (1992)
Contemplation	Board of governors' motion (March 2004)
Preparation	Consultation provided by an external professional Faculty forums and conferences Support provided by assessment coordinators
Action	Plans implemented and reported (2008)
Maintenance	Drafting of a system-wide policy

Preparation, the stage that indicates change is about to take place, often was prolonged by the challenges of agreeing upon assessment measures as evidence of learning and the development of rubrics to standardize scoring. However, consultations with the assessment coordinator, the faculty forums, and attendance at regional assessment conferences facilitated this stage.

Actually implementing the assessment measures (action) was, for some, the most challenging, because selection of a representative sample of students to assess was often difficult. Some degree programs didn't have a capstone experience, assignment, or course to assess exiting or end-of-program students. In other cases, faculty concern over what they would learn about student learning and then have to share and report publicly created a reluctance to act.

The maintenance phase is evolving. The development of a statewide policy will contribute to weaving assessment practices into the fabric of faculty work, with a predictable requirement for reporting across the three institutions. Large departments will probably settle on the development of assessment committees, whereas faculty in smaller degree programs will function as a committee.

At CCRI, where the allied health, business, chemical technology, dental, nursing, and rehabilitative health programs are accredited by external bodies, and their faculty were, therefore, already well acquainted with the assessment process, two main strategies/approaches were used concurrently to promote the cultural shift that would be necessary to carry out the mandate from our board of governors: educating the faculty and staff while altering certain campus protocols to foster a climate of student learning outcomes assessment. Accordingly, an external consultant was contracted to provide a workshop in January 2005; this was followed by a series of three more workshops that department chairs, program coordinators, faculty, and administration were invited to attend during the spring and fall of 2005. After each workshop, faculty and departments had the opportunity to work with the consultant on their individual assessment plans. These actions represented CCRI's preliminary efforts to move faculty from the pre-contemplation to the contemplation stage in Prochaska's model by means of education, contact, and discussions with role models.

By September 2005, staff from several academic departments and also from student affairs had made significant progress on the articulation of learning outcomes and gave their own presentations at an all-day workshop. In March 2006, more departments showcased their assessment progress in another workshop with the external consultant. These activities were intended to sustain CCRI's movement to the preparation stage by drawing attention to those who had made commitments to change and giving group praise and recognition to those who had made changes. That year an assessment coordinator was appointed to assist the college's various departments and schools in developing their assessment plans.

As faculty and staff were learning more about assessment and beginning to apply it to their own programs, the CCRI administration simultaneously took steps to modify certain institutional practices and establish new ones in order to favor this cultural change.

First, a student learning outcomes form was introduced as a component of program course proposals by the Curriculum Review Committee. Thereafter, every new course and program proposal would include information outlining student learning outcomes and the methods that would be used to assess student progress toward the stated outcomes. Similarly, the Academic Program Review Committee began revising their forms and ultimately included a comparable section. These required components underscored the importance of the assessment process when they were adapted by two such influential committees. It fundamentally changed the way that programs were proposed and reviewed and can be considered a key factor in the preparation stage, because these institutional changes facilitated the internalization of the basic underpinnings of assessment of student learning outcomes.

Other related actions that CCRI took include the creation of the Learning Evidence Team, a college-wide assessment committee with representation from each campus department, and the appointment of an assessment coordinator. These events modified the institutional structure and can be considered additional signs of the preparation stage in Prochaska's model. The monthly presentations that the assessment coordinator made to the Department Chairs' Council also signaled the institution's commitment to the development of a dynamic culture of assessment on campus.

For many programs, the action stage commenced with the first reports to the Academic and Student Affairs Committee of the board of governors because they had written their plans for assessment and, at that point, were beginning to operationalize them. As at RIC, this posed some challenges that needed to be tackled.

At the moment, what is critical for the maintenance stage is determining how to create other supports to assist our faculty in doing this work without overburdening them when we are operating on a very limited budget and without key staff members in various positions.

Campus Beginnings

In 2004, the three institutions were at varying stages of both the development of campus-wide assessment and regional accreditation. URI was anticipating a self-study and site visit by the NEASC. RIC was approaching the midpoint, preparing to submit a 5-year report presenting evidence of progress made in the assessment of student learning. CCRI had submitted a self-study and was anticipating a visit.

Institutional support and an introduction to the initiative were provided across the system by an external consultant contracted for 3 years of consulting services for the three institutions. The initial intention was to provide monthly meetings for working through the steps of developing comprehensive assessment plans and processes for each school. A meeting of the presidents, academic vice presidents, assistant vice presidents, deans and coordinators, and faculty with the consultant was called to share the essentials of the contract and to strategize about implementing the terms of the contract. The result of this first meeting was the acknowledgement that although faculty in the three institutions were similar in their need to develop assessment skills and processes, each school had a unique mission and organizational structure and unique beliefs about and experiences with assessment, and thus the routes or processes formulated to implement the contract would have to be different. In January 2005, the Office of Higher Education hosted a meeting for faculty from all three institutions. The presidents, academic vice presidents, assistant vice presidents, and deans, along with administrative staff from institutional research and information technology, met in a centrally located neutral environment. The commissioner of higher education introduced our consultant, who addressed assessment in a comprehensive and positive way.

Challenges to the System

As is often described in the assessment literature, the many barriers to implementing changes in faculty practice range from beliefs about teaching and research to concern about sharing data about learning. Misinterpretations of the true meaning of academic freedom, a belief that the assessment movement would vanish with changes in the administration at both the institutional and federal government levels, and comments such as "This wasn't in my job description when I was hired" characterized faculty response. In one of our institutions, a witch hunt mentality emerged and concomitant changes in administration as a result of retirements confirmed faculty suspicions that administrators were not all on the same page.

How did we confront these challenges? In order to execute the mandate for reporting to the Board of Governors for Higher Education, assessment reports were linked to the website and a stratified approval system was developed. The approval system was three tiered, consisting of Category 1 (completion of a full cycle of assessment), Category 2, (good progress, but not a complete cycle, with a requirement to report back within a year), and Category 3 (insufficient progress). The deadlines, presentations by faculty to the board, and public approval played a large part in changing faculty beliefs about the future (and present) reality of the value of assessing student learning. In the end, faculty were both surprised and impressed by the significant public interest and response to their work. Prior to meeting the deadlines for mandated reporting, the institutions engaged in activities that resulted in a massive shift in academic culture.

Key Developments at RIC That Fostered a Shift in Academic Cultures

The Committee on the Assessment of Student Outcomes was created as a special committee of the vice president for academic affairs, with the assistant to the vice president for academic affairs, the assessment coordinator, serving as chair. Committee members included representatives from each of the five academic units, the library, institutional research, and information technology. The committee scheduled and hosted regular opportunities for faculty to meet with our external consultant in small groups and on an individual basis. One of the most successful strategies that assisted faculty in embracing assessment was the faculty-sponsored assessment forums. The format for the forums was suggested by a faculty member from the Feinstein School of Education and Human Development. He suggested a modification of a process he used to evaluate student teachers, adapted from "Looking at Student Work" (n.d.).

This protocol presented guidelines for the discussion of an individual department's assessment plan. A member of the assessment committee offered to share the assessment plan of her department at the first forum. It was scheduled on a Friday at noon, an attempt to eliminate teaching schedule conflicts; however, it was acknowledged that faculty weren't likely to offer up their Friday lunch hour to assessment. Twelve faculty attended the first forum and contrary to our expectations confirmed that the Friday lunch time schedule should continue. Subsequent forums attracted 10–12 attendees.

The protocol requires attendees to assume roles. There is a facilitator, the presenter, the participants, and a knowledgeable other. The consultant assumed the role of knowledgeable other at the first forum. At subsequent forums, the assessment coordinator assumed the role. The protocol provided structure to the discussion and strict time limits as follows:

- The facilitator introduces the presenters and participants, process, timetable, and roles (5 minutes).
- The presenter introduces the focusing question, assessment plan, context, and history (15 minutes).
- Participants ask clarifying questions to get more information from the presenter (5 minutes).
- Participants pause to reflect (2–3 minutes).

- Participants present warm feedback (What's working? What's positive about the changes?), cool feedback (What's not working? What are challenges, problems, concerns?), and feedback somewhere in between related to the focusing question (8 minutes).
- Participants present feedback about other aspects of the assessment plan (7 minutes).
- The presenter summarizes what has been learned (2–3 minutes).
- The knowledgeable other provides a commentary (5 minutes).
- The facilitator asks the group to reflect on the process of using the protocol and suggests ways to improve the process for future use (5 minutes).

The presenter shares the assessment plan to the fullest extent, even if no data have been collected and the cycle is incomplete. At one forum, the focusing question was, How can we make the process more inclusive? The presenter had experienced limited involvement from her colleagues at every step of the process. She had limited feedback to drafts circulated and at faculty meetings. When this focusing question was presented, several of the participants agreed that this was an important question; they also experienced a lack of support and interest from and participation by colleagues. It is important to note that the forum was not intended to pass judgment on the status of assessment within a department or the nature of the plan, but to respond to the focusing question. Some of the valuable comments were in the form of suggestions: Rotate assessment responsibility; report results early, which might prompt a response from satisfied or dissatisfied faculty; report on assessment activities at every faculty meeting. Evaluation of the forums was positive. Faculty were pleased to hear how colleagues in other departments faced similar challenges and to share their wisdom with each other.

Key Developments at CCRI That Fostered a Shift in Academic Cultures

At CCRI, one of the defining experiences in changing the culture was the effort to assess general education goals. In 2007, the assessment of student learning outcomes at the program level was in progress, but the way to approach the assessment of general education was not entirely clear. Because no one department "owns" the general education curriculum, we realized that we needed to work in a much more interdisciplinary way in order to accomplish our goals. We chose to begin by assessing critical thinking, because it is mentioned as a learning outcome in 80%–90% of syllabi found online at the college; yet it had never been assessed. We defined critical thinking as the ability to

- Identify, analyze, and understand complex ideas
- Use information technology appropriately to locate, evaluate, and apply research data
- Draw inferences from facts
- Evaluate and present well-reasoned arguments

The Critical Thinking Project was launched in May 2007 at a 2-day critical thinking conference attended by faculty from each department at CCRI. This was considered vital because we feel that students develop their critical thinking skills in various courses over their time at our institution, so we hoped that all departments would be involved in the project. Over 70 faculty members attended, as well as several deans, the vice president for academic affairs, and the deputy commissioner for higher education. The conference culminated in 32 faculty members agreeing to participate in a pilot project to explicitly teach critical thinking in their classes, assign work that would allow students to demonstrate their critical thinking skills, and provide samples of that student work to be assessed by a committee of volunteers at the end of the 2007–2008 academic year.

During the first day of the conference, participants considered various ways to define critical thinking, as well as how to teach this skill in the classroom. They reflected on Bloom's taxonomy and also thought about the many resources presented by educational organizations, including the Foundation and Center for Critical Thinking. A panel of faculty members— from various departments including engineering, art, philosophy, and nursing—discussed the importance of critical thinking in each of their fields. Faculty then discussed ways to assess students' critical thinking skills, using classroom assessment techniques. On the second day of the conference, 32 faculty volunteers returned to discuss and plan instructional strategies for integrating the teaching of critical thinking into their courses over the following academic year. This faculty group requested a means of continuing the dialogue during the year to support the incorporation of these strategies into their courses. To facilitate communication, the conference chair, Dan Donovan, created the WebCT Critical Thinking Learning Circle, which volunteers could use to discuss ideas and assignments that were effective in their classes and also to exchange the names of useful websites and Power-Point presentations. In addition, 29 faculty participants attended several meetings during the academic year to confer about the development of the pilot project and to discuss their experiences.

Early in the spring of 2008, faculty on the critical thinking subcommittee of the Learning Evidence Team decided to undertake a pilot assessment of students' critical thinking skills as part of a college-wide assessment of general education learning outcomes. In discussing how to organize the assessment, several faculty members expressed concern about standardized testing as a method of measuring students' skills. We felt that students were not likely to take the test seriously and might not do their best if the test were taken out of context and had no relationship with any class or college requirement. A few members worried about a segment of the student population that routinely does not perform well on tests and believed that students in that segment would not be able to demonstrate their actual abilities through a standardized testing instrument. In general, subcommittee members wondered how we would get students to show up for such a test, and how representative a pool of students it would be, when only the ones who performed well on standardized tests were likely to participate.

Because of these concerns, we chose instead to use embedded assignments. We decided to adapt an assignment based on materials from the Foundation and Center for Critical Thinking that asks students to analyze the logic of an article by leading them through a series of critical thinking questions. We asked faculty members to choose articles appropriate to their disciplines and have students use the template to analyze it. Faculty then scored students' assignments, which were presented to them anonymously, on critical thinking skills. The committee decided to collect the samples at the end of the spring 2008 semester. The 112 samples came from nine courses in the following departments: business, English, legal studies, nursing, and Spanish.

A group of eight volunteers met in June 2008 to read and assess the sample assignments, using a rubric. Each assignment was rated by two evaluators and an average score was calculated for each of the five critical thinking skills. If the scores varied more than 2 points, a third evaluator was asked to read the sample, and the two closest scores were then chosen. (A third reader was needed for only a handful of assignments.) Working together in this way meant that faculty had to share their students' work with others and also disclose their assessment of the student work that they read. This made public two parts of the culture that are usually very private at our community college. This practice also introduced some faculty members to the idea of using rubrics to assess student learning outcomes and to the notion that the information learned from assessing student work can be extremely useful for refining programs.

The eight volunteers involved in gathering the assignments and rating the student samples were faculty members from business, criminal justice and legal studies, engineering, English, foreign languages, nursing, and radiology. These volunteers noted that being involved in the assessment process was helpful for developing the curriculum. It introduced new strategies for approaching critical thinking—both in the way we present it to students and in the way we assess it in our courses. Our experience in this pilot project revealed new ways to design courses, so that students could master critical thinking skills as they completed course assignments. But it also gave us new strategies for approaching the assessment of student learning from a collaborative multidisciplinary perspective.

Key Developments at URI That Fostered a Shift in Academic Cultures

URI adopted a number of formal and informal strategies—both structural and interpersonal—to modulate academic culture enough to adopt student learning outcomes assessment. Although there were a number of small assessment efforts underway in various colleges, there had been no real institution-wide progress prior to the system's mandate. Notably, URI's Faculty Senate had just approved a new general education program after a grueling 10-year debate and two failed attempts; the battle scars were just healing. As the general education program was being phased in over a 3-year period, there would be overlap with the introduction of outcomes assessment. This timing presented quite a challenge as well as an opportunity to buttress the new culture of learning that had been introduced by the president 8 years earlier. Although the administration was directly responsible for responding to the mandate, the goal was to grow the effort from both the grassroots and top-down levels.

First, the Office of the Provost and the assessment coordinator invited a small but representative and politically influential group of faculty members to attend the 2004 Association of American Colleges and Universities' Summer Institute in Utah to develop a strategic plan for introducing assessment to the campus. The resulting white paper (University of Rhode Island, 2005) identified multiple strategies that were likely to result in a thoughtful and intellectually engaged process. This document was published and presented to various faculty committees, and it foreshadowed all subsequent work in to an uncanny degree.

The overarching principle of the white paper was and remains the faculty's commitment to its students' success. Faculty-led student focus groups had revealed to the URI faculty that students, both weak and very strong, were unexpectedly challenged when asked to describe what they knew and were able to do as a result of their academic engagement over the previous years of study. They could readily recount the class sequences they had taken but were less able to summarize their learning accomplishments. This finding alarmed many of URI's faculty and staff members. From this grew a sense among the faculty that students need to be provided with a certain level of metacognition about their institution's educational scaffolding (language of accomplishment and sequencing of cognitive development) for what they are expected to have gained by the time they complete their degree program and by what various means they may do so. This rich conversation led many faculty to adopt student learning outcomes statements for their degree programs.

During the same period, the vice provost established a student learning improvement advisory committee to advise both the administration and faculty. Within a short time, the committee gained official status as a joint Faculty Senate/administration committee and was codified in the university manual. The collective wisdom and political savvy of this group have allowed them to make important strides forward, including the establishment of the Office for Student Learning and Outcomes Assessment, which is staffed by a full-time director and a part-time clerical staff member and is largely funded by external grant monies. The availability of funding for mini-grants allowed faculty and departments to engage creatively and deeply in the development of assessment mechanisms.

Cultural change came more readily once the institution was able to begin celebrating good assessment work by scheduling presentations to highlight the accomplishments of individual departments. Although assessment reports, in and of themselves, are important documents, they do not interest most people. Instead, these presentations contributed to the creation of a storehouse of strong narratives that recounted faculty concerns, actual assessment efforts, findings, and subsequent curricular amendments. The power of these stories about improving student success rates has amplified over time as the narratives get woven and rewoven into faculty dialogues.

Assessment efforts drove a thirst for student baseline data. A URI summit on student learning was held in August 2007. More than 100 faculty and staff members attended and culled through all publicly available data about the institution's students. Trends in the data were surprising. Some provided a pleasant surprise, whereas others confirmed troubling suspicions. Overall, the scarcity of general evidence about how well our students were doing prompted faculty members to advocate for committing the institution to join the Wabash National Study for Liberal Education, a longitudinal study of educational outcomes over the 4 years of a liberal arts program. The extensive data sets would be made available to the faculty for further research and assessment.

Despite the many assessment developments, it must be acknowledged that actual assessment of student work at URI would have happened much more slowly if departments and colleges had not been obliged to submit actual assessment reports to the Rhode Island Office of Higher Education. The public screening heightened awareness of the importance of outcomes assessment.

What We Have Learned Across Our Institutions

The faculty has begun to experience the true scope and utility of the assessment process. The complexity and value of this endeavor is evident and real.

Yet we need to move toward a subsequent phase of assessment that will better capture the benefits to faculty and balance the effort spent. The successful strategies described in this chapter involved committees of faculty across programs as well as the consultant. Although assessment work is best accomplished when faculty driven, additional institutional support is also required. Support can range from changing expectations for tenure and promotion to inviting participation in the assessment process at the departmental level and developing job descriptions for new hires that clearly delineate responsibility for assessment of student learning.

What is clear is that there is an unequal ability to promote and guide assessment at the departmental level that is not separate from the inability of department chairs to lead change in other areas. The application of new technology is another example where leadership ability is crucial, but not always evident. We have come to realize that outcomes assessment and faculty instructional development are tightly coupled. One can't exist productively without the other. Instructional development is course based; assessment is program based. There is now a perceived need for a center for teaching and learning where teaching strategies and best practices for assessment can be shared among faculty. At one school, the work of the assessment committee resulted in the strategic plan that makes use of a benchmark to explore the development of a teaching and learning center.

Sustainability

By the spring of 2009, all the programs in the three institutions had reported on their assessment findings. The programs that were approved as Category 2, those that had made good progress but had not completed at least one assessment cycle or closed the loop, reported again in the fall of 2009. Faculty in programs that received a Category 2 approval were noticeably chagrined and engaged in the quest to receive approval as Category 1. There were no programs that received a rating of Category 3 (insufficient progress). Does this suggest the value of grading to faculty? Perhaps. What is probably more indicative of the approval process and returning to report again is that assessment is not going away, is not a passing trend, but remains an important value of our public constituency. Are this shifting, competing, and trying to improve response of the faculty evidence of a shift in the culture toward greater estimation of assessment of student learning? Does it reflect a concern for the public's interest in what our students are learning?

To the extent possible, next steps for the Rhode Island Board of Governors for Higher Education and representatives from the three public institutions include developing a policy to describe and inform a statewide perspective on assessment of student learning outcomes. We envision a policy that will emphasize faculty responsibility for assessing student learning and also acknowledge the values and mission of each individual institution. The policy will probably require routine reporting to the Rhode Island Board of Governors for Higher Education on a 3- to 5-year cycle. Although faculty in some programs in each institution will be refining their plans and may include indirect measures of student learning, the policy will emphasize direct measures. The link between budgeting and assessment data continues to be elusive. The challenge to provide evidence that assessment findings result in the systematic allocation of institutional resources to promote institutional effectiveness remains. Over time, reporting should emphasize the results and the use of the results as the foundation for improving institutional effectiveness and achievement of the mission.

References

American Psychological Association. (2003). *Understanding how people change is first step in changing unhealthy behavior.* Retrieved from www.psychologymatters.org/diclemente.html

Looking at Student Work. (n.d.). *Protocols.* Retrieved from www.lasw.org/protocols.html

Schoeder, C. Retrieved April 29, 2009, from www.famousquotesandauthors.com/authors/caroline_schoeder_quotes.html

University of Rhode Island. (2005). *Action plan of the preliminary working group on student learning outcomes.* Draft. Retrieved from www.uri.edu/assessment/media/public/page_files/uri/documents/plans/Utah_White_Paper.pdf

About the Authors

Patricia A. Thomas is a professor of community health nursing and assistant to the vice president for academic affairs for assessment at Rhode Island College. She has been involved with assessment for many years and is invested in sharing the value of learning how and what students are learning and sharing.

Jeanne Mullaney is professor of French and Spanish at the Community College of Rhode Island and is also the assessment coordinator. She began working in assessment through a grant-funded project that involved writing desired student learning outcomes for foreign language students and designing assessments to measure their progress.

Deborah Grossman-Garber was previously the director of the Office of Student Outcomes Assessment Accreditation at the University of Rhode Island. She was recently named associate commissioner of the Rhode Island Office of Higher Education.

Also available from Stylus

Assessing for Learning
Building a Sustainable Commitment Across the Institution
Peggy L. Maki

"Maki's book offers a systematic approach to assessment that is meant to address the general questions, 'How well do we achieve our educational intentions?' and 'How well do our students learn?' . . . I consider this book to be an extremely valuable source for anyone involved in education. Its primary contribution is how it forces us to conceptualize 'assessment' as an integral part of the university system. Learning assessment is meant to be a core institutional process linked to all aspects of university life."—*Effective Teaching*

The Assessment of Doctoral Education
Emerging Criteria and New Models for Improving Outcomes
Edited by Peggy L. Maki and Nancy A. Borkowski
Foreword by Daniel D. Denecke

"It is not only informative but useful, comprising a veritable treasure trove of strategies, assessment models and research findings. The book makes an informative addition to the growing body of literature on doctoral education."—*Quality Assurance in Education* (Australia)

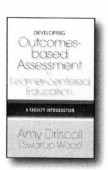

Developing Outcomes-Based Assessment for Learner-Centered Education
A Faculty Introduction
Amy Driscoll and Swarup Wood

"The personal approach of this book reads like a conversation with the authors, making it feel manageable. The case studies that begin each chapter provide a realistic perspective of the pitfalls and successes of outcomes-based education. There are many useful tools and perspectives provided throughout this book for faculty and administrators. For institutions engaging in this kind of educational approach this is an excellent resource."—*Journal of College Student Development*

Introduction to Rubrics
An Assessment Tool to Save Grading Time, Convey Effective Feedback and Promote Student Learning
Dannelle D. Stevens and Antonia J. Levi

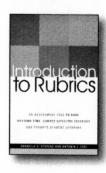

"The authors serve up the seven short chapters of this 128-page book as easy to read, delectable teaching and learning aids that can be adapted and employed with almost any post-secondary course, at any level...a handy resource with excellent potential for cultivating interdisciplinary relationships and an aid that extends the location of education beyond the classroom."—*Teaching Theology & Religion*

22883 Quicksilver Drive
Sterling, VA 20166-2102

Subscribe to our e-mail alerts: www.Styluspub.com